Contemporary
Fast-Food
and
Drinking Glass
Collectibles

Contemporary Fast-Food and Drinking Glass Collectibles

Mark E. Chase
and
Dr. Michael J. Kelly

Wallace-Homestead Book Company
Radnor, Pennsylvania

Copyright © 1988 by Mark E. Chase and Michael J. Kelly

All Rights Reserved
Published in Radnor, Pennsylvania 19089, by Wallace-
Homestead Book Company
No part of this book may be reproduced, transmitted, or
stored in any form or by any means, electronic or
mechanical, without prior written permission from the
publisher
Designed by Anthony Jacobson
Manufactured in the United States of America

ISBN 0-87069-517-7

Library of Congress Cataloging in Publication Data
Chase, Mark E.
    Contemporary fast-food and drinking glass collectibles / Mark E.
  Chase and Michael Kelly.
        p.   cm.
    Includes index.
    ISBN 0-87069-517-7 (pbk.)
    1. Advertising drinking glasses—United States—Collectors and
  collecting—Catalogs.   2. Advertising drinking glasses—United
  States—History—20th century—Catalogs.   I. Kelly, Michael, 1942–
  .   II. Title.
  NK5440.D75C48 1989
  748.8'3074013—dc19   88-28662
                                                          CIP

1 2 3 4 5 6 7 8 9 0   7 6 5 4 3 2 1 0 9 8

Contents

Index   241

Acknowledgments

A book like this is almost necessarily a collaborative effort. Information about glasses is as valuable as the glasses themselves—and often harder to come by. It has therefore occurred to us as we labored on this book, sought information, hunted glasses at salvage shops, flea markets, and even in friends' kitchen cupboards, that the "perfect" and complete collector glass book will not be written until all serious glass collectors bring all their knowledge and glasses to one central location, where glasses can be examined and traded, and knowledge can be exchanged, confirmed, and recorded. Until such an event takes place, collectors of fast-food restaurant glasses will have to rely on books like ours and hope that such individual efforts inspire others to broaden and build on the base we have created. And we writers of such books will have to rely on the willingness of fellow collectors and collector-writers to share indispensable information and glasses.

This book has been an ambitious project, an enormous undertaking. We hope that it is helpful to everyone interested in collector glasses and that it helps to stimulate interest in this exciting collectible field.

We gratefully acknowledge the cheerful and generous support of the following people, without whose aid the book would not have come together: our wives, Priscilla Kelly and Susan Chase, who were patient, supportive, and tolerant, even when we disappeared for days to attend flea markets and, especially, when our homes were converted into glass warehouses; David Cole of Newport, Washington; Michael Ferrannini of Hoosick Falls, New York; Brett and Chris Chase of Pittsburgh; Mike and Jennifer Geirhart of State College, Pennsylvania; Harold and Ruth Strang of Phoenix, Arizona; Russell Byler of Akron, Ohio; Cynthia Marshall, Ellen King and Craig and Judith Chase of Slippery Rock, Pennsylvania; Gary Kelly of Kent, Washington; Charles Kelly of Tacoma, Washington; Tom and Joan Martin of Grove City, Pennsylvania; Carol Markowski of Colorado Springs, Colorado; Peter Kroll of Madison, Wisconsin; Lance Golba of Fife Lake, Michigan; Melva Davern of Pittsburgh, Pennsylvania; Mark Carron of St. Peters, Missouri; George Cahill of the National Flag Foundation in Pittsburgh; Bob Traver of Gouldsboro, Pennsylvania. All of these people freely shared their enthusiasm and knowledge.

We also thank Carla and Alden Hart and Tim Walsh of Slippery Rock, Pennsylvania, for loaning us certain key glasses to photograph; Debra Brunken and Pam Cole of Slippery Rock and Steve Hetrick of Erie, for their assistance and advice in photography; and finally our secretaries, especially Susan Shipley, who put non-glass-related calls on hold and kept us posted on the latest glass promotions at area restaurants.

Part 1
Introduction
and
Overview

A Brief History of the Hobby

Most glass and tumbler collectors will agree that the origin of this field can be traced to the jam, cheese, and food product glasses of the 1930s and 40s, and to soft-drink companies which printed their trademarks and product designs on glasses to stimulate sales and to capture public awareness. Such manufacturers, hoping to increase the sale and popularity of their products, offered limited edition designs on the sides of their glass containers. In time, sets and series evolved and, because so many different colors and designs were available, collectors discovered the fun and challenge of putting together sets of their favorite glasses which could, after all, be used in the kitchen and dining room.

Many people are familiar, for instance, with the Disney cartoon character glasses which were offered by food product manufacturers and which were extremely popular because of the success and popularity of Disney's films in the 1930s and 40s. The multiplicity of Disney characters naturally encouraged the production and distribution of sets and series of glasses. Collectors—mostly children—simply had to have them all, and parents found that it was easier to get stubborn children to drink all their milk or juice (frequently laced with cod liver oil!) if Mickey or some other Disney character appeared on the side of the glass.

Thus, food packagers and manufacturers found an interesting way to stimulate sales, and consumers had something of permanent utilitarian and aesthetic value left after the product was used. After all, an attractive tumbler with a nice, colorful design or cartoon character was clearly superior to an empty, ugly tin can. And what about the edu-cational benefits? With nursery rhymes, brief poems, the alphabet, songs, and other juvenile fare on glasses, children sitting at the breakfast or dinner table could practice their reading skills, sometimes in advance of actual schooling.

With the precedent for decorated series of food product glasses so well established in the 1930s and 40s, it is no wonder that today there are so many different kinds of glasses out there to collect. The Swanky Swig decorated cheese containers were produced by Kraft from the 1940s through the 1950s; these sturdy little glasses (which we have chosen to omit from our listings because they are so well documented by other writer-collectors) deserve a lot of credit for their early role as collectible food containers. Their success paved the way for other kinds of collectible glasses.

Advertisers and manufacturers have always been aware of the commercial possibilities and the obvious fact that there is no other substitute for a simple drinking glass. As a result, plain, unadorned and undecorated drinking glasses are the exception rather than the rule today.

Collectors have a wealth of kinds and types to choose from and to collect, and collecting boundaries are limited only by the collector's personal preferences and tastes. They can extend to gasoline and oil company premiums, sports teams, popular cartoon characters, a specific restaurant chain, the American Bicentennial or Revolution, the American space effort, a certain soft-drink manufacturer, or any other cohesive category or area of interest.

The sheer variety of glasses available has played a large part in determining the contents of this book. The listings we have chosen to include realistically reflect current collecting enthusiasms and coincide with the actual nature of today's collecting process. As new collectors, we first thought in terms of collecting only those glasses with the names and logos of fast-food restaurants on them. Soon, however, we had to decide whether to bother with the occasional glass offerings of smaller restaurants. Next, we were faced with the problem of regional distributions. How could we even *know* about, much less get our hands on, glasses that were distributed by restaurants in other states? Like most other people with the collecting "bug," we decided to go ahead and collect as many different fast-food restaurant glasses as we could and then sort them all out later.

Once that decision was made, we had to decide whether we were going to collect glasses which bore soft drink manufacturers' names and logos. After all, it would be difficult to resist all of those cartoon character glasses with Coca-Cola, Pepsi, and 7-UP logos on them, even without a restaurant co-sponsor. And what were we to do with certain fascinating glasses not blessed with soft-drink or restaurant logos? We couldn't very well omit such beautiful glasses as The Sunday Funnies series, which has no restaurant or soft drink associations, nor could we exclude from our collections such sets as Battlestar Galactica, Smurfs, Popples, and Chipmunks just because they lacked restaurant or soft drink sponsorship.

One kind of glass led to another. Certainly, by the time we thought of doing a book on the subject, we no longer regarded the variety of glasses as a liability, and the presence of logos and definite sponsorship a necessity, because we realized that collectors were indeed already collecting practically every kind of glass currently circulating.

We therefore went with the flow, and we discovered by collecting that the "connections" or progressions between types of glasses were quite logical. For instance, the 1986 Pizza Hut Flintstone Kids set led back to Welch's early sixties Flintstone jam glasses. Recent comic-book or real-life heroes led back to older ones, such as Davy Crockett. Major restaurants like McDonald's led to smaller franchises like Taco Time and Skipper's. Fast-food restaurants led to "slower" food restaurants like Eat'nPark, Pappan's, and Joe DiMaggio's.

The giants of the soft drink industry led to 7-UP, Mountain Dew, R.C. Cola, Dr Pepper, and Hires. Glasses promoting soft drinks led to glasses by Keebler, Hershey's, and Kellogg's, promoting food. Glasses led to cups, pitchers, and carafes, because many of these items share the same design or sponsorship or simply "belong" together as members of sets or series. Johnny Hart's Arby's B.C. Ice Age set led to Hart's non-sponsored B.C. type glassware. Gary Patterson's Pepsi Sports series led to his nonsponsored glasses and cups. Coca-Cola Holly Hobbie led to American Greetings Holly Hobbie. McDonald's Camp Snoopy set led to the nonsponsored Peanuts glasses. 7-UP Ziggy glasses led to various unsponsored Ziggy glasses. The Coca-Cola National Flag Foundation set led to the non-Coke National Flag Foundation set, etc. Obviously, this list could be extended, but we hope that what we have mentioned here is sufficient to help collectors better understand what we included in this book—and why.

Systematic gathering of information on all the different types and variations of glasses has only seriously begun in the last few years. There have always been collectors, but it was not until fairly recently that a large number of them actually began to compile, exchange, and examine information about the glasses. It is a sad fact that many, perhaps most, glass manufacturers kept few or poor records on the types and quantities of glasses manufactured and distributed. It is no doubt true also that promoters, advertisers, and food product manufacturers originally considered their designed or otherwise decorated glasses to be relatively ephemeral; that is, they probably expected most of the glasses to be broken or discarded fairly soon after distribution, and probably never dreamed that people would be building permanent collections of these glasses, prizing them, and passing them on to future generations. It is equally likely that they could never have foreseen books dedicated solely to, say, Swanky Swigs or Welch's jam glasses.

The modern collector who wants to know as much as possible about the glasses he is collecting has much to do and many obstacles to overcome. People are already beginning to forget when and where they got certain unsponsored and undated glasses or sets of glasses. Even restaurant managers and employees tend to forget when certain promotions were held or, indeed, *if* they were held. Parent companies and national headquarters kept poor records and are unable or unwilling to provide collectors with the kinds of information they want.

Reliable information is precious and often extremely difficult to collect and verify. This is the case for many reasons, one of the most obvious being the regional nature of many glass promotions. Glasses abundant in a certain state or area of the country may never have been heard of in other states or areas of the country, even when they were distributed by franchise giants like Mc-Donald's or Arby's. Many promotions were extremely limited, and some simply failed or were cut short.

Other promotions, like many of McDonald's, were national; huge numbers of glasses are involved—too many, evidently, for the corporations themselves to keep track of. Certain specific glasses or cartoon characters met with disfavor or, even worse, public indifference. And sets which were planned, but only reached the prototype stage, never to be released to the public, further complicate the modern glass historian's job and frustrate the avid collectors who know about these glasses but can never hope to obtain them. And then there are the glasses, both singles and sets, that are rare simply because large numbers were never produced. All of these factors contribute to the essential appeal and challenge of glass collecting.

Today, the successful collector is a person who travels widely to flea markets, thrift shops and collectible shows; who corresponds and trades with a good number of other collectors from all parts of the United States; and who literally exhausts all channels in an attempt to find glasses for his collection as well as information about them.

It becomes slightly easier to follow the evolution of collector glasses when we get to the late 1940s and early 1950s. With television came popular children's shows like Howdy Doody, and Welch's jellies and jams were successfully promoted and sold in small $7\frac{1}{2}$ ounce glasses featuring the Doodyville characters with catchy little rhymes praising Welch's products. In the mid-fifties, similar small food glasses bearing Davy Crockett lore, jingles, and adventures corresponding with the popular television serial appeared. Then the early sixties brought a second wind for jam glasses when Welch's began to issue its Flintstone series with a seemingly endless number of color and bottom embossment combinations. This Welch's jam glass phenomenon continued into the 1970s with The Archies, Warner Brothers, and NFL sets.

During the 1960s, gasoline companies even got into the collector glass act by issuing glasses with their logos on them, as well as glasses with regional attractions, sports teams and players, and famous Indians. Glasses commemorating various World's Fairs and even the United States' space missions are also popular with the public.

In the early 1970s, fast-food restaurants began to offer cartoon or comic character tumblers to patrons who purchased a soft drink. Soon, the major national franchises adopted this successful promotion technique, usually with the sponsorship of a soft-drink manufacturer. The 1973 Pepsi Collector Series of eighteen glasses featuring Warner Brothers cartoon characters was one of the earliest and most popular large-scale promotions. This success led to other promotions which soon spread to a large number of chains, especially those associated with a specific soft drink. The results are quite apparent now: there is hardly an existing cartoon character who hasn't been publicized and immortalized on the sides of a drinking glass!

It is safe to say that our country's bicentennial year, 1976, and the accompanying review and reappreciation of our history, was mainly responsible for an accelerated production and issuance of collector glasses. This surge in glass production essentially began in 1974 when Libbey Glass, the National Flag Foundation, and Herfy's Restaurants distributed their Historic Flags sets, and it continued with Bicentennial commemorative sets issued by franchises such as Arby's, Burger Chef, Burger King, and Wendy's, and by soft-drink companies such as Coca-Cola.

Looking back, we are now able to see that 1975 to 1980 were the peak production years for collector glasses. The cost of such promotions has increased from the 22¢ per glass that the 1976 Arby's Bicentennial Series and the 1976 Pepsi-Warner Brothers Interaction Series originally cost the distributor, to something nearly twice that. With minimum case order requirements and other complications, many franchises simply do not want the trouble of running an extended promotion, even though it is an established fact that such promotions significantly stimulate and increase business.

Rising costs have no doubt been responsible for a greater number of plastic drinking container promotions, and collectors are sure to have noticed that in the past few years the restaurants that are still issuing glasses from time to time (McDonald's, Arby's, and Pizza Hut) are charging more for them. Perhaps increased business at restaurants which use glass promotions, books such as this one, collector glass clubs and the publicity which such organizations could potentially generate, and articles on glasses in collectors' publications will combine to create a climate in which collector glass promotions are regular, much-anticipated events. We strongly feel that these glasses have now firmly established themselves as part of our popular culture and that they deserve to be treated with serious regard because of their commercial, historical, and cultural relevance.

Pricing and Condition

As with most any collectible, condition is a key factor in determining value and collectibility. Most collectors want only the best specimens available and, after they have seen the best, the second or third best has little or no appeal. With collector glasses, brightness of color is absolutely desirable. Color is the first quality that the viewer notices when examining a collector glass. Close to color in importance is strong, clear lettering. Imperfect or missing letters detract significantly from the value and appeal of a glass because they are almost always immediately apparent. Finally, on a top-quality glass, colors are always within their outlines, and there are no scratches or rim chips.

The automatic dishwasher and its detergent are a collector glass's worst enemy (second only to the USPS and UPS for those of us who insist on shipping glasses for one reason or another—but more on this subject later). One trip through the dishwasher and a "mint" glass becomes a "good" glass. Repeated trips through a dishwasher result in "a" glass. In other words, the high gloss that is evident on new ("mint") glasses is very susceptible to the detergent and hot water action of today's efficient dishwashers, and serious collectors will not buy or trade such glasses, nor will they want them in their own collections unless they happen to be extremely rare and unusual. With a plentiful supply of "mint" or near-mint glasses still available, it makes little sense to bother with faded ones.

In Part 2, we attempt to provide realistic price ranges for collector glasses. Besides condition, several other factors determine the actual buying and selling prices for glasses. These factors include the popularity or regional availability of a particular series, the sponsor or distributor of a particular series and, of course, the rareness or scarcity of a particular issue. Basically, universal economic laws of supply and demand operate in the glass collecting field. What is difficult to find in one area may be easy to find in another. The individual collector ultimately decides what a glass or set of glasses is worth to him, based on his own interests and collecting goals. Through extensive contacts with other collectors throughout the United States and through our own experience buying, selling, and trading, we have arrived at realistic price ranges for the glasses we list in this book. Naturally, there are going to be anomalies and discrepancies in a field as new as this one. We are fully aware that on any given day at any given flea market or yard sale, a collector may be lucky enough to purchase a given amount of rare collector glasses for practically nothing, but such happy events are fairly uncommon and not especially significant when it comes to influencing general trends and everyday buying and selling prices. If you are a serious collector and you need or want any of the glasses we have listed in this book, you will not be far off the glass's "real" value if you buy somewhere within the price ranges we suggest. If you have a chance to buy it for less, congratulations! That happens frequently in every collectible field, and everyone loves a bargain and deserves one once in a while.

Care and Storage of Glasses

We have already cautioned collectors to refrain from running their glasses through dishwashers. If glasses must be washed, it is best to use a mild pH-balanced dishwashing solution and warm water. Glasses should then be dried with a cotton polishing cloth for that extra sparkle. It is best not to wash glasses too often. We all know the old saying about taking the pitcher to the well: eventually, the unexpected or the inevitable will happen. It is also wise to keep glasses out of direct, prolonged sunlight, which will eventually subdue the colors.

The storage of collector glasses presents its own special problems. Most collectors are proud of their collections and want to display them, but such displays are often impractical for several reasons. For one thing, even a "fair" or "good" collection may easily contain from 500 to 600 different glasses, and an "excellent" one might comprise 1200 to 1500 glasses. Since a collector would want to show off each individual glass, it would not be effective to arrange glasses more than one deep on a shelf. The good news is that each linear foot of shelving can accommodate four glasses; so, for example, an 8-foot-wide by 5-foot-high shelf system with 7 inches between shelves can accommodate 256 glasses. Larger shelf systems could be built, depending on the availability of wall space.

Some collectors find it necessary to store their glasses, and there are several safe options for doing this. Probably the most convenient and safest way to store glasses is in cardboard, twelve-compartment liquor boxes. Glasses housed in these boxes do not need to be wrapped, and if the fronts of the boxes are clearly labeled (we suggest taping a piece of 8½" × 11" paper to the box and labeling it with a marking pen), it is an easy matter to locate and examine glasses when necessary. Being able to locate glasses quickly is important when comparing new acquisitions to old ones. Collectors who wrap their glasses in newspaper and pack them in boxes cannot easily locate a specific glass, and the kind of handling that newspaper wrapping and unwrapping requires often leads to accidents and breakage. In addition, we have found that newspaper tends to make the glasses dirty. Finally, if the glasses are wrapped up and unsystematically stored, it will be extremely difficult for you to show them off to uninterested friends and fellow collectors.

While storing glasses in sturdy compartmentalized liquor boxes is convenient, there is one drawback: space. Boxes take up substantial room and, if a collector has a thousand glasses in his collection, he will need to have room for 83 boxes. Duplicates, which every serious collector has on hand, compound the storage problem. Many collectors' homes are not spacious enough to accommodate quantities, and we know from experience that many collectors' spouses therefore demand that the glasses go outside to the barn or to the garage, or in some lucky cases, to the basement. If there is an "up" side to such blatant discrimination, it is that glasses are rarely affected by freezing temperatures and they can be safely stored in unheated buildings in boxes in the coldest climates. Needless to say, storage and display problems must be solved by the individual collector.

Inventory Systems

Normally, collectors will want to know fairly early in the collecting process exactly what glasses they have—and where—so they will establish some sort of system for keeping accurate track of them. Many advanced collectors have established computerized databases identifying the type, quantity, condition, and location of glasses in their collections.

Simpler systems can work just as well. Many collectors find it convenient, for instance, to establish a 4" × 6" notecard for each set of glasses and then to alphabetize the notecards according to restaurant, product, or soft-drink sponsor (essentially the way we have arranged this book). Informal as it is, such a system is potentially as accurate as a computer database, and it has the advantage of being portable: a good thing when one sets out on the flea market trail and especially if a collector needs to quickly verify what he has and what he needs.

Regardless of the system you use, it is important to keep it up to date and to enter new acquisitions as soon as you get them so that you will always have a current listing.

Shipping Glasses

Shipping is an unavoidable evil for collectors who trade with or sell to geographically distant fellow collectors. It would be wonderful if we didn't have to commit our precious glasses to the temporary care of package handlers and conveyors, but this is the only practical way for most collectors to add to their collections. This fact admitted, there is only one solution to the shipping problem: pack as if your glass's "life" depended on it—because it does!

We recommend double boxing a smaller box inside a larger one and, further, that the two boxes be separated and insulated from each other with Styrofoam pellets, crushed newspaper, or large bubble wrap. We advise that the inner box be a sturdy one with dividers; twelve-compartment liquor boxes are excellent to use for inner boxes. Put a layer of Styrofoam pellets in the bottom of each compartment, and then insert each bubble-wrapped glass (the small bubbles are ideal for glasses packed this way) into a compartment and fill the remaining space with Styrofoam pellets or crushed newspaper. Do not pack the glasses into the compartments too tightly; it is important that they have room to move. If they do not have some space to move in, a blow to any outside glass is sure destruction for its inner companions, since there will be a chain reaction inside the box. Next, tape this box up with filament tape, and cover its top with a 2 to 3-inch layer of Styrofoam pellets and a piece of bubble wrap for good measure. Finally, tape the outside box shut with filament tape. When you shake the box, you shouldn't feel much movement within it, and you shouldn't hear much either. You'll know when you have packed the boxes just right; and, as you pack more and more boxes, you'll find ways to improve on your strategies to ensure safe delivery of your glasses.

Adding to a Collection

It sounds too obvious, but glasses can be found wherever people drink liquids, and that is everywhere. Yard sales, garage sales, estate sales, church bazaars, flea markets, thrift shops, Salvation Army, Goodwill, and St. Vincent DePaul stores, antique and collectible shops and cooperatives—all are good sources of collectible glasses.

Specialized collectible shows will always have glasses, especially if the show themes are Pepsi, Coke, sports, Disneyana, superheroes, or other cartoon-related subjects. And, of course, let's not forget the latest collectible glasses offered by fast-food franchises around the country. If you have a lot of nerve, there's always the glass cupboard in your friends' kitchens. . . .

Production Errors and Variations

With such large quantities of glasses being produced, it is logical to assume that a certain number of flawed glasses occasionally escape the notice of glass company employees and quality control people. Such glasses do make it to the end of the line and are boxed and shipped to restaurants, where they are distributed over the counter to customers who are in too much of a hurry to examine them carefully for flaws. These glasses are showing up on the collectible market and provoking some discussion regarding their value. Usually these glasses are missing one of their colors, or some portion of their design or printed material, such as a character's name or factual background information, and sometimes even the restaurant logo or copyright information. Such glasses are interesting, but we believe they belong to the oddity category. Their departure from manufacturing norms should not be unduly valued, since they represent something neither the manufacturer nor the distributors intended.

Variations are quite another thing, and a fair number of interesting ones exist. The 1973 Pepsi Collector Series of eighteen characters, for instance, has a large number of them, and other smaller sets and series often have several glasses in them which fall into the variation category. These variations involve "small" design changes, color changes, omissions, and inclusions. We feel that it is adequate to let collectors know that these variations do exist without going into great detail and without making fine distinctions about desirability and value since the average collector will probably not encounter a significant number of them.

How to Use the Listings

Sequence

In Part 2, we have alphabetized the names of sponsors, restaurants, distributors, general and specific subjects, food and beverage manufacturers, personalities, companies, events, and other categories. Such an arrangement, we believe, is natural and user-friendly. In addition, we have compiled a comprehensive index which will help readers locate specific information within the text quickly.

The arrangement of glasses presented a few problems, having to do with co-sponsored glasses. We had to decide which would take precedence in our general overall alphabetical listing: the soft drink or the restaurant. This dilemma applied especially to the prolific giants in the collector glass business, Pepsi-Cola and Coca-Cola. We decided that since Pepsi and Coke have issued so many glasses, we should list all of them under those name brands even if they shared sponsorship with a restaurant on the glass. It seemed to make sense, for example, to list our sole Coca-Cola Arctic Circle glass under Coca-Cola rather than creating a separate category for Arctic Circle, and this decision holds for several similar cases. However, we chose to create a separate restaurant listing for Elby's since the Coca-Cola set they recently issued involved a set of four glasses.

Perhaps the Burger King/Star Wars Trilogy/Coca-Cola sets illustrate the classification "problem" most clearly. Where should these glasses be listed? We decided to favor the restaurant because it is national and there are many collectors who concentrate solely on Burger King collectibles. A similar decision was necessary in the case of Arby's 1979 Norman Rockwell Winter Scenes, which were co-sponsored by Pepsi. Since Arby's is national and issues a great number of collector glasses, we decided to list these glasses under that heading rather than Pepsi. So what the reader/collector will find in this book is an overall alphabetical listing which includes restaurants, soft drink companies, food manufacturers, events, sports, personalities, themes, etc.

Major national restaurants and soft drink brands which have established themselves as integral collecting categories take precedence over "smaller" collectible categories. When co-sponsors seem to have equal importance, as in the Arby's and Burger King cases cited above, we tend to favor the restaurant, but we have provided cross-references to the "other" sponsor. We therefore advise collectors to look under all the major headings for cross references to other headings and to refer to the index frequently where all headings, titles, sponsors, key words, and names contained on glasses are listed.

Within each major alphabetical category, we have further alphabetized subcategories grouping similar subjects together. Individual glasses or series are chronological where they have the same title. In the specific listings for each glass or set of glasses, we have attempted to list the issue and/or copyright dates when such information is available. These dates appear in parentheses and can be considered reliable and firm. When precise dating information is unavailable on the glass itself but known to us in other ways, we place the likely date in brackets.

Every glass listed has an identification code consisting of two letters and a number (e.g., all Coca-Cola glasses have a CC prefix, all Arby's glasses an AR prefix). We hope this will make identification of glasses easier in discussions or correspondence; you can check the number in this book to be *certain* which glass is being described. Sets with two different glasses, such as the 1976 and 1978 Dr Pepper Star Trek issues, are given individual numbers, the first set listed in [brackets], the second set in (parentheses).

Physical Descriptions

We generally begin the physical description with the height of the glass in inches or with some other significant measurement or specific observation on shape or design, and go on to the number of glasses in the set and the colors of the glasses. We describe the "front" of the glass first, if it has a discernible front, and we proceed from the glass's top to its bottom. We continue this procedure with the reverse side. We attempt to convey in our text a sense of the actual lettering configurations on the glasses by separating various horizontal levels with slash marks (/) and by referring to color and print size in brackets. We have taken pains to quote all printed material on glasses exactly, so when readers encounter quotation marks in our text, they can be sure that the material within them is accurately reproduced from the glass even though it occasionally strikes them as awkward or grammatically incorrect.

Photographs

It is very challenging to photograph glasses effectively, and we experimented with a number of approaches. In order to eliminate undesirable and confusing backside show-through in the photographs, we filled the glasses with salt or sand, depending on the glasses' colors, in order to highlight glass designs and lettering. When it seemed appropriate and when we had sufficient duplicate glasses, we included a backside view, and we normally positioned this glass in the middle. We also made it our practice to coordinate glass photographs and textual listings in a left-to-right, top-to-bottom manner.

Where to Find More Information

Collectors can gather and exchange information about glasses, using an increasing number of sources. Many regional and national collectible publications are beginning to include columns on collector glasses, among others "The Daze" (Box 57, Otisville, MI 48463), a national publication on china and glass, and the "Collector Glass News" (P.O. Box 308, Slippery Rock, PA 16057), a quarterly newsletter with informative articles on a variety of glass collecting issues and topics. The authors are interested in hearing from collectors who have information to share or questions to ask about collector glasses, and we can be contacted by writing to P. O. Box 308, Slippery Rock, PA 16057. Please include a self-addressed stamped envelope if you would like a reply.

Part 2
Collectible
Glasses:
The Listings

AAFES (Army & Air Force Exchange Service)

E.T. The Extra-Terrestrial (1982). A set of four 5$\frac{15}{16}$" glasses featuring key themes and scenes from the popular film. Title of scene appears in white at bottom of glass. The reverses of all four glasses are identical: near the top, E.T. and child's hands touching, and below that the words "E.T./The Extra-Terrestrial/ © 1982 Universal City Studios, Inc. All rights reserved./*A trademark of and licensed by Universal City Studios, Inc." Near the bottom appears the brown "aafes" logo and, in very small brown print, the words "Army & Air Force Exchange Service." Appealing glasses with nice design and color. Value: $3–$5.

To the spaceship (boy carrying E.T. in bicycle basket) **[AA1]**

"I'll be right here" (E.T. and boy on bicycle in sky with moon in background) **[AA2]**

"Be good" (girl with E.T. dressed up as little girl) **[AA3]**

"E.T. Phone Home" (boy and E.T. in woods, phonograph) **[AA4]**

Mt. St. Helens Volcano (1980). A 5$\frac{9}{16}$" glass commemorating the May 18, 1980, eruption of Mt. St. Helens. On the front of the glass the mountain is shown in blue, white, and black with a black cloud above it. Beneath the mountain in large white capitals is the word "VOL-CANO," followed by "Mt. St. Helens/ 18 May 1980/Washington." On the reverse in white, this description of the eruption appears: "Mt. St. Helens, dormant for 123 years,/returned to life the morning of May 18, 1980./The explosion, 'heard round the/world', blew 2,000 feet off the top of the/mountain sending steam and ash more/than 60,000 feet into the atmosphere." Beneath this there is a list of subsequent 1980 eruption dates followed by a question mark. Finally, near the bottom of the glass, there is a shield-shaped AAFES logo with "Army & Air Force/Exchange Service" across its middle. [AA5] Value: $3–$5.

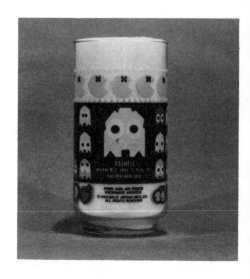

Pac-Man (1980). A set of four 5⅝" glasses spotlighting the four "ghosts" that Pac-Man is so intent on devouring. These colorful glasses have a black wraparound center panel which is full of small red, yellow, pink, and blue ghosts. On one section of the panel, one of the four ghosts appears by himself in an enlarged version. Below him is his nickname and a reference to his personality. Directly below this information in black are the words: "Army And Air Force/ Exchange Service/© 1980 Bally Midway Mfg. Co./All Rights Reserved." This AAFES information appears as a break

in the glass's bottom border which consists of the Pac-Man game's fruit motifs. The top border consists of the standard yellow and red Pac-Man name and six yellow Pac-Man figures. Rings of small white squares encircle the glass and serve to define the border. Definitely cheery barometers of the early eighties, and difficult to find. Value: $4–$6.

Bashful—Nicknamed "Inky," is real shy and may run away. [AA6]
Pokey—Nicknamed "Clyde," slow but tries his best. [AA7]
Speedy—Nicknamed "Pinky," is pink and he's fast. [AA8]
Shadow—Nicknamed "Blinky," is always close behind. [AA9]

American Greetings

Holly Hobbie

Christmas. This 5¾″ Christmas glass flares outward at the top and bottom, and it has a thick base. In the center there are a little girl and a smaller brother or sister, a cat, and Santa Claus with a backpack full of toys. The split caption in red reads: "Love is the magic/of Christmas." Below and to the left of the front design there are the words: "© American Greetings Corp." and under Santa's feet there are these words: "Holly Hobbie ®." There is no date. **[AG1]** Value: $2–$4.

Series Tumblers. Not exactly a "set" so much as a continuing issue of glasses by American Greetings Corporation which features the almost too adorable, bonneted (and therefore faceless), busy little girl, Holly Hobbie. On these 5½″ to 5⁹⁄₁₆″ glasses, Holly is depicted either in a pose or engaged in an outdoor activity, and brown-lettered joyful affirmations of life or optimistic injunctions to enjoy life appear above Holly's head, below her, or in some cases the caption begins above and continues onto the bottom. In small brown letters near the bottom of each glass appear the words : "© American Greetings Corp." followed by a date, and at the bottom, off to the right appears the "Holly Hobbie" registration symbol. The colors on these glasses are usually soft blue, pink, yellow, green, and white. People either adore or detest Holly, but collectors do collect these glasses! One thing you can be sure of: just when you think you have them all, another one will turn up! Value: pre-1976 glasses, $3–$5; post-1976, $2–

$4; canisters, $4–$5.

"The time to be happy is now" (caption below; Holly in pink swinging; 1967) **[AG2]**

"Life's a picnic . . . enjoy it" (split caption; Holly in yellow climbing over fence with picnic basket; 1969) **[AG3]**

"Start each day/in a happy way" (split caption; Holly in patchwork dress holding flowers; 1972) **[AG4]**

Simple pleasures are life's finest treasures (4¾" canister; beige lace design with brown lettering; one side has saying, the other a picture of Holly with parasol; dated 1976). This is the largest of three lidded canisters in the set. **[AG7]**

Life is filled with/sweet surprises (split caption; Holly in pink dress gathering flowers in apron; 1977) **[AG8]**

The world is full of happy surprises (caption above; Holly and friend with geese; 1978) **[AG9]**

Special friends give the heart a lift (caption above; Holly and friend with a yellow balloon; 1978) **[AG10]**

Fun is doubled when you share it (caption above; Holly being pulled in red wagon by little boy; 1978) **[AG11]**

The smile of a friend is as warm as the sun. (caption above; Holly in yellow with basket of flowers, white picket fence; MCMXXX. This glass is different from all of the above. It is slightly flared at the top, the front design continues around both sides to the back, the name "Holly Hobbie" appears in large brown letters on the bottom front, the American Greetings information is on the reverse, and the date [1980] is in Roman numerals.) **[AG12]**

SPECIAL ENTRY: Anonymous Holly Hobbie. "Love is the nicest gift of all" (a $5\frac{5}{8}$" glass which to all appearances looks like a normal Holly Hobbie glass, but instead of an American Greetings rights statement, we have only "© WWA. Inc." on the lower left bottom of the glass. The name "Holly Hobbie" appears beside Holly's feet without a registration symbol. But the most obvious difference of all is that Holly is facing us, and we can see her face and yellow hair! In addition, she is wearing a hat, and not a bonnet. Our conclusion is that this glass definitely predates American Greetings' ownership of Holly

18 American Greetings

Hobbie rights. (caption below; Holly in green dress with apron, holding flowers, flowers in hat; no date). **[AG25]** Value: $2–$4.

Strawberry Shortcake

It's The Berries! (1980). A 5⅞″ barrel-shaped glass featuring two Strawberry Shortcake girls working in their strawberry garden and harvesting huge strawberries. In the background are cute little details like a large house shaped like a strawberry and a pink puppy hiding behind a bushel basket containing two enormous strawberries. Beneath the main design are the words: "It's the berries!" and "© American Greetings Corp. MCMLXXX." **[AG38]** Value: $1–$3.

Mug (1980). 4½″ white milk glass cup in pink, green, and white with the name "Strawberry/Shortcake" in pink and just to the right of that a freckled Strawberry Shortcake doll-like character sitting on a large pink strawberry. Seven additional background strawberries adorn this cup. Near the bottom under the main strawberry are the words: "© American Greetings Corp. MCMLXXX." **[AG35]** Value: $1–$2.

Strawberry Shortcake (1980). A tiny 3⅞″ barrel-shaped glass featuring little Miss Strawberry Shortcake carrying a very large strawberry and a watering can on the front and an actual strawberry shortcake in a dish on the reverse. Below the front design are the words: "© American Greetings Corp. MCMLXXX." The words "Strawberry Shortcake" appear in red, arched over the front and reverse scenes. All of this is in the standard Strawberry shortcake colors: pink, red, white, and green. **[AG36]** Value: $1–$2.

"There's more/where this came from!" glass (1980). A 5⅛″ slightly barrel-shaped glass featuring the Strawberry Shortcake doll carrying a large strawberry in her basket. There is a pink cat-doll tugging at her apron strings and above the cat in pink the words that give this glass its name: "There's more/where this came from!" Near the bottom appear these words: "© American Greetings Corp. MCMLXXX." Colors: red, pink, green, and white. **[AG37]** Value: $1–$2. *(See also Coca-Cola)*

Annie Green Springs

Wine Cooler Glasses. $5\frac{9}{16}''$ pedestal-base glasses which promote the flavored wine coolers of Mt. Valley Wine Company of San Francisco. Each glass has two identical panels which resemble the product's label. The background panels are beige and feature the brand name "Annie/Green/Springs" in large colored letters followed by the name of the drink's flavor, and finally by the words "Serve Cold." "Mt. Valley Wine Co. San Francisco, Calif." appears at the bottom of each panel in small print. Presumably there are as many glasses in the set as there are Annie Green Springs Cooler flavors. Value: $1–$3.

Annie Green Springs Berry Frost (blue lettering) **[AS1]**

Annie Green Springs Country Cherry Brand (red lettering) **[AS2]**

Arby's

Characters, Personalities and Themes

Actors Collector Series (1979). This set of six smoke-colored glasses commemorates some of the film industry's most famous and lovable actors, actresses, partnerships, and groups in both silent and "talkie" films during the golden age of cinema. On the back of each glass is the name of the actor(s), the title and date of the movie, the series number (e.g., "Take: 1 of 6") and the words "Arby's Collector's Series," followed by the date, 1979. Value: $2–$4.

Charlie Chaplin, Take: 1 of 6, "The Gold Rush," 1925 **[AR1]**

Abbot and Costello, Take: 2 of 6, "In the Foreign Legion," 1949 [AR2]
Laurel and Hardy, Take: 3 of 6, "Wrong Again," 1929 [AR3]
Mae West, Take: 4 of 6, "I'm No Angel," 1933 [AR4]

Little Rascals, Take: 5 of 6, "Little Rascals," 1920's [AR5]
W. C. Fields, Take: 6 of 6, "My Little Chickadee," 1940 [AR6]

B.C. Ice Age Collector Series (1981).

Issued in 1981, this set of six 5¼" glasses features the B.C. characters of cartoonist Johnny Hart in characteristic poses or humorous activities. These tankard shaped glasses have an unusual rippled effect, in keeping with the "age" these glasses pretend to depict. The characters are not named on the glasses; familiarity with the comic strip is assumed. Several smaller versions of these glasses exist, but while the characters are the same, there are design differences and no lettering to identify them as Arby's (see also "Johnny Hart"). On the reverse of the Arby's glasses are the words: "Arby's B.C. Ice Age Collector Series, Field Enterprises. Inc. 1981." (The names that we assign the characters are taken from Arby's promotional material.) Value: $3–$5.

Anteater (Zot-Yikes) [AR10]
BC [AR11]
Fat Broad (Woman with Snake on Club) [AR12]
Grog (Man Pouring Liquid into Ear from Shell) [AR13]
Thor (Man Riding Wheel) [AR14]
Wiley (Man Leaning on Club, Ball Coming) [AR15]

Bicentennial Collector Series [1976].

This set of ten glasses was issued early in 1976, and it features P.A.T. Ward, Harvey Cartoon, Leonardo TTV, and Walter Lantz cartoon characters humorously involved in famous historical events of the American Revolution. Each glass comes in two sizes, an 11-ounce 5⅛" glass and a 16-ounce 6¼" glass, for a total of twenty different glasses. These glasses, which also appear without the Arby's logo and with variations in color, are difficult to find, and a complete set in excellent condition would therefore be an unusual discovery. Value: $4–$6. *Note:* Numbering for 11-oz. glasses is in brackets; numbers of 16-oz. glasses in parentheses.

Bullwinkle To The Defense **[AR20] (AR30)**
General Bullwinkle Crosses The Delaware
  [AR21] (AR31)

Casper And Nightmare's Midnight Ride **[AR22]**
  (AR32)
Dudley Takes Tea At Sea **[AR23] (AR33)**
George By Woody **[AR24] (AR34)**
Hot Stuff Makes It Hot For The Redcoats
  [AR25] (AR35)
Never Fear—Underdog Is Here **[AR26] (AR36)**
Woody Has Spirit **[AR27] (AR37)**
Rocky In The Dawn's Early Light **[AR28]**
  (AR38)
Underdog Saves The Bell **[AR29] (AR39)**

Looney Tunes Collector Series (1980). A set of six 6″ glasses, each of which features a popular Warner Brothers cartoon character on the front, with its best-known expression in a "balloon." On the back is the name of the character in a rectangular bar and a small star with the character's head inside it. In small print: "Arby's Collector Series™ and © Warner Bros. 1966," with the

exception of Daffy Duck, which has a 1980 date. This 1980 set closely resembles the Pepsi Looney Tunes single-character set of seven issued the same year. Value: $3–$5.

Bugs Bunny (What's Up/Doc?) **[AR50]**
Daffy Duck (You're Disspicable!!) **[AR51]**
Porky Pig (That's All Folks) **[AR52]**
Sylvester (Sufferin'/Succotash!) **[AR53]**
Tweety (I Tawt I Taw A/Puddy Tat!) **[AR54]**
Yosemite Sam (I'll Gets That/Varmint!!!) **[AR55]**

Monopoly Collector Series (1985). A set of four 4¾" glasses, each of which features a quarter of the Monopoly gameboard. On each of these colorful glasses are the words: "Arby's 1985 Collector Series" and centered on the front below each corner the words, "CPG 1935, 1984." Value: $4–$6.

Just Visiting **[AR60]**
Free Parking **[AR61]**
Go to Jail **[AR62]**
Collect $200 **[AR63]**

Pac Man Collector Series [1980–1982]. This 4⅝" glass depicts the popular early 80s video game, which features Pac-Man relentlessly pursuing fleeing "ghosts" through a complex electronic maze. "Arby's Collector Series © 1980 Bally Midway Mfg. Co. All Rights Reserved" appears on the bottom reverse. Distributed in the early 80s to capitalize on the popularity of the game. **[AR 70]** Value: $1–$3.

Thought Factory Collector Series (1982). This 1982 set of four 4¾" glasses features cartoonist Gary Patterson's satiric potshots at skiers, golfers, pool players, and tennis players. The title of each cartoon appears in white on the front of the glass under the cartoon. On the back near the bottom are the words: "Arby's Collectors Series, 1982 Thought Factory." Value: $3–$5.

Luck Out (Tennis) **[AR80]**
Dedication (Golf) **[AR81]**
First Flake (Skiing) **[AR82]**
Pool Shark (Pool) **[AR83]**

The Wizard of Id Collector Series (1983).

A set of six $5\frac{1}{4}''$ tankard-shaped, rippled glasses very similar to the 1981 Ice Age Collector Series. The glasses in this series are intensely rippled, and as a result they are quite fascinating and eye-catching. The character's name appears in black below the character. On the reverse near the bottom in black and red appears specific information about the series: "the [black] WIZARD [red with black outlines] of [black] ID [red with black outlines]/Arby's ® Collector Series/© Field Enterprises, Inc. 1983 [black]." These glasses are infrequently encountered and not well known, probably because they were not very widely distributed. Value: $5–$7.

Wizard **[AR90]**
Bung **[AR91]**
Sir Rodney **[AR92]**
King **[AR93]**
Larsen E. Pettifogger **[AR94]**
Spook **[AR95]**

Zodiak Series (1976).

A set of twelve $6\frac{1}{4}''$ glasses issued in 1976 featuring the twelve astrological signs in various colors. The back of each glass has the inclusive dates of each sign, as well as a brief astrological description and the name of the set's designer, "Beverly." The glasses are dated 1976, preceded by the initials "K. M. A." These glasses tend to be very "regional," and it is therefore difficult to acquire a set of twelve. (A $4\frac{3}{4}''$ non-restaurant version of this set is available also; see "Zodiak.") Value: $3–$5.

Aries (the Ram) **[AR99]**
Aquarius (the Water Bearer) **[AR100]**
Cancer (the Crab) **[AR101]**
Capricorn (the Goat) **[AR102]**
Gemini (the Twins) **[AR103]**
Leo (the Lion) **[AR104]**
Libra (the Balance) **[AR105]**
Pisces (the Fishes) **[AR106]**
Sagittarius (the Archer) **[AR107]**
Scorpio (the Scorpion) **[AR108]**
Taurus (the Bull) **[AR109]**
Virgo (the Virgin) **[AR110]**

Currier and Ives

Currier and Ives Collector's Series (1978). A set of four 4⅝" glasses dated 1978 and featuring famous winter scenes from original Currier and Ives prints. "Currier and Ives" appears in white on the front below each print. On the back, the title of the print appears, and below that: "Arby's Collector's Series 1978" followed by the series number (in this set "1 of 4," etc.) and "Courtesy of the Museum of the City of New York." Value: $2–$4.

The Road in Winter, 1 of 4 **[AR120]**
Winter Pastime, 2 of 4 **[AR121]**
American Farm in Winter, 3 of 4 **[AR122]**
Frozen Up, 4 of 4 **[AR123]**

Currier and Ives Collector's Series. A set of four 4⅝" undated and unnumbered glasses with popular Currier and Ives winter scenes as the subject. The title of each print appears on the front of the glass below the print and above the words "Currier and Ives." On the back of each glass appear the words "Arby's Collector's Series" and below that "Courtesy of the Museum of the City of New York." Probably most attractive of the three Currier and Ives sets because of color combinations and detail. Value: $2–$4.

The Sleigh Race **[AR130]**
American Homestead Winter **[AR131]**
Christmas Snow **[AR132]**
Winter in the Country—Getting Ice **[AR133]**

Currier and Ives Collector Series (1981).
This set of four 4⅝" glasses is dated 1981, but the individual glasses are not numbered. The prints are the same winter scenes that appeared on the earlier 1978 set. "Currier & Ives" appears on the front below each print, and on the back is the title of the print above "Arby's Collector's Series 1981." Value: $2–$4.

The Road in Winter **[AR140]**
Winter Pastime **[AR141]**
American Farm in Winter **[AR142]**
Frozen Up **[AR143]**

Decorated Glassware and Mugs

Christmas Collection (1983–1987).
Each Christmas since 1983 Arby's has issued beautiful Christmas Holly and Berry design tumblers and stemware. All of these glasses have the rippled effect of the Arby's B.C. Ice Age glasses, as well as 22-karat-gold rims. Each glass is labeled, for example, "Arby's [date] Christmas Collection." Value: $2–$3.

1983 5" Tumbler (same shape as Arby's B.C. glasses) **[AR150]**
1984 5" Tumbler (same shape as Arby's B.C. glasses) **[AR151]**
1985 6¾" Stemware **[AR152]**
1986 6¾" Stemware (except for date, same as 1985) **[AR153]**
1987 5¾" Tumbler (slightly flared top) **[AR154]**

Pittsburgh Steelers Mug [1982]. This 5½" handle mug commemorates the Steelers' 50th season. Not dated, but we know that 1933 was the first year of the franchise. The front of the mug says "Steelers 50 Seasons Gold Cup," and the back names the sponsors: "Arby's, Dr Pepper, and WPXI Channel 11." **[AR170]** Value: $2–$4.

Stained Glass Design with Arby's Name [1975–1978]. Comes in two sizes: 5¼" and 6". There is also a matching pitcher which is difficult to obtain. This is an early issue, probably dating from 1975–1978. Value: glasses, $1–$2; pitcher, $5–$7.

Stained Glass, 5¼" **[AR165]**
Stained Glass, 6" **[AR166]**
Pitcher **[AR167]**

Stained Glass Mug. A 3"-high milk glass mug with a stained glass design. "AR-BY'S" appears on each side of the mug in large green letters against a black-and-white leaded glass window background. A lighter green stained glass bar with white flowers appears at the top and bottom of the stained-glass design. Unusual colors for Arby's. The bottom tells us that this mug is heat proof and made by Federal Glass. Date is uncertain. **[AR175]** Value: $1–$3.

Stars and Stripes design [1976]. 6½", red, white, and blue; slightly flared at top. Probably issued during the Bicentennial year. **[AR160]** Value: $2–$4.

Norman Rockwell

Norman Rockwell Summer Scenes (1987). This set of four 6¼″ glasses came out in the summer of 1987 and featured some of Rockwell's most popular summer scenes from *Saturday Evening Post* covers. The artwork reproduced on these glasses is less formal and realistic than the earlier set (see **[AR200–205]**), more folksy and nostalgic. The title of the *SEP* cover appears in black below the print.

On the back in a frame is the title of the print, the date of the *SEP* cover, and a commentary on the print. Rockwell lovers will notice immediately that "No Swimming" is a repeat of #2 in the earlier six-piece set. Value: $1–$3.

Gramps at the Plate (1916) **[AR180]**
No Swimming (1921) **[AR181]**
Sunset (1926) **[AR182]**
Gone Fishing (1930) **[AR183]**

Norman Rockwell Winter Scenes (1979). Issued in 1979, a set of four 4″ glasses with Pepsi logos featuring Norman Rockwell's charming vision of children enjoying winter activities. Each glass is numbered and contains on the reverse the title of the print, the date it appeared (in parentheses below), the series number (e.g., "One of Four"),

and the words "Arby's Collector Series," below which are the words "Art from the Archives of Brown & Bigelow, 1979." Made by Libbey Glass Co. Value: $3–$5.

A Boy Meets His Dog, One of Four (1959) **[AR190]**
Downhill Daring, Two of Four (1949) **[AR191]**
Chilling Chore, Three of Four (1963) **[AR192]**
Snow Sculpturing, Four of Four (1952) **[AR193]**

Saturday Evening Post/Norman Rockwell Collector Series. This set of six 6⅛" undated, sequentially numbered glasses features six of Rockwell's most beloved *Saturday Evening Post* covers. The artwork on these glasses is realistic and nicely detailed. These glasses are hard to find in mint condition since the white background color is easily scratched. On the back in white lettering are the title of the cover print, its date, an interesting commentary, the words "Arby's Collector's Series," and the number of each glass (e.g., "One of Six").

Probably issued in the early 1980s. On the "leapfrog" glass there is a variation of the color of the boy's shirt and vest. On some of the glasses the shirt and vest are red, and on others, they are yellow. Red is the most common. Value: $2–$4.

Knuckles Down, One of Six **[AR200]**
No Swimming, Two of Six **[AR201]**
Catching the Big One, Three of Six **[AR202]**
The Champ, Four of Six **[AR203]**
The Spooners, Five of Six **[AR204]**
Leapfrog, Six of Six **[AR205]**

A&W Family Restaurant

A&W Bear. An orange, brown, and white 5¾" glass with the A&W "Family Restaurant" logo on one side and the well-known A&W bear on the other. The bear has his back turned to the viewer, and he is looking over his shoulder with his arms stretched out, in effect holding up the glass and its contents. No date. **[AW1]** Value: $1–$3.

The Great Root Bear Series. A set consisting of a pitcher and tumblers, probably issued in the mid seventies, featuring the A&W "Root" Bear in the traditional A&W orange and brown colors. The pitcher is 8" high at the spout, and the A&W "Root Bear" design is the same on both sides. Under the spout about half-way down the pitcher are the white words: "The Great/Root Bear," and below that, near the bottom of the pitcher, is the orange, brown, and white A&W logo. The 6¼" glass is similarly designed: the "Root Bear" in orange and brown on each side and "The Great/Root Bear" in white below the design. Between the panels near the bottom is the orange, brown, and white A&W logo. This pitcher and glass set is uncommon and is probably a very regional issue. Values: **[AW2]** glasses, $5–$7; **[AW3]** pitcher, $10–$12.

Mugs. From the very beginning, A&W has been synonymous with mugs, and over the years there have been quite a few of them. (In the early days, the mugs weren't for sale, and they weren't given away: one had to appropriate them!) We list a few of the many that are now available at flea markets and salvage shops.

$3\frac{3}{16}''$ *Baby Handle Mug.* This early mug, which was used for complimentary servings of A&W Root Beer for children, holds about 3 fluid ounces. The logo is orange, and the letters in "A & W/Root Beer," as well as the traditional arrow, are clear. When the glass is filled with root beer, the letters and arrow are brown, thus completing the traditionally colored A&W logo. **[AW20]** Value: $3–$5.

$3\frac{1}{16}''$ *Baby Handle Mug.* This little Anchor Hocking mug has the traditional A&W logo in red against a clear background. It says "A & W/Ice Cold/Root Beer." More recent than the preceding mug. **[AW21]** Value: $2–$4.

$3\frac{3}{16}''$ *Baby Handle Mug.* This mug bears A&W's most recent logo, a map of the United States with the A&W initials in an oval in the middle of the map. The colors are orange, brown, and white. **[AW22]** Value: $1–$3.

Bally

Ceramic Pac-Man Mug. A $3\frac{1}{2}''$ white ceramic mug showing Pac-Man chasing the four ghosts. The design is by "Houze" whose name appears inside the light blue game maze lines. "© Midway" and "TM of Midway Mfg. Co." appear in the lower left corner of the maze. Colors are dark red, yellow, blue, pink, and black. On the bottom of the mug, "Grindley England" is embossed. **[BA1]** Value: $2–$4.

Ms. Pac-Man (1981). A 6" glass, slightly flared at the top and featuring Ms. Pac-Man being pursued by Mr. Pac-Man on the front panel. On the reverse, the game maze appears in light blue. On the front,

Ms. Pac-Man is depicted wearing high heels, and she has a bow on her head. Appearing vertically, just to the right of the front panel, are the words: "© 1981 Bally Mfg. Co. All Rights Reserved." The colors on this glass are light blue, yellow, orange, and red-orange. There is also a 3⅜" version of this glass. 6 " glass [BA5]; 3⅜" glass [BA6] Value: $2–$4.

Pac-Man Mug. A 5½" glass mug with a wraparound game maze design in light blue, red, orange, pink, yellow, orange-brown, and black colors. The "Pac-Man" logo appears in yellow at 45 degrees across the panels on each side of the mug, and frenzied ghosts are hurrying out of harm's way. In the corner of the left panel appear these small words in blue: "© Midway" and "TM Of Midway Mfg. Co." Near the top of this same panel, the name "Houze" is present. Presumably this is the artist's name. There is no date. [BA10] Value: $2–$4.

Pac-Man (1982). Bally's popular video game characters are captured on three similarly designed glasses. Below the front design on each glass appear the words: "© 1982 Bally Midway Mfg. Co./ All Rights Reserved." Colors are black, yellow, red, and orange.

3⅜" slightly flared tumbler with game maze on reverse. Pac-Man chasing four ghosts. [BA15] Value: $2–$4.

6" glass, Pac-Man chasing two ghosts while carrying one and eating another, "Pac-Man" banner outlined in red, game maze on reverse. [BA16] Value: $1–$3.

5½" mug, same central character design as the 6" glass, but banner is not outlined in red, and instead of the maze, the front design is repeated on the back. [BA17] Value: $1–$3.

Baseball

Baltimore Orioles [1984]. A set of six 6" slightly flared glasses in orange, black, and white featuring Baltimore Orioles players. On the front of each glass, the player is shown with his signature below him in black. Below this is an orange, white, and black band which encircles the glass. In the white band are these words in black: "Make Your Great Comeback in 1985." On the reverse, the player's number appears in large orange, black-outlined letters, followed by the player's name in black, and then by a brief paragraph summarizing the player's 1984 baseball accomplishments. Below this, the name "Baltimore Orioles" appears in orange. Then the series number appears in black (e.g., "Four In A Series Of Six"), and finally there is a Major League Baseball Players logo which interrupts the orange, white, and black bands. The players' likenesses are very good on these glasses, and the colors are attention getting. Value: $4–$6.

#8 Cal Ripken, Jr., One In A Series Of Six **[BB1]**
#24 Rick Dempsey, Two In A Series Of Six **[BB2]**
#33 Eddie Murray, Three In A Series Of Six **[BB3]**
#34 Storm Davis, Four In A Series Of Six **[BB4]**
$19 Fred Lynn, Five In A Series Of Six **[BB5]**
#52 Mike Boddicker, Six In A Series Of Six **[BB6]**

Johnny Bench's Home Plate Restaurant. A $3\frac{3}{16}$" bowl-shaped glass with "johnny bench's Home Plate" in white on a black home plate; a red, white, and black cartoon of Bench waiting for the ball and defending home plate against a sliding player; and, on the third section of this glass, Johnny Bench's signature in red. That's it. Every baseball collector should have one. **[BB9]** Value: $2–$4.

Joe DiMaggio's. A simply designed $3\frac{7}{8}''$ water glass made by Libbey, depicting a baseball player at bat. "Joe Di-Maggio's" appears in script to the batter's left on a 45-degree angle, and "San Francisco" appears in print near his feet to his right. Blue is the sole color on this restaurant glass. There is no date. **[BB10]** Value: $1–$3.

Major League Baseball Players Association. $6\frac{1}{4}''$ glasses featuring major league baseball players on the front. Beneath each player appears his name, position, team, a notable career fact, signature, and at the bottom of the glass the words: "© Major League Baseball Players Assn." To his right is the MLB logo in black, and on the reverse appears a black-bordered, frosted box of his statistics in black print. Yellow stars with blue lines above and below encircle the top of the glass. Unknown number of glasses in series. Value: $5–$7.

George Brett [1977] **[BB15]**

Pittsburgh Pirates

"Just Between Friends" Pirates/KDKA Glass Mug. A $5\frac{1}{2}''$ glass mug in yellow and black showing the old Pirates logo with "Pittsburgh Pirates" directly below it in black. On the reverse in black on a yellow panel are the words "just between friends." "KDKA Radio 1020 Group W" appears near the bottom in black on a yellow background. An uncommon mug, probably dating from the early seventies. **[BB25]** Value: $4–$6.

Ralph Kiner. A $5\frac{1}{16}$" round-bottom glass featuring Pirate star Ralph Kiner in red in the batting position against the white background of Forbes Field. Kiner's signature appears in red below his left arm, and this is the only writing on the glass with the exception of the "P" on his cap. This glass could go back to 1953 when Kiner left the Pirates, or it could be a slightly later glass which looks back to Kiner's Pittsburgh playing days. This glass may be part of a larger set. **[BB30]** Value: $3–$5.

Pirates. A $6\frac{1}{2}$" pedestal-base glass with a black and gold Pittsburgh Pirates logo on the front. On the reverse in black and gold are a baseball with a star on it, and beneath that the words "JOIN THE/FAMILY 2/KDKA-TV." **[BB35]** Value: $1–$3.

Pirates '75. An orange and black $6\frac{1}{2}$" glass celebrating the Pittsburgh Pirates and sponsored by KDKA-TV2. Front and back of glass are identical: a large " '75" in black and gold with a Pirate in the center of the "5." Gold "KDKA-TV2"

borders encircle both top and bottom of glass. **[BB40]** Value: $3–$5.

Pirates " '76". A red, white, and blue $6\frac{1}{4}$" glass sponsored by KDKA-TV2 to honor the Pittsburgh Pirates during the Bicentennial year. Identical design on both sides: a red, white, and blue baseball with stars and stripes on it. Above the baseball in red are the words: "Pirates '76," and, at the bottom, alternating red and blue "KDKA-TV2" logos encircle the glass. **[BB41]** Value: $3–$5.

Pirates 81. A 6⅜" pedestal glass with small black and gold panels on each side. On one side there is an "old" rectangular Pirate logo and on the other a TV screen image of a Pirate batter with "Pirates 81" above it and "KDKA-TV2" below it. **[BB46]** Value: $3–$5.

Pittsburgh Pirates. A 5 9/16" thick-bottomed glass made by Continental Can Company. On the front is the Pirate logo in gold and black with the words "Pittsburgh/Pirates" below it in black. On the reverse there is a 2" black square with a large gold "P" in it. At the top and bottom on the front and reverse there are gold bars with black outlining. **[BB50]** Value: $2–$4.

"We're The Champs" Mug. A 5½" mug featuring the front page of the *Pittsburgh Post-Gazette* for October 18, 1961, and the headlines: "We're The Champs/ Blass, Clemente Stop Orioles, 2–1." **[BB55]** Value: $2–$4.

World Champs 1960—Pittsburgh Pirates. A 5" glass from the 1960 Championship year of the Pittsburgh Pirates. The front of the glass is yellow and black with the words "WORLD CHAMPS/ 1960/PITTSBURGH PIRATES." A Pirate with crossed bats highlights the center of the glass. The reverse reads "BEAT 'EM BUCS" across the top in black letters. A yellow scorecard gives information on the home and visiting teams, the score, and the winning pitcher. The reverse is completed with two cartoon baseball players pitching and hitting along with the words "Pittsburgh all the way" in black. **[BB60]** Value: $6–$8.

World Champions 1979. A 4⅛" highball glass in black, white, and gold celebrating the 1979 World Series champions. One quarter of the glass features a black and gold Pirates logo with

"World/Champions" above it in black and "1979" below it in black. The other three-forths of the glass contains a facsimile page from *The Pittsburgh Press* for Thursday, October 18, 1979. Above the newspaper's masthead are seven Pirates fan cartoons with the scores of each of the seven games. In large black print on the bottom half of the glass are the headlines: "Willie, 'Family'/Win It All." To the right of these headlines are a picture of the team celebrating and the beginning of the lead article by Dan Donovan, *Press* Sports Writer. **[BB70]** Value: $3–$5.

Batman

Batman Glass. This is a processed food glass in blue and gray dating from the mid to late sixties. Batman is pictured on the front in a pugilistic pose, and above his head is the word "ZOK!" To his right is the word "CRAACK," and below him is the word "WHACK!" Beneath his feet in blue are the words: "© National Periodical Publications, Inc." On the reverse of this glass near the top "BATMAN" appears in large gray letters against a blue "bat" background figure. Beneath this in a blue-lined frame are the words: "With Robin The Boy Wonder." There is no date and no printed information regarding a specific food product. Robin The Boy Wonder is a companion glass. Value: $6–$8.

Batman **[BT1]**
Robin the Boy Wonder **[BT2]**

Batman Mug. A $3\frac{3}{8}''$ white milk-glass mug with blue designs which are almost identical to the Batman glass above. On the front of the mug, Batman is doing his "Zot! Whack! and Craack" routine. The reverse, too, is like the glass, except the words "© National Periodical Publications, Inc." appear below the "Batman/With Robin The Boy Wonder" panel. There is no date. There is also a companion Robin mug. Value: $4–$6. (*See also Pepsi*)

Batman [**BT10**]
Robin [**BT11**]

Battlestar Galactica

Battlestar Galactica (1979). A set of four $5\frac{15}{16}''$ glasses featuring the main characters from the popular but short-lived television series. The name "Battlestar Galactica" appears at the top of each glass in red letters, and the character appears on the front with selected programmatic details. On the reverse appears the glass's title and a brief explanation of the character's role in the series. Each of these character summaries is in a different color. Beneath this account appear the following words in black: "© 1979 Universal City Studios, Inc. All Rights Reserved/* a trademark of and licensed by Universal City Studios, Inc." Desirable glasses and therefore a difficult set to complete. Value: $4–$6.

Apollo (white lettering on reverse) [**BG1**]
Cylon Warriors (blue lettering on reverse) [**BG2**]
Starbuck (pink lettering on reverse) [**BG3**]
Commander Adama (red lettering on reverse) [**BG4**]

Bicentennial Glasses

Bicentennial Celebration: 1776–1976.
A 5½″ glass in yellow, red and brown with Paul Revere on his midnight ride on the right side of the glass and the Old North Church on the left. The words "BICENTENNIAL CELEBRATION/1776–1976" are in brown letters across the bottom. **[BI1]** Value: $2–$4.

Declaration of Independence. 3¼″ red and blue with 1776–1976, Liberty Bell, eagle and flag, and banner with the following words: "Bicentennial Observance of Signing the Declaration of Independence." This glass has a thick rim and may have been a food container. **[BI2]** Value: $1–$3.

3½″ brown and beige with gold rim. This glass has a wraparound parchment design with the Liberty Bell and the dates 1776–1976 on the front, and a generous portion of the top of the Declaration of Independence on the reverse. **[BI3]** Value: $2–$4.

5¼″ red, white, and blue "Happy Birthday America!". This glass features crossed American flags of 1776 an 1976 along with those dates, and the words "Happy Birthday America!" between red and blue bars. On the reverse there is a black line drawing of the Capitol in Washington. **[BI4]** Value: $2–$4.

5⅝″ historical/patriotic scenes. This Libbey glass features a number of Revolutionary War motifs and events: Minuteman, forging of the Liberty Bell, Paul Revere's ride, Washington crossing the Delaware, and Lexington/Concord. Colors: blue, black, gold, red, frost. **[BI5]**Value: $2–$4.

$6\frac{1}{8}''$ *Tankard.* The design on this tankard is quite simple: an etched Liberty Bell with the dates 1776 and 1976 on either side of it. **[BI6]** Value: $3–$5.

Big Boy

Big Boy 50th Anniversary. A heavy $6\frac{1}{4}''$ glass in red, white, black, and gold celebrating Big Boy's 50th anniversary. Similar diamond designs on both sides, but one is dated 1936 and shows a chubby "Big Boy," while the other is dated 1986 and shows a slim, running "Big Boy." The words: "Where America's/Been Getting Together for 50 Years" appear on the top sides of both diamonds, and the name "BIG BOY" appears in a banner on the bottom of each diamond. "50th Anniversary" in gold letters appears at the right center of the diamond. **[BY1]** Value: $1–$3.

Shoney's Big Boy Restaurant. A $3\frac{3}{4}''$ water glass with red words and designs. "Shoney's" is positioned just above "Big Boy/Restaurant," and to the right of both is the "Big Boy" in his traditonal checkered overalls carrying a hamburger on a platter. In all likelihood this is an early pre-independent Big Boy glass. **[BY5]** Value: $3–$5.

James Bond

007 Collector Series. A series of attractive 4″ glasses focusing on the James Bond films. Each colorful glass features an important film scene with smaller motifs and details in the background. A blue band with black-lined borders encircles each glass, and on the reverse the title of the film appears in large black letters within this band. In white in the center of the reverse side is a brief summary of the film's story line and information about the main characters. Below in white are the words: "Roger Moore Is James Bond 007/007/Collector/Series/[date] Danjaq S.A." Lively, interesting glasses with exceptional detail. Difficult to find. Unknown number of glasses in set. Value: $4–$6.

The Spy Who Loved Me (James Bond and Major Asamova, aquacar, aquasled, submarine), 1977 **[BD1]**

For Your Eyes Only (Bond skiing, sniper, motorcyclists, helicopter), 1981 **[BD2]**

Moonraker (Bond in spacesuit, Holly Goodhead, shuttle, space station), 1979 **[BD3]**

A View To A Kill **[BD4]**

Burger Chef

Bicentennial Presidents and Patriots Collector's Series (1975). The earliest known dated issues from this hamburger chain. Each 5¼" glass has a president's or patriot's likeness on the front with a brief biographical sketch below it. On the reverse in a frame topped by an eagle there is a humorous exchange between Burger Chef and Jeff, which makes reference to the president or patriot. The words "© 1975 Burger Chef Systems, Inc." appear below. These glasses are, appropriately, red, white, and blue, and all of them are difficult to find. Value: $6–$8.

Benjamin Franklin **[BC1]**
Thomas Jefferson **[BC2]**
John F. Kennedy **[BC3]**
Abraham Lincoln **[BC4]**
Paul Revere **[BC5]**
George Washington **[BC6]**

"Breakfast at Burger Chef" Milk Glass Mug. This 3½" red and white coffee cup has on it the words "Breakfast at Burger Chef" and "It's a Good Morning Feeling" with a Burger Chef logo between the two phrases. These cups are infrequently encountered and may be an earlier issue than any of the glasses. **[BC10]** Value: $2–$4.

Burger Chef & Jeff (1975). A 5 9/16" glass featuring Burger Chef's characters, Burger Chef and Jeff, standing beside each other in blue aprons with white polka dots. The names "Burger Chef" and "Jeff" appear in red on their chefs' caps, and their names appear again below each character's feet in black. The design is the same on both sides of the glass. Between the two panels near the bottom of the glass, these words appear in black: "Burger Chef Is A Trademark/ Of Burger Chef Systems, Inc./ Copyright © 1975 Burger Chef Systems, Inc./ Printed In USA." **[BC12]** Value: $3–$5.

Endangered Species Collector's Series (1978). This much-sought-after set of four 5⅝" glasses is not only beautiful, but it deserves our respect because it is probably the first example of fast-food glasses used to educate the public and to focus attention on an environmental issue of great importance. The front of each glass features the animal, and the reverse has at the top the words "Endangered Species, 1978 Collector's Series" followed by both the Latin and common names of the animal, a paragraph of information on the animal from the World Wildlife Fund, and the Burger Chef logo at the very bottom. The Giant Panda and Bald Eagle are more difficult to find than the Tiger and Orang-Utan. Values: Panda and Eagle, $7–$9; Tiger and Orang-Utan, $5–$7.

Tiger (Panthera tigris) **[BC15]**
Orang-Utan (Pongo Pygmaeus) **[BC16]**
Bald Eagle (Haliaeetus leucocephalus) **[BC17]**
Giant Panda (Ailuropoda melanoleuca) **[BC18]**

National Football League (NFL) Collector Glasses (1979). These smoke-colored and relatively plain 5⅝" glasses feature a football helmet in profile with a NFL team's name or logo within it and the team's name below it. On the reverse is a NFL shield logo and, at the bottom of the glass, the words "Burger Chef Collector Glasses 1979." Like all Burger Chef collectibles, not easy to find. Number of glasses in set not known at this time. Value: $2–$4.

Cincinnati Bengals **[BC25]**
New York Giants **[BC26]**
Pittsburgh Steelers **[BC27]**
Green Bay Packers **[BC28]**
Cleveland Browns **[BC29]**
Washington Redskins **[BC30]**
Philadelphia Eagles **[BC31]**
Seattle Seahawks **[BC32]**

Burger King

Pedestal Glasses

"Burger King, where kids are king" **[1975–1976].** This is a 5½" glass with the Burger King picture between the two [above] phrases. On the back beneath the Burger King logo are the words, "Home of the Whopper." Colors: red, orange, black, and white. **[BK1]** Value: $3–$5.

"1776–1976 Have It Your Way Collector's Series" (1976). A set of four 5½" glasses identical in shape to the

"Home of the Whopper" glass above, the fronts of these glasses boldly feature the bicentennial dates, beneath which are represented well-known symbols of the American Revolution. The "Three Patriots" glass listed below, for instance, is inspired by Archibald Willard's well-known 1870s painting "The Spirit of '76." The backs of these glasses are the same, but the words "Have It Your Way Collector's Series" vary in color. These are fairly difficult glasses to find. Value: $4–$6.

Liberty Bell (red lettering) **[BK5]**
Three Patriots Playing Drums and Fife (orange lettering) **[BK6]**
Eagle and Shield (black lettering) **[BK7]**
Crossed Flags (blue lettering) **[BK8]**

Promotional Characters

Broadmoor Glass Mug (1977). This rather dainty 2⅞" clear glass mug was given to Burger King employees who attended the 1977 Burger King convention at the famous Broadmoor in Colorado Springs. Etched near the top is the Burger King logo, and beneath it are the words "The Broadmoor/October, 1977." On the bottom are the words: "Garrick Glass" and "Made In France." **[BK15]** Value: $5–$7.

"The Marvelous Magical Burger King" (1978). This series of glasses promotes the individual food products of Burger King. They are not frequently encountered and may be earlier editions of the better known 1979 Collectors' Series. We believe there are four in the set, and the ones we know about are as follows.

Milkshakes. A 6¼" red, white, and yellow glass which features the Burger King conjuring up a batch of milkshakes (same design on front and back). On a red panel at the bottom of the glass are these verses: "I've got the magic/That it takes/To put the shiver/In the shakes." At the extreme bottom of the glass are the words "© 1978 Burger King Corporation." **[BK20]** Value: $5–$7.

French Fries. A 6¼" blue, red, gold, and white glass which features the Burger King making French fries. At the top of the glass in white are the words: "The Marvelous Magical/Burger King." Below this the Burger King is spinning French fries and making them stand on end. On the blue panel which encircles the bottom of the glass are these verses in gold: "It isn't luck/It isn't chance/Magic makes my/French Fries dance." The same design appears on both sides.

In small brown letters at the bottom of the glass are the words: "© 1978 Burger King Corporation." **[BK21]** Value: $5–$7.

Hamburgers. "See these burgers?/Watch them spin!/My magic fun/will make you grin" (gold panel, red lettering) **[BK22]** Value: $5–$7.

Onion Rings. "I'll turn onions/into rings/Then make a chain/do magic things." Green panel at bottom. **[BK23]**

1979 Burger King Corporation Collectors' Series. This set of five 6" round-bottom glasses introduces Burger King's answer to McDonald's promotional characters. Each glass features a character in a sequence of three actions and clever Burger King product-related rhymes. The words "© 1979 Burger King Corporation Collectors' Series Made in U. S. A." appear between two of the panels. The appeal of these characters was relatively brief, but the glasses are becoming difficult to find and quite desirable. Value: $4–$6.

Marvelous Magical Burger King **[BK30]**
Burger Thing **[BK31]**
Duke of Doubt **[BK32]**
Wizard of Fries **[BK33]**
Sir Shake-A-Lot **[BK34]**

Special Regional Promotions

Mark Twain Country Series (1985). A set of four 5" glasses commemorating Mark Twain and the novels he wrote in Elmira, New York. Each glass has a colorful scene on the front, and they originally came in a cardboard Burger King carrying case with "Mark Twain Festival Summer 1985" printed in black. On the reverse of each glass is a brief explanation of the front illustration (see below), and near the bottom of each glass in black are the words, "'Mark Twain Country,' Series 1985." A black Burger King logo appears below that caption. The glasses are not numbered, so we describe them and picture them in the positions they occupied in the carrying case. This Libbey set was definitely a special limited regional promotion, and these glasses are not well known, though they certainly deserve to be. Value: $8–$10.

Mark Twain. A well-known likeness of Mark Twain appears in white, flesh, and black, and to either side of him is a green wreath with a bow at the bottom. Near the bottom there are two boys with fishing poles looking up at Twain. There are a river boat and river in the background. Below this scene in black are these words: "Horseheads, N. Y. Home of ZIM." This is probably a reference to the artist who designed this set. On the reverse in black these words appear: "Mark Twain celebrates his/150th birthday November/30, 1985. Twain wrote his/famous classics in El-mira,/New York, and is buried in/that city as well." **[BK35]**

Tom Sawyer. A barefoot boy with straw hat and fishing pole is depicted sitting on a riverbank. Colors are blue, green, flesh, brown, and black. The reverse reads as follows: "Tom Sawyer is another of/the many beloved charac-/ters who sprang from/Mark Twain's mind while/spending peaceful, crea-/tive summers in Elmira,/New York." **[BK36]**

Huck Finn. On this glass Huck Finn is depicted displaying a rabbit which he has shot with his rifle, which he holds with his left hand.

Colors are brown, black, green, and yellow. On the reverse are these words: "The American Edition of/Adventures of Huckleber-/ry Finn was first published/in 1885, one hundred years/ago. Huck Finn was/created by Mark Twain in/his Elmira, New York/ study." **[BK37]**

Octagonal Study. Twain's study is depicted in brown in the center of this glass, and there are green trees in the background. On the reverse are these words: "Mark Twain's fa-mous/classics like Adventures of/Huckleberry Finn and/Tom Sawyer, were written/in this octagonal study in/Elmira, New York." **[BK38]**

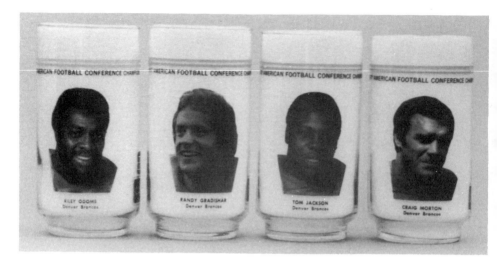

Sports

American Football Conference Champions (1977). This is a Burger King/Dr Pepper set featuring individual players from the Denver Broncos. These glasses have double orange bands around the top and a black and white photograph of each player, along with the Dr Pepper, Burger King, and National Football League Players logos. Exact number of glasses in this set is unknown at this time. Value: $3–$5.

Riley Odoms **[BK40]**
Randy Gradeshar **[BK41]**
Tom Jackson **[BK42]**
Craig Morton **[BK43]**
Lyle Alzado **[BK44]**
Haven Moses **[BK45]**

Detroit Tigers '88 (May, 1988). A set of four 6" round-bottom glasses featuring the Tiger mascot in four action scenes promoting the 1988 Detroit Tigers baseball team. The Tiger mascot scenes are in orange, dark blue, orange-yellow, and white. "Tigers '88" appears on the front of three glasses, and "Tigers 1988" appears on the other. On the reverse near the bottom of the glass is a bright red and orange-yellow Burger King logo. Value: $2–$4.

Tiger Catching Fly Ball **[BK80]**
Tiger At Bat **[BK81]**
Tiger Holding Scoreboard **[BK82]**
Tiger Waving Pennant In Stadium **[BK83]**

Dr Pepper/Dallas Cowboys [1977]. This issue of 5⅝" glasses commemorates the Dallas Cowboys. Blue and grey bands and stars encircle the top of each glass, and single players are spotlighted. There is a single action scene next to which appears the MSA copyright. Total number of glasses in this set is unknown at this time. These are probably 1977 glasses, since 1977 was the first year Donovan started for Dallas and the last year Herrera played for them. Value: $3–$5.

Bob Breunig **[BK50]**
Billy Joe DuPree **[BK51]**
Harvey Martin **[BK52]**
Efren Herrera **[BK53]**
Drew Pearson **[BK54]**
Pat Donovan **[BK55]**
Randy White **[BK56]**
Cliff Harris **[BK57]**
Robert Newhouse **[BK58]**
Golden Richards **[BK59]**
D.D. Lewis **[BK60]**
Charlie Waters **[BK61]**

Dr Pepper/Dallas Cowboys. A 6¼" NFL Players glass with the same logos and colors of the smaller set above. On this glass there are additional action scenes which occupy more space than they do on the smaller version. Date is uncertain, as is number of glasses in set. Value: $4–$6.

Roger Staubach **[BK65]**

Star Wars Trilogy

The Empire Strikes Back Collector Series (1980). A set of four $5\frac{7}{8}$" round-bottom glasses similar in shape to the Star Wars set below, but slightly heavier in construction. Characters from the film appear on the front, and a synopsis of film action relating to each appears on the back. There is a Coca-Cola logo and the words "Collector Series™ © Lucasfilm Ltd. (LFL) 1980 Made in U. S. A." on the reverse. There seems to be a plentiful supply of these glasses. Value: $2–$4.

Lando Calrissian **[BK94]**
Luke Skywalker **[BK95]**
Darth Vader **[BK96]**
R2-D2/C-3PO **[BK97]**

Return of the Jedi (1983). Having run its course, the *Star Wars* film series terminates with this film. Again, there are four 5⅝″ glasses similar in design to their predecessors: nicely depicted characters, a brief review of the relevant action, Coca-Cola logo, and the words "™ & © Lucasfilm LTD. (LFL) 1983 All Rights Reserved The Coca-Cola Company Authorized User." These rather fragile glasses are at this time readily available. Value: $2–$4.

Intergalactic Gangster Jabba the Hutt **[BK98]**
At the Ewok Village **[BK99]**
In the Emperor's Throne Room **[BK100]**
In the Tatooine Desert **[BK101]**

Star Wars (1977). A Coca-Cola/Burger King set of four 5⅝″ glasses which feature the main characters from the popular 1977 film in appealing colors. A brief summary of each character's history and role in the film appears in a rocket-shaped frame, beneath which are the words "© 1977 Twentieth Century-Fox Film Corporation, Limited Edition." These glasses are fragile, and the colors seem especially vulnerable to fading; add to this their relative scarcity, and you have an extremely desirable and quickly appreciating set. Value: $5–$7.

Darth Vader **[BK90]**
Luke Skywalker **[BK91]**
Chewbacca **[BK92]**
R2-D2/C-3PO **[BK93]**

Burgermaster

Burgermaster Glass. A 5⅝″ glass promoting Burgermaster Restaurants. The name "BURGERMASTER" appears in red letters at a 45-degree angle above a crude straight-line drawing of a long-horned steer in brown on both sides of the glass. Encircling the glass at the bottom is a brown stone wall. That's it. No date. Burgermaster is a West Coast hamburger outfit. **[BG1]** Value: $1–$2.

Cabbage Patch Kids

Cabbage Patch Kids (1984). A 5¼″ slightly flared glass featuring the famous Cabbage Patch Dolls in action. The name "Cabbage Patch Kids" appears in black over a boy kid who is standing on his head. To the right of him we have a girl "kid" roller skating and under her the words "© 1984 O.A.A.Inc." To her right, we have a girl kid jumping rope. Colors: red, yellow, black, and flesh. There is also a matching pitcher which completes the set. Value: glasses **[CP1]**, $1–$2; pitcher **[CP2]**, $3–$5.

Campbell's

Campbell's Soups Salute America Mug (1976). A 3½" white ceramic mug with colorful depictions of a young boy and girl posing as Uncle Sam and the Statue of Liberty. Opposite the handle inside a ring of blue stars are these words in red: "Campbell's/Soups/Salute/ America." "Made in Brazil" appears on the bottom. **[CA1]** Value: $3–$5.

Campbell's Tomato Soup. A 4" red, white and gold glass with identical markings to a Tomato Soup can, complete with recipes and instructions on the reverse. **[CA5]** Value: $3–$5.

Al Capp

1949 4¾" Set. Early set of eight glasses featuring Al Capp's Dogpatch characters in one color pictures and line drawings."© UFS/1949" appears at bottom of each glass to the right of the character's name. Available, but not plentiful. Value: $6–$8.

Lil Abner (red) **[AC1]**
Daisy Mae (pink) **[AC2]**
Lonesome Polecat (blue) **[AC3]**
Mammy Yokum **[AC4]**
Marryin' Sam/Sadie Hawkins (turquoise) **[AC5]**
Pappy Yokum (green) **[AC6]**
Shmoos (orange) **[AC7]**
Unwashable Jones **[AC8]**

1949 5¼" Set. The same set as above, but in a slightly larger size. Value: $7–$9.

Lil Abner **[AC9]**
Daisy Mae **[AC10]**
Lonesome Polecat **[AC11]**

Mammy Yokum **[AC12]**
Marryin' Sam/Sadie Hawkins **[AC13]**
Pappy Yokum **[AC14]**
Shmoos **[AC15]**
Unwashable Jones **[AC16]**

1975 6¼" Set. A set of six Al Capp glasses with a slightly different lineup of characters. Value: $6–$8.

Lil Abner **[AC20]**
Daisy Mae **[AC21]**
Joe Btsptflk **[AC22]**
Mammy Yokum **[AC23]**
Pappy Yokum **[AC24]**
Sadie Hawkins **[AC25]**

Care Bears

Care Bears (1986). A set of four 5¹⁄₁₆" glasses featuring the Care Bears. On the front of each glass is a pastel-colored bear in a joyful pose. Each bear's stomach has on it an illustration which is indicative of the bear's name, which appears in white nearby. On the reverse in white, there is a phrase or sentence which reflects the particular bear's personality. Each glass is liberally sprinkled with red hearts and yellow stars. On the reverse, near the bottom, in white are the words: "© 1986 Those Char-

acters From Cleveland, Inc." These bears are very similar to the American Greetings/Pizza Hut issue (*see Pizza Hut*). There is also a small 2" set of these glasses **[CB5–8]**. Value: $1–$3.

Bedtime Bear (blue, with half moon and star on stomach)/Dreaming up fun! **[CB1]**
Cheer Bear (pink, with red, pink, and yellow rainbow on stomach)/Have a rainbow day! **[CB2]**
Good Luck Bear (green, with shamrock on stomach)/Good luck is everywhere! **[CB3]**
Share Bear (purple, with ice-cream soda with two straws on stomach)/Happiness is for sharing **[CB4]**

The Centsible Place

Love is . . . (1975). A set of six 5⅞" round-bottom glasses featuring cute little bare-bottomed children in various situations which give rise to philosophical pronouncements on what love is. Each side of the glass is different. At the top there is a red and blue band containing the words "The [red] Centsible [blue] Place [red] love is . . . [blue]." In the center of each panel are small male and female creatures doing things which illustrate the definitions appearing in blue at the bottom of the glass. Appearing vertically on one side of the glass between the panels in pink are the number of the glass and the words: "Copyright Los Angeles Times 1975." These glasses look good on the same shelf with Hallmark Shirt Tales and Charmers, Strawberry Shortcake, Holly Hobbie, Cabbage Patch Kids, Peanuts, etc. These glasses closely resemble the Pizza Hut "Love Is . . ." set and, for that matter, all other "Love Is . . ." glasses. The titles in this set are the same as the plain (unsponsored) "Love Is . . ." set. (See under Pizza Hut, Love is . . .) Value: $2–$4.

#1 . . . whatever you make it.
    . . . sharing even the hard times. **[CP1]**
#2 . . . an autumn walk through the woods.
    . . . tickling his nose with a long piece of grass. **[CP2]**
#3 . . . telling her she's as lovely as the day you were married.
    . . . making marriage last 75 years. **[CP3]**
#4 . . . that first kiss in the morning.
    . . . watching the sun sink into the sea. **[CP4]**
#5 . . . telling him how much his golf game has improved.
    . . . listening again how he made the hole in one. **[CP5]**
#6 . . . telling him his paint job is marvelous when it isn't.
    . . . holding the ladder while he paints the ceiling. **[CP6]**

Christmas

The Twelve Days of Christmas. A set of twelve glasses available in three different sizes and shapes: a 6¼" tapered Brockway-style glass; a 5½" not-quite-so-tapered version; and a 5" round-bottom glass. The designs and colors are the same on all three sets, but the 5" set seems to have several serious correspondence problems (see below). The main motif common to all the glasses is the "Twelve Days of Christmas" song. On the front of each glass is a scene corresponding to the appropriate verse in the song. The colorful depictions appear in potted trees with a banner near the bottom proclaiming the day. On the

reverse, centered within a three-piece holly frame, are the actual words of the song for the particular day. There is no date, and except for the $6\frac{1}{4}''$ and $5\frac{7}{8}''$ Pepsi sponsored sets, no maker or sponsor. These are beautifully designed glasses that could actually be used during the Christmas holidays without embarrassment. The smaller glasses seem to be harder to find than the larger. Value: $6\frac{1}{4}''$, $1–$3; $5\frac{1}{2}''$, $2–$4; 5", $2–$4.

$6\frac{1}{4}''$ and $5\frac{1}{2}''$ sets

1st Day (A Partridge In A Pear Tree) **[CH1]**
2nd Day (Two Turtle Doves) **[CH2]**
3rd Day (Three French Hens) **[CH3]**
4th Day (Four Colly Birds) **[CH4]**
5th Day (Five Gold Rings) **[CH5]**
6th Day (Six Geese A-Laying) **[CH6]**
7th Day (Seven Swans A-Swimming) **[CH7]**
8th Day (Eight Maids A-Milking) **[CH8]**
9th Day (Nine Drummers Drumming) **[CH9]**
10th Day (Ten Pipers Piping) **[CH10]**

11th Day (Eleven Ladies Dancing) **[CH11]**
12th Day (Twelve Lords A-Leaping) **[CH12]**

5" set. A comparison of the 5" set with the $6\frac{1}{4}''$ and $5\frac{1}{2}''$ sets results in some disturbing and confusing discrepancies. 5" glasses #9, #10, and #12 have been confused with the same numbers in the $6\frac{1}{4}''$ set—unless, that is, there are several different sets of lyrics for the song.

1st Day **[CH15]**
2nd Day **[CH16]**
3rd Day **[CH17]**
4th Day **[CH18]**
5th Day **[CH19]**
6th Day **[CH20]**
7th Day **[CH21]**
8th Day **[CH22]**
9th Day **[CH23]**
10th Day (Ten Lords A-Leaping) Should be Ten Pipers Piping **[CH24]**
11th Day **[CH25]**
12th Day (Twelve Drummers Drumming) Should be Twelve Lords A Leaping **[CH26]**

Coca-Cola

Bicentennial Issues

Heritage Collector Series From The Coca-Cola Company [1976].

A set of four 6⅛" glasses issued for the Bicentennial and celebrating Revolutionary War heroes. Each glass has a wraparound scene on a parchment design, a likeness of the hero with a famous quotation, a brief historical account, and the words "Heritage Collector Series from the Coca-Cola Company." Value: $2–$4.

Patrick Henry, "Give Me Liberty or Give Me Death" (1775) **[CC170]**

Paul Revere, "The Regulars are Out" (1775) **[CC171]**

George Washington, "Times that Try Men's Souls" ("Words by Thomas Paine of Army's Winter Hardships and Crossing of Delaware River, 1776") **[CC172]**

John Paul Jones, "I Have Not Yet Begun to Fight" (1779) **[CC173]**

Heritage Collector Series from the Coca-Cola Company [1976].

This single-issue glass in blue and green has wraparound patriotic scenes, including Archibald Willard's "Spirit of '76" (see

also Burger King's "Have It Your Way" Collector's Series) and Revolutionary War motifs with the date 1776 in blue 4" numerals also wrapped around the glass. There are three variations: a 5" size and a 5⅝" size with the words "Heritage Collector Series from The Coca-Cola Company," and a 5⅝" glass with the words "and Herfy's Restaurants" following the Coca-Cola logo. Value: 5" **[CC180]** and 5⅝" **[CC181]** without Herfy's logo, $2–$4; 5⅝" **[CC182]** with Herfy's logo, $4–$6.

Heritage Collector Series from the Coca-Cola Company (1976). This set of sixteen colorful 6" glasses depicting America's history was issued in conjunction with the National Flag Foundation in Pittsburgh, Pennsylvania, made by Anchor Hocking, and distributed by Herfy's Restaurants in Washington, Oregon, and northern California in 1975 and 1976. According to the "Premium/Incentive Business" bulletin for November, 1975, the promotion began in May, 1975, at 73 Herfy's outlets. Initially, eight glasses were available over an eight-week period, but the 671,000 glass supply was exhausted after only six weeks. "To encourage consumers to complete the set, a matching pitcher was liquidated at 99 cents," and 22,300 pitchers were sold. Each glass features an historic flag and complementary scene on the front, with a detailed historical account of this flag and related events on the back, along with the words "Heritage Collector Series From The Coca-Cola Company." The copyright dates of the flags also appear on the back of each glass; they appear in pairs and range from 1968 to 1976. An additional eight glasses were issued in the fall of 1976 to bring the total to 16. The flag paintings on these round-bottom glasses were done by Don Hewitt under a commission from The National Flag Foundation, and the designs are the same as those that appear on the National Flag Foundation set of eighteen glasses. This beautiful set is somewhat difficult to complete, and the pitcher is downright tough to find. (See also National Flag Foundation.) Value: glasses, $4–$6; pitcher **[CC190]**, $15–$20.

Alamo **[CC191]**
Bennington **[CC192]**
Bunker Hill **[CC193]**
California Bear Flag **[CC194]**
Commodore Perry **[CC195]**
Cowpens **[CC196]**
First Stars and Stripes **[CC197]**
General Fremont **[CC198]**
Grand Union **[CC199]**
Green Mountains **[CC200]**
Iwo Jima **[CC201]**
Promontory Point **[CC202]**
Rattlesnake **[CC203]**
Star Spangled Banner **[CC204]**
Taunton **[CC205]**
Washington's Cruisers **[CC206]**

Spirit of 1776 Series [1976]. A set of four $5\frac{9}{16}''$ glasses with a wooden tavern sign format featuring scenes and personalities from the Revolutionary War. The colors are brown, black, gold, and cream. Each glass is divided into three panels, and Archibald Willard's "Spirit of '76" occupies one panel on each glass. Near the bottom of the glass, "Heritage Collector Series From The Coca-Cola Company" appears in cream-colored letters. There is no date. These glasses are much more difficult to find than the taller Coke Heritage Series above. Value: $4–$6.

Betsy Ross & Old Glory/Washington Crossing the Delaware **[CC210]**
Paul Revere/Writing The Declaration of Independence **[CC211]**
The Minutemen **[CC212]**
Nathan Hale **[CC213]**

Characters and Personalities

America on Parade [1976]. A single-issue $6\frac{1}{8}''$ glass featuring Mickey Mouse, Goofy, and Donald Duck in a cartoon parody of Archibald Willard's famous painting "The Spirit of '76," which also appears on the single-issue Coca-Cola/Herfy's 1976 Heritage Collector Series glass above. Below the three Disney characters are the words "America on Parade" in a banner. Centered on the reverse are the words "Limited Edition Bicentennial Series," a red Coca-Cola logo, and the words "it's the real thing." **[CC220]** Value: $3–$5.

Buck Rogers (1979). A set of four glasses featuring Buck Rogers series characters. These are seldom-seen glasses. Value: $8–$10.

Buck Rogers **[CC225]**
Draco **[CC226]**
Twiki **[CC227]**
Wilma Deering **[CC228]**

Disneyland Limited Edition. A set of six rather delicate 5⅛" glasses featuring Disney characters at Disneyland. Each character appears in his/her traditional colors in a familiar pose in the center of the glass next to a white Disneyland logo. Each character's name appears in black below the character followed by the words "at/Disneyland." "© Walt Disney Productions" appears in small black print below that. On the reverse of each glass, "Limited Edition" ap-

pears in white lettering above a red "Enjoy Coca-Cola" wave logo, and "it's the/real thing" appears in white below the logo. There is no date. This is a colorful, desirable set which is difficult to complete and is also available in a Disney World version. Value: $8–$10.

Donald Duck **[CC229]**
Dumbo **[CC230]**
Goofy **[CC231]**
Mickey Mouse **[CC232]**
Minnie Mouse **[CC233]**
Pluto **[CC234]**

King Kong (1976). A set of four 5⅝" glasses commemorating highlights in the 1976 film revival of *King Kong*. Distributed by Burger Chef in the east, there is also a Cinema Classics variation with film frames encircling the top of the

glasses (see *King Kong Limited Edition*, below). King Kong appears on the front in an action scene, and a brief explanation appears on the reverse inside a frame of broken chains which also contains the boxed Coca-Cola logo. Below this are the words "© 1976 Dino De Laurentiis Corporation Limited Edition." Value: $3–$5.

Skull Island **[CC235]**
Giant Serpent **[CC236]**
New York Subway **[CC237]**
Twin Trade Towers **[CC238]**

King Kong Limited Edition (1977). A 5⅝″ glass promoting the Dino De Laurentiis King Kong film. On the front of this glass, there is a yellow and black outlined oval featuring King Kong breaking his chains and bars. The name "King Kong" appears in red letters at the bottom of the oval. On the reverse, within a broken net and chain frame, there is "King Kong" in red, followed by two paragraphs which explain the cinematic action. Because this glass is not well known, we quote this information in its entirety: "As master of Skull Island the/intrepid King Kong reigned supreme./Only his desire for Dwan, the blond/sacrifice, and the combined might/ of civilization could defeat this/giant of the motion picture screen./Forty-three years after the/original release, the 'new' King Kong/reaffirms his role as one of the 'big-/gest' stars in film fantasy." Below this text is a square red "Enjoy Coca-Cola" logo, and at the bottom of the glass in small gray print are the words

"Limited Edition." Below King Kong's foot on the front are the small gray words: "© 1977 Dino De Laurentiis/Corporation." Near the bottom and to the left of the red King Kong name are the small gray letters: "© D.D.L.C." Perhaps the most unusual feature of this glass is the gray and black film strip which encircles its top. On the reverse, just above the red King Kong name, "Cinema Classics" appears in black on the film strip. This glass is therefore probably part of a "Cinema Classics" set, and these glasses are not frequently encountered. **[CC250]** Value: $5–$7.

Kollect-A-Set Series (1975). A set of six 5⅞″ glasses featuring the well-known Popeye characters. Identical images on front and back, with the name of the

character in black below the character. A square Coca-Cola logo in a box appears on one side, and "© King Features Syndicate, Inc. 1975" appears on the other. This is an attractive set and a popular favorite with collectors. Value: $4–$6.

Popeye **[CC260]**
Olive Oyl **[CC261]**
Brutus **[CC262]**
Swee' Pea **[CC263]**
Rough House **[CC264]**
Wimpy **[CC265]**

Mickey's Christmas Carol (1982). A set of three 6⅛" glasses, slightly flared at the top, featuring Disney characters acting parts in Charles Dickens' *A Christmas Carol.* The Disney characters appear on the front of each glass beneath the arched words "Mickey's Christmas Carol," and "© 1982 Walt Disney Productions" appears below the character. On the reverse, the title of each glass and the words "The Coca-Cola Company" appear inside an oval Christmas wreath. Value: $5–$7.

Scrooge McDuck As Ebenezer Scrooge **[CC280]**
Goofy As Marley's Ghost **[CC281]**
Mickey Mouse And Nephew Morty As Bob Cratchit And Tiny Tim **[CC282]**

Pittsburgh Pirates (1988). A set of four 6" glasses featuring a total of eight Pittsburgh Pirate baseball players. *See also Elby's.*

Star Trek "The Motion Picture" [1980]. A set of three 5⅝" glasses featuring the classic *Star Trek* characters in the popular motion picture. The front panels feature the subjects beneath "Star Trek The Motion Picture" in red letters. On the back of each glass appear the title of the glass, a brief account of the film story, and the words "The Coca-Cola Company © PPC." A difficult set to complete. Value: $8–$10.

Captain James T. Kirk, Mr. Spock, Dr. "Bones" McCoy **[CC290]**
USS Enterprise **[CC291]**
Commander Decker **[CC292]**

Star Wars (1977). A set of four 5⅝" glasses identical to the Burger King/Coca-Cola set, with the exception of having only the Coca-Cola logo in the center of the reverse. This set is more unusual than its Burger King conterpart. (*See Burger King* for full listing). Value: $7–$9.

Darth Vader **[CC294]**
Luke Skywalker **[CC295]**
Chewbacca **[CC296]**
R2-D2/C-3PO **[CC297]**

Urchins (1976–1978). A set of six 5¾" glasses highlighting the recreational pastimes of American Greetings' "Urchins," freckled, precocious creatures who are probably Holly Hobbie's first cousins. Each glass has a three-colored border with flowers at the top, and the colors vary from glass to glass. Next, in the front center of each glass we have the Urchins preoccupied with idyllic play and an optimistic injunction or Urchin-style truism beneath. On the reverse, below the floral border, appears in brown the name "Urchins," followed by "© American Greetings Corp. 1976 [four glasses] or 1978 [two glasses]." Below this is the square white "Enjoy Coca-Cola" logo and "Limited Edition." On

either side of the Coke logo there are brightly colored flowers, and on the right a small bird flutters. These glasses are not particularly abundant and, if you collect Coca-Cola, you simply have to have them. Value: $5–$7.

"Serve up sunshine with a smile" (Urchin playing tennis/orange caption/1976) **[CC300]**
"Good friends score a perfect hit!" (Urchins playing baseball/red caption/1976) **[CC301]**
"Friends make life more fun" (Urchins roller-skating/yellow caption/1976) **[CC302]**
"Good fun is par for the course" (Urchins playing golf/blue caption/1976) **[CC303]**
"A little fun goes a long, long way." (Urchin riding bicycle/purple caption/1978) **[CC304]**
"Life is fun . . . plunge right in!" (Urchin preparing to dive into pool/white caption/1978) **[CC305]**

Co-Sponsored Glasses

Arctic Circle. A 5½″ stained glass and filigree design in black, white, and plum. The front says "Enjoy Coca-Cola" and the reverse says "At Your/Arctic Circle." **[CC325]** Value: $3–$5.

Bacardi Rum Pitcher. A 9¼″ pitcher in red and white. "Enjoy Bacardi rum & Coca-Cola" appears on one side, and "Enjoy Bacardi and Coke" appears on the other. Vertically, just to the right of the "Enjoy Bacardi rum" side, are the small red words: "Bacardi Imports, Inc., Miami, Fla. Rum 80 Proof." **[CC330]** Value: $8–$10.

Casa Olé Mexican Restaurant. A colorful 6″ tumbler with cactus motif and the words "10th Anniversary Casa Olé" on one panel and "Decimo Anniversario Casa Olé" on the other. "Enjoy Coca-Cola" appears between two cacti toward the bottom. **[CC335]** Value: $1–$3.

Clancy's (1976). 5½" stained glass and filigree design in blue, black, and white with the words "Clancy's 1776–1976" on the front and "Enjoy Coca-Cola" on the back. **[CC340]** Value: $1–$3.

Collegiate Crest Collection From The Coca-Cola Company. 6⅛" glasses with college logos in black enclosed within a black circle, name of university below; on the reverse, the university's nickname and the words "Collegiate Crest Collection From The Coca-Cola Company." Total number of glasses in set is unknown at this time. Value: $3–$5.

Wake Forest University (Winston-Salem, NC) **[CC345]**
Concordia College (River Forest, IL) **[CC346]**
University of Wisconsin—Milwaukee **[CC347]**
University of Wisconsin—Oshkosh **[CC348]**

Dag's 30th Anniversary (1985). A 6¼" handled fountain glass with "Enjoy Coca-Cola" in white on one side and "Dag's/ 30th Anniversary/1955–1985" on the other. The Dag's design is oval in shape, with tiny white light bulbs forming the oval, and all the lettering is red except for "Anniversary," which is white. This glass has a small Libbey's symbol on the bottom, as well as the word "Canada." **[CC390]** Value: $1–$3.

Godfather's Pizza Carafe. This 8⅝" carafe contains two red and black floral filigree-bordered panels, each of which has a leaded glass center window. One panel features the Godfather's Pizza logo in black and white, and the other features a black and white "Enjoy Coca-Cola" logo. The overall design motif is the same as that which appears on Shakey's/Coca-Cola glass **(CC440)**, the Coca-Cola flare **(CC570)**, and Coca-Cola pitcher **(CC571)**. **[CC395]**, Value: $1–$3.

Hardee's. Essentially the same glass as Clancy's (above) but with plum, black, and white as the colors. "Hardee's" appears on one panel and "Enjoy Coca-Cola" on the other. **[CC400]** Value: $1–$3.

Kroger (1983). Classic 5½" flared shape with brown and beige colors, poster of young lady in oval sipping Coke on front. On the reverse is a Kroger grocery wagon drawn by two mules, a grocery-man, and below this the words "1883–1983 Kroger 100th Anniversary Limited Edition from Kroger and The Coca-Cola Company." **[CC420]** Value: $2–$4.

McCrory Stores, Inc. Christmas Glasses. These cheerful Christmas glasses were available in larger McCrory stores with cafeterias. Value: $3–$5.

Santa, sleigh loaded with presents, same scene front and back, Coca-Cola logo, "McCrory Stores, Inc." (no date) **[CC430]**

Santa in sleigh drawn by reindeer over house, full moon and comet, "Enjoy Coca-Cola Trademark," "McCrory Stores, Inc." (no date) **[CC431]**

Santa waving in sleigh drawn by reindeer, Rudolph on ground looking up, "Enjoy Coca-Cola Trademark," "McCrory Stores, Inc. 1983." **[CC432]**

Santa with bag of presents, elves, and tree, "Season's Greetings" in large red letters over tree, "Enjoy Coca-Cola" logo, "McCrory Stores 1882–1982 100th Anniversary." **[CC433]**

Jack in the Box Hamburgers. 5½" stained glass and filigree design in blue, black, and white with "Jack in the Box Hamburgers" on the front and "Enjoy Coca-Cola" on the back. This particular glass also comes with yellow, green, or red as the predominant color, so these glasses can be considered a set of four. **[CC410]** Value: $2–$4.

Shakey's Pizza. A 6" glass in red, black, and white with delicate filigree and stained glass panels. In a round panel on the front is a Shakey's sign with the words "Shakey's Pizza Parlor World's greatest pizza" and below that in white the words "Refill me free." On the back in an identical circular panel is the familiar "Enjoy Coca-Cola" trademark. **[CC440]** Value: $1–$3.

Whataburger. A 6¼" classic fountain glass design with a handle on the side. This unusual glass has a rich aqua color

and looks as much like a mug as it does a glass. On one side in white are the "Enjoy Coca-Cola" logo with the word "COWBOY" below it, and on the other, also in white, the "Enjoy Coke" trademark with the word "WHATABUR-GER" below it. **[CC450]** Value: $1–$3. (See also Whataburger)

Whataburger Poinsettia Christmas Glass. A 6" glass in red, green, white, and black which flares outward at the top and features two poinsettias on a leaded window grid. At the top of the leaded window panel there are three bands (red, white, and green) which serve as a border, and at the bottom, two bands (red and white) encircle the glass. On the side opposite the poinsettias, "Enjoy [white]/Coca-Cola [black and white]/Trade-mark®." [white] appears above "Whataburger" [white]. **[CC453]** Value: $2–$4.

Yellow Rose Coca-Cola Classic Flare (1986). A 5½" flare glass in yellow, green, white, and black featuring a wraparound leaded window design with three yellow roses in the middle. On the reverse appears the following: "Enjoy [white]/Coca-Cola [black and white]/Classic [white]." "WHATABURGER" appears in black centered below this logo. **[CC455]** Value: $2–$4.
(*See also Whataburger*)

Events and Places

The Four Seasons. This is a Canadian set featuring the four seasons. It is in demand and not easy to find. Value: $6–$8.

Winter **[CC470]**
Spring **[CC471]**
Summer **[CC472]**
Fall **[CC473]**

Historical Mission Series From The Coca-Cola Company. A set of six 5⅝" glasses commemorating historic Spanish missions in the western United States. The front of each glass features a drawing of the mission on a tattered parchment scroll background, with the name of the mission and its location below. On the reverse is a square parchment frame containing information on the mission, and below that are the words "Historical Mission Series From The Coca-Cola Company." This is a difficult set to complete. Value: $5–$7.

Mission San Juan Bautista [CC460]
Mission Santa Barbara [CC461]
Mission San Carlos Borromeo [CC462]
Mission San Gabriel Arcangel [CC463]
Mission San Antonio de Valero (The Alamo) [CC464]
Mission San Xavier Delbar [CC465]

Knoxville World's Fair (1982). This classic 5½" flare glass was distributed by McDonald's in 1982 to commemorate the World's Fair in Knoxville, Tennessee. Value: $4–$6. (*See also McDonald's* for full listing.)

National Sports Festival (1982). A 5½" red, white and blue flare issued by Coca-Cola and Steak N Shake, commemorating the National Sports Festival. The front pictures the festival logo in red, and in white the words "National Sports Festival/Indianapolis/July 23–31 1982/An activity of the/U.S. Olympic Com-

mittee" in blue. On the reverse in red: "The National Sports Festival is/the highest level of national/competition for an amateur/athlete, established by the United/States Olympic Committee to aid/ in selecting the members of the/Pan American and U.S. Olympic/Teams." Continuing beneath in white lettering, the glass reads "COMMEMORATIVE GLASS LIMITED EDITION/Distributed exclusively by/Coca-Cola/and/Steak N Shake." [CC480] Value: $4–$6.

The Taste of Victory Los Angeles Olympic Tumbler (1981). This rather fragile, simply decorated 5⅜" glass has a red and white band encircling it one inch from the rim. On this band there are 16 squares, each of which contains a symbol representing an Olympic event. Below the band are the words "The Taste of Victory!", a Coca-Cola logo, and an Olympic logo containing the words "© 1980 L. A. OLY. COM." On the reverse below the band appear the words "© 1981 L.A. OLY. COM." [CC490] Value: $3–$5.

Fountain Glasses

Banded (short). A heavy $4\frac{1}{8}''$ glass with red, blue, yellow, and green half-inch bands encircling it, each band being interrupted by the words "Coca-Cola" in the same color as the band. 3" diameter mouth. A modern glass, very colorful. **[CC500]** Value: $2–$3.

Banded (tall). Same colors and design as above glass, but $6\frac{1}{4}''$ tall and narrower ($2\frac{3}{4}''$ mouth). **[CC501]** Value: $2–$3.

Coke Adds Life. A $4\frac{15}{16}''$ glass with a red and green stained glass design. Four panels encircle the upper part of the glass, and identical panels oppose each other. One panel features the modern wave logo "Enjoy Coca-Cola," and the other features "Coke" in black-outlined white letters followed by "adds life to . . . /everything nice." Thin bands of see-through green stained glass sections encircle the glass at the top and bottom of the panels. **[CC510]** Value: $2–$4.

"Drink Coca-Cola" Flare. This small, delicate flare bears the Federal Glass Company's imprint on the bottom, and it holds a scant 6 ounces. The frosted white lettering says "Drink/Coca-Cola," and near the bottom of the glass is a small line or bar which was probably used for measuring the syrup. This is an unusual early glass prized by collectors. **[CC520]** Value: $8–$10.

Drink Coca-Cola Stained Glass Design. This $5\frac{1}{2}''$ tumbler in lime, plum, black, white, and pearl has nearly its entire surface covered with a beautiful stained glass design. The plum-colored band near the top has the small black word "Drink" above the words "Coca-Cola" in white. **[CC530]** Value: $1–$3.

black leaded window background panel; the panel is bordered at top and bottom by green and black bands which encircle the glass. Below the pearl oval band, there is a green and black tulip design band which encircles the glass. **[CC531]** Value: $1–$3.

Drink Coca-Cola Stained Glass Design, Round Bottom. This $5\frac{7}{8}$" round-bottom glass in red, green, white, black, and pearl resembles CC530, but on this glass the band of pearl ovals which encircles the glass is near the bottom. At the top of the glass, "Drink/Coca-Cola" appears in black and white on a red and

Enjoy Coca-Cola Floral Design. A $5\frac{9}{16}$" glass with an overall floral and filigree design in red, orange, white, yellow, and brown. On opposing sides of the glass there are brown filigree ovals with "Enjoy [white]/Coca-Cola [brown and white]/Trade-mark [white]" within them. Below the ovals, large brown-outlined flowers in various intensities of white, yellow, red, and orange comprise the background of the glass. **[CC535]** Value: $2–$4.

"Enjoy Coca-Cola" Goblet. A modern 6" goblet with red lettering as follows: "Enjoy Coca-Cola" in red script on one side, and "Enjoy Coke" in print on the other. **[CC540]** Value: $1–$3. ⌐|

mid-seventies date quite likely. The same design also appears on a $5\frac{7}{8}''$ round-bottom glass. There is also a matching 9" pitcher. Value: $6\frac{1}{8}''$ **[CC550]**, $2–$4; $5\frac{7}{8}''$ **[CC551]**, $2–$4; 9" pitcher **[CC552]**, $5–$7.

"Enjoy Coca-Cola" Stained Glass/Filigree. A $6\frac{1}{8}''$ glass identical in size and shape to "America on Parade" and to the four-glass Coca-Cola "Heritage Collector Series" [1976] glasses. This glass is red, green, black, and white. "Enjoy Coca-Cola" appears in black-outlined white against a red and black stained glass/filigree background. Black-bordered green crossed leaves serve as borders at the top and bottom of the design. The design is the same on both sides. The shape of this glass makes a

Flared Glass Reproduction. The classic shaped $5\frac{1}{2}''$ flare in brown and beige with an old-fashioned picture of a lady in an oval frame sipping a Coke on the front.

On the reverse there is an oval frame containing these words: "A 16 OZ. RE-CREATION OF THE ORIGINAL FLAIR GLASS FEATURING A DESIGN FROM THE TURN OF THE CENTURY . . . " Below the oval appear the words "THE ARCHIVES, The Coca-Cola Company." Note: Students of English will note that "FLAIR" is misspelled. **[CC560]** Value: $1–$3.

Flared Glass Reproduction—Oval Panel. A brown and beige $5\frac{1}{2}''$ flare with an oval Coca-Cola Archives poster on the front. The oval has fancy filigree work around it and shows a lady in a hat holding a glass of Coca-Cola in her right hand and two straws in the other. "Drink/Coca-Cola/Trade-mark ®" appears near her left shoulder. On the reverse, there is an oval with scrollwork at top and bottom. The following information appears in brown letters within this oval: "A/16 OZ./Re-Creation/Of The/Original/Flair Glass/Featuring/A Design/From The/Early Part/Of The/Century . . ./The Archives,/The Coca-Cola Company." This glass is very similar to CC560. They both share the "Flair" misspelling, and they are both "Recreations" from the Coca-Cola Archives. **[CC561]** Value: $1–$3.

Flared Stained Glass Design. The standard flared glass, with stained glass and filigree designs in black, white, and red. "Enjoy Coca-Cola" appears on front and back. There is also a matching $9\frac{3}{4}''$ pitcher. Value: glass **[CC570]**, $1–$3; pitcher **[CC571]**, $4–$6.

Fountain Glass, Classic (red lettering—short). A $4\frac{15}{16}''$ modern fountain glass reproduction with red lettering, "Coca-Cola" in script on one side and "Coke" in print on the other. **[CC575]** Value: $1–$2.

Fountain Glass, Classic (red lettering—tall). A 6½″ modern fountain glass reproduction with red lettering (a larger version of the glass listed directly above), "Coca-Cola" in script on one side and "Coke" in print on the other. **[CC576]** Value: $2–$3.

Fountain Glass, Classic (red lettering—extra tall). A 6¹⁵⁄₁₆″ fountain glass with red lettering, as the two glasses immediately above, but huge in comparison. This glass holds over a quart of your favorite beverage. Modern, interesting, and you don't see too many of them. **[CC577]** Value: $3–$5.

Fountain Glass, Classic (white lettering). Same size and design as above, but clear glass with white logos on opposing sides: "Enjoy Coke" on one side and "Enjoy Coca-Cola" on the other. A modern reproduction available in 6″ **[CC580]** and 5″ **[CC581]** versions. Value: $1–$2.

Fountain Glass—Genuine Coca-Cola Drinkware. A classic 6⅛″ frosted fountain glass with "Coca-Cola" in red encircled by "Genuine Drinkware" in blue. An interesting modern glass. **[CC590]** Value: $2–$3.

Fountain Glass—German. A 5" fountain in white lettering reading "Trink/Coca-Cola/Schutzmarke/Koffeinhatige Limonade." **[CC600]** Value: $3–$5.

Fountain/Handled. This is a 6¼" heavy fountain glass with handle. On one side of the glass is a white "Enjoy Coca-Cola" logo, and on the other is a white "Enjoy Coke" logo. The word "Canada" is embossed on the bottom. This glass closely resembles the "Whataburger" glass **[CC450]**, as well as Dag's **[CC390]**, and the same things can be said about all of them. We wonder who came up with this design idea? **[CC610]** Value: $1–$3.

Fountain Glass—Multiple Language. This 5" fountain glass has the "Enjoy Coca-Cola" trademark in five different languages: English, Japanese, Hebrew, Chinese, and Arabic. The lettering is white. Modern and interesting. **[CC620]** Value: $3–$5.

Fountain Glass—75th Anniversary (1977). This 5" fountain glass was issued to commemorate Coca-Cola's 75th anniversary in 1977. All lettering and designs on the glass are gold. On the front there is the "Enjoy Coca-Cola" trademark, and beneath this is a round anniversary design which contains these words: "1902–75 Years Of Bottled Refreshment—1977/75th Anniversary [large numbers in middle]/Meridian Coca-Cola Bottling Company." On the reverse, "Enjoy Coke" appears in gold letters. This is a very beautiful glass. **[CC630]** Value: $4–$6.

have been a candle glass. Whatever it is, it is unusual. **[CC650]** Value: $2–$4.

Holly and Berry Christmas Glass. A beautiful 6″ Christmas glass in red, green, black, and pearl featuring holly leaves with red berries within a stained glass design. "Enjoy Coca-Cola" appears front and back in pearl within a red and green stained glass band. **[CC640]** Value: $1–$3.

Hurricane Glass. A 6$\frac{9}{16}$″ hurricane-style glass with red, gold, black, and white "Enjoy Coca-Cola" and "Enjoy Coke" trademarks on opposite sides. This may

1913 Calendar Girl Flare. This 5$\frac{1}{2}$″ flare features a lady in a black hat drinking a Coke. On her left shoulder appear the words: "Drink [black]/Coca-Cola [red]/Delicious/And/Refreshing [black]." Below the red-bordered panel are these words in black: "1913 Coca-Cola Calendar Girl." This glass may be part of a set of six. **[CC660]** Value: $3–$5.

Poinsettia Christmas Glass. This beautiful 6″ tumbler has a frosted panel containing small Christmas toys in clear glass running around its middle and identical ovals on front and back with poinsettias in bloom and the "Enjoy Coca-Cola" trademark. **[CC670]** Value: $1–$3.

Red and White Ribbon Glass (small curved base). Almost identical to the glass listed above in design, but this $5\frac{1}{4}$″ glass has a small base, and the word "Enjoy" above "Coke" and "Coca-Cola." In addition, on this glass, the word "Trade-mark" with a small registration symbol appears below the name "Coca-Cola." Like its near kin above, fairly common now, but who knows about the future. **[CC690]** Value: $1–$2.

Red and White Ribbon Glass (straight sides). A heavy $5\frac{1}{2}$″ red and white glass with three vertical logos, two saying "Coca-Cola" and one saying "Coke," separated by three vertical wavy white Coca-Cola ribbons. Fairly recent and plentiful. **[CC680]** Value: $1–$2.

Script Glass. Same size, shape, and colors of the above glass, but this glass is covered with various sized and colored Coca-Cola names. Modern and pleasant to look at. **[CC695]** Value: $2–$3.

Script Straw Holder. A 32-ounce, 7⅝" glass with a white plastic cap, same colors and design as the above glass. Intended as a straw holder to complement the tall script glass (above), this glass and the three above it appear to be members of one set. A welcome, unusual piece. **[CC700]** Value: $3–$4.

Smoke-Glass Flare. This 5½" flare is smoke colored, and it has the "Enjoy Coke" and "Enjoy Coca-Cola" trademarks on opposing sides. This is a heavy glass, and it is quite appealing. **[CC705]** Value: $1–$3.

Stained Glass Design. 5" variations of the Hardee's glass with "Enjoy Coca-Cola" on front and back. **[CC710, CC711]** Value: $1–$3.

Tab. A 7" hourglass-shaped glass promoting one of Coke's early forays into the diet softdrink market. A rather plain glass, but irresistible to the hand. In small white letters the word "Enjoy" appears over the "TAB Trade-Mark" in yellow. Television commercials touted Tab's dietary virtues, and the glass's pinched middle is supposed to suggest a trim waistline. A novel, clever glass. **[CC715]** Value: $2–$3.

32-Ounce Glass. A one-quart capacity glass with two red vertical Coke trademarks and one vertical red "Enjoy Coca-Cola" trademark. A modern glass. **[CC720]** Value: $2–$3.

Tulip Flare. A $5\frac{7}{16}$" red, green, black, and white flared glass with a stained glass window design featuring a red tulip above the "Enjoy Coca-Cola" logo. Same design on both sides. Recent, but beautiful. **[CC725]** Value: $2–$3.

20-Ounce Straight-Sided Glass. This is a large, heavy $6\frac{1}{8}$" straight-sided glass with "Enjoy/Coke" on one side and "Enjoy/Coca-Cola" on the other. Lettering is in white. On the bottom of the glass there is a frosted Anchor Hocking symbol. **[CC730]** Value: $2–$4.

Holly Hobbie

Bouquets of Joy. A set of six Holly Hobbie glasses which have optimistic sayings and upbeat advice. Value: $4–$6.

Make Every Day A Sunshine Bouquet **[CC1]**
Love Makes The World A Beautiful Place **[CC2]**
Happiness Is Just Being Yourself **[CC3]**
Today Can Be The Start Of Something Good **[CC4]**
Life Is Filled With Sweet Surprises **[CC5]**
Let Joy Blossom In Your Heart **[CC6]**

Country Kitchens. A set of six glasses with recipes for healthy attitudes. Value: $4–$6.

Love Is The Little Things You Do **[CC40]**
Life Is Simply Delicious **[CC41]**
Treat Yourself To A Happy Day **[CC42]**
Don't Forget To Add The Love **[CC43]**
Nice Surprises Are The Spice Of Life **[CC44]**
6th glass: **[CC45]**

Happy Talk. A set of six 5⅞" glasses, each featuring Holly and a friend under an arched "Happy Talk" saying. Below and to the left of the Holly Hobbie characters appear the words "© American Greetings Corp." On the reverse are the words "Holly Hobbie Happy Talk" arched over the white boxed "Enjoy Coca-Cola" trademark. "Limited Edition" appears below the Coke logo and is part of a floral band which encircles the bottom of the glass and has brown lines above and below it. In Canada, this set was issued with a Taco Time logo. Value: $2–$4.

Happiness is meant to be shared **[CC50]**
The easiest tasks are those done with love **[CC51]**
Friendship makes the rough road smooth **[CC52]**
The happiest times are those shared with friends **[CC53]**
A good example is the best teacher **[CC54]**
Love is the little things you do **[CC55]**

Holly Hobbie Christmas (1982). A set of three 5¹¹⁄₁₆" glasses. Holly appears engaged in a Christmas activity below an arched caption. Below Holly and to the left are the words "© American Greetings Corp. MCMLXXXII." A plain hollyberry band encircles the bottom of the glass. On the reverse is an arched title in red, above the square red "Enjoy Coca-Cola" logo, and below that are the words "Limited Edition," interrupting the band. These glasses have a square bottom with a button base. Value: $2–$4.

Share in the fun of the season! (front); Holly and Robby Sledding (reverse) **[CC10]**
Wishing you the happiest of holidays! (front); Holly Hobbie Picking Christmas Holly (reverse) **[CC11]**
Holidays are meant to be shared (front); Holly Telling a Story (reverse) **[CC12]**

Holly Hobbie Christmas, Limited Editions. From 1977 to 1980, Holly Hobbie Merry Christmas Limited Edition glasses were issued in sets of four. Each glass in each set was numbered, so these glasses are comparatively easy to identify. Value: $4–$6.

1977: #1 **[CC20]**
    #2 **[CC21]**
    #3 **[CC22]**
    #4 **[CC23]**
1978: #1 **[CC24]**
    #2 **[CC25]**
    #3 **[CC26]**
    #4 **[CC27]**
1979: #1 **[CC28]**
    #2 **[CC29]**
    #3 **[CC30]**
    #4 **[CC31]**
1980: #1 **[CC32]**
    #2 **[CC33]**
    #3 **[CC34]**
    #4 **[CC35]**

Holly Hobbie and Robby Twelve Days of Christmas (1979). A set of four $5\frac{3}{4}''$ glasses in red, green, white, and black, featuring Holly Hobbie and Robby engaged in various holiday activities. Holly and Robby appear on the front center of each glass. Above them in red are these arched words: "The Twelve Days Of Christmas." Below and to the left of Holly, "© American Greetings Corp. 1979" appears in small brown letters. Below Robby, "Holly Hobbie®" ap-

pears in small brown print. On the reverse, "Merry Christmas" appears in red, arched over a red square "Enjoy/Coca-Cola" logo. Directly beneath the logo, "Holly Hobbie And Robby/Limited Edition/1979" appears in white, followed by the series numbers: 1, 2, 3, or 4 of 4. Near the bottom of each glass, there is a line of music in red and green with one forth of the lyrics to the song printed above it in white. Value: $4–$6.

1 Of 4 (Days 1–3) **[CC36]**
2 Of 4 (Days 4–6) **[CC37]**
3 Of 4 (Days 7–9) **[CC38]**
4 Of 4 (Days 10–12) **[CC39]**

Merry Christmas Limited Edition. These $5\frac{5}{8}''$ Christmas glasses feature Holly Hobbie on the front with an arched seasonal saying above her. In small letters below Holly are the words "© American Greetings Corp." After a space and to the right are the words "Holly Hobbie®" In some cases, there is a date after the word "Corp." This date appears in parentheses (below) after the title of such glasses. On the reverse the words "Merry Christmas" appear in an arch above a square red "Enjoy Coca-Cola" logo. Below the logo are the words "Limited Edition" in white. Note: These glasses all share the same 2" base (like the Coke "Kollect-A-Set") and should not be confused with Holly Hobbie glasses that belong to numbered sets or with Holly Hobbie glasses which have a different type of base. A holly and berry design band encircles the bottom of these glasses; however, sometimes there are brown lines above and below the holly-berry band. An asterisk(*) after the title of the glass indicates a plain holly-berry band, and a dagger(†) indicates a brown-bordered band. Value: $2–$4.

Merry Christmas (undated set of three). Holly Hobbie is $2\frac{7}{8}"$ to $3\frac{1}{8}"$ high; each word of caption begins with an upper case letter, [1983].

There's A Special Glow At Christmas* **[CC60]**
Have A Happy Holiday!* **[CC61]**
It's Time For Christmas* **[CC62]**

Merry Christmas (undated set of three). Holly Hobbie is $3\frac{1}{4}$" to $3\frac{3}{8}$" high; words in captions begin with lower case letters except for word "Christmas," [1982].

Christmas is love with all the trimmings† **[CC65]**
Christmas is the nicest time of all† **[CC66]**
Christmas is a gift of joy† **[CC67]**

Merry Christmas (1977). Holly Hobbie and friend in each scene; words in captions begin with lower case letters except for word "Christmas."

Christmas is fun for everyone† **[CC70]**
Christmas is here . . . the nicest time of the year† **[CC71]**
Christmas brings a world of happy things† **[CC72]**

Merry Christmas (1981). A set of four glasses with more cheery descriptions of Christmas. Dates are in Roman numerals. Value: $2–$4.

A Gift Of Love Especially For You **[CC80]**
Dreams Can Come True **[CC81]**
Magic In Your Heart **[CC82]**
Happiest Days **[CC83]**

On Parade. A set of four Holly Hobbie glasses with sayings. Value: $4–$6.

It's Friends That Make This Land So Grand **[CC90]**
It's A Grand Old Day For Being Happy **[CC91]**
Make Every Day A Celebration **[CC92]**
Three Cheers For Friendship **[CC93]**

Simple Pleasures. A set of six $5\frac{7}{8}$" glasses featuring Holly Hobbie and her friend enjoying pleasurable activities. The predominant colors on these glasses are green and blue. The caption is in brown and arched above the glass's central scene. The floral band which encircles the bottom of the glass is blue and green and has brown lines above and below it. The words "© American Greetings Corp." [on some glasses followed by

"1973"] appear below and to the left of the front design, and "Holly Hobbie®" appears below and to the right of the design. On the reverse, "Holly Hobbie Simple Pleasures" appears in brown, arched above the white-boxed "Enjoy Coca-Cola" logo. "Limited Edition" interrupts the band just below the logo. These glasses are difficult to find. Value: $4–$6.

Good friends are like sunshine **[CC100]**
Make every day a picnic **[CC101]**
Fill your day with happiness **[CC102]**
Treat the world with tenderness **[CC103]**
Good times are for sharing **[CC104]**
Simple pleasures are the sweetest **[CC105]**

Norman Rockwell and Haddon Sundblom

Norman Rockwell Saturday Evening Post Santas. A set of three 6" glasses, each featuring a "Reproduction of an Original Painting of Christmas by Norman Rockwell from The Saturday Evening Post." Specific information about each Santa appears in a white holly and berry oval on the reverse, and the copyright date of each Santa appears near the bottom of each glass. Value: $2–$4.

December 4, 1920 (Santa with Ledger) **[CC150]**
December 2, 1922 (Santa and Elves in Workshop) **[CC151]**
December 4, 1926 (Santa Studying Globe) **[CC152]**

Reproductions of Original Paintings by Norman Rockwell. A set of three 5⅝" glasses which feature the companionship of boy and dog in idyllic settings and picture-perfect nostalgia. In an ornate oval on the back of each glass appear these words: "Reproduction of an original painting by Norman Rockwell from the Archives of The Coca-Cola Company." There are two glass styles. Both are the same height, but one has a small 2" diameter base and a 2½" inside mouth diameter; the other is heavier, with a 2½" button base and a 2⅝" inside mouth diameter. The artwork on the larger version is not as clear as that on the smaller version, and there are minor but noticeable differences in color. Value: $2–$4.

Boy with fishing pole, dog, and Coke **[CC155]**
Boy with begging dog, hoe, and Coke **[CC156]**
Boy holding sandwich and Coke, dog watching **[CC157]**

Haddon Sundblom Santas from The Archives of The Coca-Cola Company. These two sets of three glasses each chronicle the artistic achievements of Haddon Sundblom. Depictions of Santa drinking Coke in various contexts appear on the front of each 6" glass; on the reverse, within an oval holly and berry frame, is the specific historical information as well as the old circular Coca-Cola logo. Value: $2–$4.

One of three Series 1 (1961) **[CC130]**
Two of three Series 1 (1960) **[CC131]**
Three of three Series 1 (1947) **[CC132]**
One of three Series II (1943) **[CC133]**
Two of three Series II (1946) **[CC134]**
Three of three Series II (1948) **[CC135]**

Country Time Lemonade

Country Time Lemonade. A $5\frac{15}{16}''$ round-bottom glass with the same Country Time Lemonade design (label) on each side. This pretty glass has a frosted background with a black-outlined yellow border. At the top of the arched panel are the small black words "General Foods." Below that in large letters appears the "Country Time" brand name. In the center of the panel are a whole lemon and a half lemon in yellow, along with green leaves. Below the lemons appear the words "Lemonade/Flavor Drink." There is no other writing or date and this is probably a mail order premium. **[CT1]** Value: $2–$4.

Norman Rockwell. A set of four 5⅞" glasses featuring famous Norman Rockwell *Saturday Evening Post* covers. Each print appears on a white background panel with fancywork corners. On the reverse on an identically sized white panel appears the title of the print, then the words "By Norman Rockwell," then an interesting and fairly lengthy account of the *SEP* cover with quoted reflections from the artist himself. Below this are the words: "As Appeared On The/Saturday Evening Post/[date of issue]/© [year] Curtis Pub. Co." Below that at the bottom of the panel is the "Country Time/[lemon logo]/Lemonade/Flavor Drink" logo. These glasses were probably mail-order premiums, and they are pretty difficult to find. Value: $4–$6.

Low and Outside (SEP, August 5, 1916) **[CT5]**
The Big Moment (SEP, January 25, 1936) **[CT6]**
Grandpa's Girl (SEP, February 3, 1923) **[CT7]**
The Rocking Horse (SEP, September 12, 1933) **[CT8]**

Currier & Ives

Coffee Mugs. A set of four 3½" glass coffee cups with nicely detailed Currier & Ives winter prints on the front, in brown with silver and white, or in black with silver and white. On the reverse in a fancy frame is the title of the print beneath which are the words: "From A Lithographic Print/By Currier & Ives." No date, but the original box the black set came in tells us that these cups were made by Carlton Glass in Mt. Clemens, Michigan, and that they were sold by Sears. The catalog number is on the box: "63469–01/3552/Mugs/1-Set 4 Pak # Currier & Ives." On the bottom of each mug is the name "Luminarc." There is also a coffee pot with the same design. The prints on the black set possess clearer detail than the prints on the brown set. Value: cups, $1–$2; coffee pot **[CI1]**, $3–$5.

(See also Arby's and Kraft)

American Homestead/Winter **[CI5]**
Home To Thanksgiving **[CI6]**
The Old Homestead/In Winter **[CI7]**
Winter In The Country/"The Old Grist Mill" **[CI8]**

Dad's Root Beer

Dad's Black Cow Glass. A 5" red and yellow glass with a slight bulge at the top. On the front in red letters just below the bulge appear these words: "Don't Say Root Beer/Say . . ." followed by a yellow and red Dad's sign/logo with the words "Reg. U. S. Pat. Off." On the reverse are these words: "Have A [yellow]/DAD'S/Black/Cow [red]/ . . . It's Delicious [yellow]." Near the bottom there is a red line which rings the glass, and at two points opposite each other the line is broken by "1 oz.," which appears in yellow. This glass was almost certainly a commercial fountain glass used for the serving of root beer floats or what used to be called "black cows." It probably dates to the early fifties. **[DA1]** Value: $6–$8.

Dairy Queen

Collector Series (1976). A set of three $5\frac{1}{2}$" glasses in red, white, blue and yellow. The front of each glass shows a young cowboy and cowgirl, a horse, and a villain. The reverse displays a large Dairy Queen logo in front of a typical Dairy Queen-style store. **[DQ1]** Value $4–$6.

Houston Oilers (1979). A $5\frac{1}{2}$" glass in "Oiler" blue with red and white accents. The front of the glass shows a large Oiler's helmet with outline lettering reading "HOUSTON OILERS." The reverse reads "Houston Oilers/1959–1979" in blue letters. These words are encircled with a blue wreath and the words "Commemorating 20 years of

sides of glass. The late seventies is a reasonable issue date. **[DQ15]** Value: $1–$3.

Sundae Cup. In shape resembling a flower pot, this $3\frac{3}{16}''$ glass was given to purchasers of Dairy Queen sundaes. On the front center is the Dairy Queen logo in red, and on either side of it there are red daisies in decreasing sizes progressing around toward the rear of the glass. On the base of the glass in red appear these words: "® US PAT OFF. AM. D.Q. Corp. COPYRIGHT 1981 AM. D.Q. CORP." Plastic seems to have replaced this unusual item at Dairy Queen. **[DQ20]** Value: $2–$3.

Professional Football." A red Dairy Queen logo and AFL football logo complete the reverse. **[DQ10]** Value $5–$7.

Little Miss Dairy Queen. A $5\frac{5}{8}''$ glass with Little Miss Dairy Queen dressed in Dutch costume, and to her right a red and white Dairy Queen logo. There is no date, but below Little Miss Dairy Queen are the words: "® Trademark of Amer. D.Q. Corp." Colors: red, white, blue, and yellow. Same design on both

Davy Crockett

The Backwoods Boy. The front of this $4\frac{5}{8}''$ glass features Davy [red] holding a rifle, against a wilderness background. The name "Davy Crockett" appears above him in yellow. Near the bottom of the glass, "The Backwoods Boy" appears in green print. On the reverse, at the top in yellow are the words "Born 1786—Limestone, Tennessee." The red central panel continues around the glass and includes a log cabin and tree. This delicate glass has a Libbey's imprint on the bottom, but there is no date. **[DC1]** Value: $8–$10.

Events In the Life of Davy Crockett.

This is a set of six 4¼″ jam glasses celebrating legend and fact in the life of Davy Crockett. The glasses come in a variety of colors—orange, blue, white, and red—and each glass has a wraparound scene depicting Davy in action. Below this scene there is a rustic white wooden sign with the name "Davy Crockett" on it, and on the lower reverse opposite this sign in white is a two-line rhyming couplet which comments on the depicted action. There is no date, but these are mid-fifties issues, and they are scarce and desirable. Value: $6–$8.

Davy was a Happy Boy/With Flintlock Rifle for a Toy. **[DC5]**

Ol' Grumpy Bear made his Mistake/a fight with Davy Sealed his Fate. **[DC6]**

Steady Nerves and Trigger Squeeze/Davy Wins it in a Breeze. **[DC7]**

When Davy Met an Indian Foe/He Dealt Him Just One Mighty Blow. **[DC8]**

Davy had a creed that said/Be sure you're right then go ahead. **[DC9]**

Davy Fought this War You See/So Texas People Could be Free. **[DC10]**

Indian Fighter/Hero of Alamo 1786–1836.

These 5″ glasses have wraparound scenes in brown and yellow depicting events in the life of Davy Crockett. At the bottom of each glass there is a rustic animal hide sign which has on it the following words: "Davy Crockett/ Indian Fighter—Hero Of Alamo/1786– 1836." These mid-fifties glasses are infrequently encountered and very desirable. Unknown number of glasses in set. Value: $6–$8.

Indians by Campfire/Davy on Horse **[DC15]**
Davy and Friend in Canoe/Davy on Horse
  [DC16]
Davy Fighting Bear/Indian on Bluff Watching
  [DC17]
Davy Fighting Mexican Soldier **[DC18]**
Davy Standing with Rifle **[DC19]**

Milk Glass Mug. A 3⅜" white milk glass mug with a brown wraparound scene showing Davy Crockett with rifle on his horse leading a covered wagon drawn by oxen. A horseman with rifle follows the wagon, and there is a prairie background. **[DC30]** Value: $3–$5.

Large Ribbed Davy Crockett Glass. This 5¹⁵⁄₁₆" glass has dark red wraparound scenes from the life of Davy Crockett on the top half and bold vertical ribbing on the bottom half. On the top Davy is depicted paddling a canoe with a friend; at the bow of the canoe is a hide plate with the following words on it: "Davy/ Crockett/Indian Fighter/Statesman/Hero Of Alamo/1786–1836." On the reverse, there is an Indian on a galloping pony. There is no date, but there is an Anchor Hocking imprint on the bottom. There are probably other glasses which accompany this one. **[DC25]** Value: $5–$7.

Pitcher. This 8¼" pitcher features a brown and pearl star-betopped wraparound panel, showing Davy and his Indian companion gazing off into the distance. In the background there are mountains and trees and a log cabin. "Davy Crockett" appears in brown under the spout. In the lower right corner of the panel, a 1955 copyright date appears. This pitcher is rare. It probably has companion glasses. **[DC35]** Value: $15–$20.

Tri-Panel Davy Crockett Star Glass. This 5" glass has three panels depicting events in the life of Davy Crockett. At the top of each panel the name "Davy Crockett" appears with a star at either side of it. The panels depict the following actions: Davy fighting a bear, Davy riding a galloping horse, and Davy and an Indian looking off into the distance. Below Davy and the Indian there is a 1955 copyright date. The scenes on this glass are white, but there are probably several other glasses in other colors in the set. This glass is virtually identical in size and design to **[DC38]**, but it has a one-color design and lacks the frosted background panel. **[DC40]** Value: $5–$7.

Domino's Pizza

Domino's Pizza. A 4⅛" frosted design glass with three Domino's Pizza logos on it. No date. **[DO1]** Value: $1–$3.

Dr Pepper

Cherub's Kiss. A $5\frac{1}{2}''$ stained glass filigree design glass in blue, white, pink, black, and flesh colors. The front panel contains an oval with a boy and girl kissing on the seashore. "Dr Pepper/ King of Beverages" appears above them. On the reverse panel, under the same "Dr Pepper/King of Beverages" logo, there is a white circle with the following information in pink capitals: "Cherub's Kiss/An Appealing/Lithograph Art Piece/ Designed To Capture/The Fancy Of Youth,/Was A/Popular Dr Pepper/Advertisement./Circa 1900." This engag-

ing glass is no doubt part of a historical Dr Pepper poster series, and its leaded window design is very similar to the King of Beverages "turn of the century lady" glass **[DP25]**. **[DP1]** Value: $2–$4.

Dr Pepper. A modern $5\frac{3}{16}''$ red, white, and dark red glass with two identical panels. On the upper left of the panel, "Dr Pepper" appears in white letters inside a small red oval. In the center of the dark red panel in large white, almost vertical, letters appears the name "Dr Pepper," and under the name is a red bar. **[DP5]** Value: $1–$3.

"Happy Days" Collector Series (1977). A set of six $6\frac{1}{8}''$ glasses featuring the pop-

ular television program's characters. Each character's name appears in large red and black letters above the character's portrait, and below that in black are the words "© 1977 by Paramount Pictures Corporation." On the reverse near the bottom appears the white Dr Pepper oval logo and below it the words " 'Happy Days' Collector Series." Another difficult set to complete. The Fonz/motorcycle glass is the most difficult to locate. An interesting footnote: the copyright date and information which appear directly below the Fonz's motorcycle are in much smaller, significantly less bold lettering. Also, on the Fonz/motorcycle glass, the word "Corporation" is centered below the word "Paramount." The design differences in this copyright information raise the question: was this second Fonz glass an afterthought? There is also a seventh glass featuring Fonz on his motorcycle in front of Arnold's restaurant. On this glass, Fonz's name appears in stick letters below the motorcycle. This glass may also have been an afterthought, since its design does not conform to the rest of the set. Like the Fonz/Motorcycle glass, this one is difficult to find. Value: Fonz/Motorcycle and Fonz/Arnold's, $6–$8; others, $3–$5.

The Fonz **[DP10]**
The Fonz (same title as above but depicted sitting on yellow motorcycle) **[DP11]**
The Fonz (sitting on motorcyle in front of Arnold's) **[DP12]**
Richie **[DP13]**
Joanie **[DP14]**
Ralph **[DP15]**
Potsie **[DP16]**

King of Beverages (1977 & 1978). A very colorful 6" glass in red, green, black, white, and pearl. A red leaded glass design appears at the top within which are the words "Dr Pepper, King of Beverages." A green and black Greek key band circles the middle of the glass. Below this band is a Currier and Ives

type winter homestead, ice skating scene with the date 1978 (front and back). There is a Dr Pepper glass very similar to this one which is dated 1977. 1977 **[DP20]**; 1978 **[DP21]**. Value: $3–$5.

King of Beverages. Generally similar to the glass above, but undated and smaller ($5\frac{5}{8}$"), blue, pink, black, white, and brown being the colors. Same design front and back: within a fancy oval frame there is a turn-of-the-century lady in hat sipping Dr Pepper through a straw. An intricate leaded glass window design covers the glass. **[DP25]** Value: $2–$4.

Pizza inn Pitcher. A heavy 9" pitcher

with red lettering. On one side are the words "Be a Pepper" with the "Drink Dr Pepper" logo below it, and on the other the words "Pizza inn" with a cook tossing pizza dough in the air. **[DP30]** Value: $6–$8.

Star Trek Collector's Series by Dr Pepper (1976). A set of four 6⅛" glasses featuring the Enterprise and the three principal *Star Trek* characters. The name of the character appears on the front above the likeness. On the reverse appears a brief biography of the character over the words "Star Trek Collector's Series by Dr Pepper [logo]." Below the logo are the words "© 1976 Paramount Pictures." This is a very desirable set, difficult to complete. The Enterprise is especially hard to locate. A second, less common, set with the same four glasses but additional background artwork was issued in 1978. Value: 1976 McCoy, Kirk, Spock, $8–$10; 1976 The Enterprise, $12–$15; 1978 McCoy, Kirk, Spock, $12–15; 1978 Enterprise, $16–$20.

[1976] (1978)
Dr. Leonard McCoy **[DP31] (DP35)**
Captain James T. Kirk **[DP32] (DP36)**
Mr. Spock **[DP33] (DP37)**
The Enterprise **[DP34] (DP38)**

Wendy's/Cleveland Browns (1981). A set of four 6¼″ glasses in red, orange, and brown celebrating the 1981 Cleveland Browns. A red band with "Wendy's" appears at the top of the glass. Below appears the player's head in a star with his name and number. Behind that is an action scene of the player, the name of his position, and his signature. Below that appear the words "© 1981, Wendy's. All rights reserved." Value: $4–$6.

Brian Sipe #17 **[DP40]**
Doug Dieken #73 **[DP41]**
Lyle Alzado #77 **[DP42]**
Mike Pruitt #43 **[DP43]**

Eat'nPark

Pittsburgh Marathon (1986). A 5⅝″ barrel-shaped glass with small pedestal base commemorating the 1986 Pittsburgh Marathon. There are thin gold bands encircling the glass above and below the black line drawing of male and female runners, Pittsburgh's "Golden Triangle," and the city's skyline. "Pittsburgh/[black bar with wavy gold line]/Marathon '86" appears just above the central scene, and a small black "Eat'nPark" logo appears in the center of the back of the glass. **[EP1]** Value: $1–$3.

Elby's

Elby's [Pittsburgh] Pirates (1988). A set of four 6" glasses with a crease at the bottom and a slightly flared top. One side of the glass features the newest Pirate logo in orange, white, black, and red. The name "Pirates" appears at the top of this diamond-shaped logo in black-outlined orange letters. The other side features two Pirate players with their signatures and names printed below them in black. Just below the players and the logo are two black lines, ¾" apart, which encircle the glass. Between them in orange appear the "Elby's" name and the Coca-Cola script trademark. These glasses were distributed in western Pennsylvania in April and May of 1988 by Elby's Family Restaurants, and they are quite handsome. Value: $2–$4.

Jim Gott and Jose Lind **[EL1]**
Mike LaValliere and Barry Bonds **[EL2]**
Bobby Bonilla and Doug Drabek **[EL3]**
Mike Dunne and Andy Van Slyke **[EL4]**

The Electric Company

Rita the Director. A 4¾" glass featuring Rita Moreno from the once popular PBS children's television program *The Electric Company*. Rita is depicted on the front of the glass shouting through a megaphone. On the reverse in large yellow letters appear the words: "Rita the Director," and below these appears "The Electric Company" logo in black and yellow. In small black letters at the bottom of the glass appear the words: "© 1977 Children's Television Workshop." Probably part of a set. Colors: brown, black, gold, pink. **[EC1]** Value:

$1–$3.

Endangered Species

Endangered Species Series. Not to be confused with the Burger Chef Endangered Species set, these $4\frac{11}{16}''$ glasses are interesting and attractive in their own right. Nothing on the glasses helps to identify their provenance or date, but there is a semicircular logo with the words "Endangered Species Series" above it and the name of the endangered species below it. Color and artwork are very appealing. There are eight glasses in the set. Value: $2–$4.

Cape Mountain Zebra **[ES1]**
African Elephant **[ES2]**
Whooping Crane **[ES3]**
Prairie Dog **[ES4]**
Giant Panda **[ES5]**
Columbia White-Tail Deer **[ES6]**
Bengal Tiger **[ES7]**
Bald Eagle **[ES8]**

Exxon

Tiger Glass. A $5\frac{3}{16}''$ glass with an orange and black tiger on it. The tiger occupies the whole glass. There is no writing of any kind, but the tiger is easily remembered because he was used in Exxon's "put a tiger in your tank" commercials. **[EX1]** Value: $1–$2.

Tiger Glass. A $5\frac{3}{16}''$ glass similar to the one above, but with the Exxon tiger's head on one side and the phrase "Put a tiger in your tank" in eight different languages on the reverse. This glass also comes in a $3\frac{1}{4}''$ version. $3\frac{1}{4}''$ **[EX4]**; $5\frac{3}{16}''$ **[EX5]**. Value: $1–$2.

Fantasy Glasses

Fantasy Adventures. A set of four 6″ glasses with a cartoon character depicted in some type of fantasy adventure. Each glass comes in a single color trimmed in white. These are probably food containers from the 50s. Value: $2–$4.

Spaceman/Blue [FY1]
Indian/Yellow [FY2]
Pirate/Orange [FY3]
Island Native/Green [FY4]

Farrell's

"Farrell's Is Fabulous Fun" Mug. A $5\frac{1}{8}$″ heavy glass mug featuring a couple in black and white enjoying sundaes at Farrell's. Below them in black letters framed by musical notes are the words: "Farrell's/Is/Fabulous/Fun." [FA1] Value $1–$3.

Football

Fridge Fever. A 5⅛" glass issued to make more money for William Perry, otherwise known as "The Refrigerator." On the front, #72 is running toward us with the ball. His signature appears in orange below his cleats. On the reverse, the word "Fridge" appears in large black letters topped with ice, and below that is the word "Fever" also in large black letters but with orange heatwaves rising from the top of the letters. That's it. No date or maker is mentioned. **[FB1]** Value: $1–$3.

National Collegiate Champions Nebraska Cornhuskers (1971). A 6½" pedestal-based glass in red and white celebrating the 1970–1971 National Collegiate Champions. The same design appears on both sides: a red and white Nebraska helmet with "National Collegiate Champions/1970–1971" above it and "Go Big Red" below it. "Nebraska Cornhuskers" appears at the top and bottom of the glass in red and white bands which encircle the glass. **[FB5]** Value: $3–$5.

National Professional Football Hall Of Fame. A 6⅝" Libbey glass in red, white, and blue promoting the Football Hall of Fame in Canton, Ohio. At the top of the glass is a red band with "National Professional Football Hall Of Fame" in white. In the center of the glass, the Hall Of Fame buildings appear in blue on a white background. "Canton, Ohio [white star] Cradle Of Pro Football" appears in white on a blue band at the base of the glass. The only other writing on the glass is "No. 1/Collector's Item" which appears in very small clear glass lettering at the bottom right of the center panel. **[FB7]** Value: $1–$3.

NFL Helmet Handle Mug. A heavy $5\frac{1}{2}''$ smoke-colored mug which has small colored helmets of the 28 National Football League teams. Each team's name appears in black print beneath its helmet. There is an NFL logo among

the helmets on each side of the mug. There is no date. **[FB8]** Value: $2–$4.

NFL Smoke-Colored Glasses [1979]. These undated, unsponsored bowl-shaped glasses come in two sizes: $3\frac{3}{16}''$ and $4\frac{1}{4}''$. In appearance and design, they look like they belong to the 1979 Burger Chef NFL glass set, and it is probably safe to say that they date from that year and were made by the same maker and designed by the same designer. Each glass has a helmet viewed from the side, with the name of the team below it on one side and on the other an NFL shield logo. The helmet, team name, and logo, as on the Burger Chef glasses, appear to be etched or frosted. We assume that there are as many glasses in each size as there were NFL teams in 1979, but we picture and list only a selection. This is probably a gasoline station promotion. It would be a formidable task to assemble a complete set of these glasses. The $4\frac{1}{4}''$ glasses are more difficult to find than the smaller size. Value: $3\frac{3}{16}''$, $1–$2; $4\frac{1}{4}''$, $1–$2.

$3\frac{3}{16}''$

Cleveland Browns **[FB10]**
Denver Broncos **[FB11]**
Kansas City Chiefs **[FB12]**
Los Angeles Rams **[FB13]**
Miami Dolphins **[FB14]**
New Orleans Saints **[FB15]**
New York Giants **[FB16]**
Philadelphia Eagles **[FB17]**
Washington Redskins **[FB18]**

$4\frac{1}{4}''$

Cleveland Browns **[FB40]**
St. Louis Cardinals **[FB41]**

Pittsburgh Steelers

NFL Superbowl Champions. A set of four $5\frac{1}{2}''$ mugs celebrating the four Superbowl victories of the Pittsburgh Steelers. On the front of each mug in the center is a gold football with the number of the Superbowl in Roman numerals and the Steelers' logo. Above the football are the words "NFL/Superbowl," and below it, "Champions." On the Superbowl XIII and XIV mugs, the dates 1978 and 1979 appear below the word "Champions." On the Superbowl IX and X mugs, there is no date in this location. On the reverse of each mug,

the number of the Superbowl appears at the top, followed by the score of the game, division playoff scores, and regular season scores. Colors: black and gold, of course! A gold rim gives this mug a touch of class. Value: $2–$4.

Superbowl IX (Pittsburgh 16, Minnesota Vikings 6) **[FB100]**
Superbowl X (Pittsburgh 21, Dallas Cowboys 17) **[FB101]**
Superbowl XIII (Pittsburgh 35, Dallas Cowboys 31) **[FB102]**
Superbowl XIV (Pittsburgh 31, Los Angeles Rams 19) **[FB103]**

NFL Team Helmet. This $3\frac{15}{16}''$ glass features a Steelers helmet in black and gold with a red, white, yellow, and blue Steelers logo on it. The name "Steelers" appears below the helmet in large black letters. On the reverse in black appears the NFL logo. This glass closely resembles the frosted Mobil helmet glasses, but this glass does not have the Mobil name or the frosted panel, and the helmet is 2" high (rather than $1\frac{3}{4}''$), and the Steeler's name is $\frac{1}{8}''$ larger than it is on the Mobil glass. This glass was distributed by gasoline stations in Pittsburgh; total number of glasses in set is unknown at this time. **[FB110]** Value: $1–$3.

Pittsburgh Steelers (1976). A series of $6\frac{3}{16}''$ glasses honoring selected Steeler greats. A Steeler player's face appears on the front of each glass, with his signature at an angle slightly below. Gold bars with black outlines appear at the top and bottom, front and reverse, of each glass. On the reverse the player's number appears in large frosted numerals. Below that, in black, appear the player's name, position, height, weight, birthdate, and college. Below this information is a frosted NFL Player's logo and the 1976 MSA copyright date. Simply designed but essential for sports collectors, and Steeler fans have caused a shortage of these glasses in the Pittsburgh area. Unknown number of glasses in set. Value: $3–$5.

#12 Terry Bradshaw **[FB70]**
#20 Rocky Bleier **[FB71]**
#27 Glen Edwards **[FB72]**
#34 Andy Russell **[FB73]**
#47 Mel Blount **[FB74]**
#56 Ray Mansfield **[FB75]**
#58 Jack Lambert **[FB76]**
#59 Jack Ham **[FB77]**
#75 Joe Greene **[FB78]**
#78 Dwight White **[FB79]**

Franco Harris **[FB80]** (*Note:* This glass is slightly different—the player has no number, and the black and gold bar on the bottom reverse has "1250/wtae stereo 96" inserted in the middle. We have also seen a Terry Bradshaw glass without Bradshaw's number and with the same WTAE logo. There are either two versions of each glass (and therefore two distinct sets) or possibly only several were selected for the WTAE logo).

Steelers72/wtae Glass Mug (1972). A $5\frac{1}{2}''$ glass mug in yellow and black. One side has on it in yellow a pass receiver being tackled, and the other features a receiver making a diving catch. "Steelers72" is superimposed in black on both pictures. Near the bottom of the diving receiver side, black-outlined yellow "wtae" [radio station] letters appear, and beneath them "radio 1250" appears in black. A nice early mug. **[FB115]**Value: $5–$7.

Garfield

Garfield "All Star" Mug (1978). A $3\frac{5}{8}''$ ceramic mug showing Garfield operating a sailboard. Above him, "ALL STAR" appears in yellow. Jim Davis' name appears at the bottom of the mug. On the bottom are the words: "GARFIELD: © 1978/United Feature Syndicate, Inc./Licensee Enesco." **[GA1]** Value: $3–$5.

Garfield/Soda Bottle. A 5" glass featuring Garfield drinking a bottle of what looks like Coca-Cola; whatever the beverage is, it is shooting out of his ears, and the word "GOOSH" consequently

appears above his head. Jim Davis' name appears in black directly below Garfield. On the reverse there are three additional empty bottles and below them in black the words: "GARFIELD: © 1978 United Feature Syndicate, Inc." Colors: green, orange, black, and white. There is something likable about this ridiculous cat. **[GA5]** Value: $1–$2.

Garfield/"Wheee". A 6" glass with Garfield riding ice cubes across the front with the words "Wheee" above his head. The trail of water leads around to the reverse with an empty ice cube tray and extra cube. Below the tray in black letters are the words: "Garfield: © 1978 United Feature Syndicate, Inc." **[GA10]** Value: $2–$3.

Godfather's Pizza

The Goonies (1985). A set of four $5\frac{5}{8}$" glasses featuring characters and scenes from the film *The Goonies*. While these glasses do not bear the Godfather's Pizza logo, they were distributed by Godfather's; several glasses we have found have a sticker on the bottom with these words: "Free Pitcher of Coca Cola when you buy a medium or large Godfather's Pizza now through 9/30/85." The front of each glass has a crucial film scene on an antique map/parchment background. The reverse carries these messages in black: "The Goonies" [film title and logo]/ "Amblin/Entertainment" [logo], "TM&C 1985 Warner Bros. Inc." Beneath this is the title of the scene on the front of each glass, below which are the words "Collector Series." Available in the West, scarce in the East. Value: $3–$5.

Sloth and the Goonies **[GO1]**
Sloth Comes to the Rescue **[GO2]**
Goonies in the Organ Chamber **[GO3]**
Data on the Waterslide **[GO4]**

Seattle Supersonics/NBA Players Association. $5\frac{5}{8}''$ glasses, each featuring three members of the Seattle Supersonics basketball team. Each glass has yellow and green bands at top and bottom, a National Basketball Players Association logo, a Godfather's Pizza logo, and a green and yellow Seattle Supersonics logo. Value: $4–$6.
(See also Coca-Cola)

James Donaldson, David Thompson, Danny Vranes **[GO10]**
Phil Smith, Fred Brown, Mark Radford **[GO11]**
Gus Williams, Lenny Wilkens, Jack Sikma **[GO12]**
Greg Kelser, Lonnie Shelton, Ray Tolbert **[GO13]**

Guiness Book of World Records

Guiness Book of World Records (1976). These are $5\frac{1}{2}''$ pedestal-base glasses, each of which has three panels on which Guiness world records are featured. The top of each panel names the specific record, the center of the panel illustrates the record in cartoon fashion, and the bottom of the panel explains the record in detail. Each glass has two dominant colors, and the center cartoon on each glass includes these two colors on a pearl background. "© 1976 Sterling Publishing Co., Inc. New York" appears in pearl-colored print vertically between two of the panels. The number of glasses in the set is unknown at this time. Value: $2–$4.

Longest Shower, Largest Guitar, Message In A Bottle (green and yellow) **[GU1]**
Modern Dancing, Largest Wig, Apple Peeling (red and blue) **[GU2]**

Hallmark

Charmers (1975, 1976). A set of four $5\frac{1}{16}$" glasses in black and white, slightly flared in design. The focus of each glass is a white panel meant to put us in mind of a greeting card. On the panel, charming little children are depicted in black line drawings doing cute things. At the bottom of the "card" appears an optimistic obviousism. At the top of the "card" on the left is the name "Charmers," and on the right the words "by Hallmark." Appearing vertically on the right bottom of each panel is the copyright information: "© [1975 or 1976] Hallmark Cards, Inc." Value: $1–$3.

It's good to take some time to do/whatever makes a happy you. (Charmer carrying basket of flowers on arm, 1976) **[HA1]**

Thankfulness grows/where thoughtfulness shows. (Boy and girl Charmers smooching, boy presenting corsage, 1975) **[HA2]**

Try your best/to see the best in others. (Charmer laying cement, puppy making tracks in it, 1976) **[HA3]**

When there's love in the home,/there's joy in the heart. (Charmer hanging up "Home Sweet Home" sign, 1975) **[HA4]**

Shirt Tales (1982). Hallmark's animal characters, the "Shirt Tales," appear on at least three glasses and a decanter.

$3\frac{3}{8}$" Glass. This slightly flared glass features five of Hallmark's "Shirt Tales" characters distributed evenly around the glass. To the right of Digger (mole) who is holding a "Shirt Tales" sign, are Bogey (monkey), Pammy (panda), Rick (raccoon), and Tyg (tiger). Beneath Rick in small black letters appears the copyright information: "© 1980, 1981, 1982 Hallmark Cards, Inc." Cute and colorful, with subject matter appealing to children. **[HA10]** Value: $1–$3.

6" and $5\frac{1}{2}$" Glasses. The 6" glass is also slightly flared. This glass features the Shirt Tales characters playing in and around a tree which wraps around the glass. A Shirt Tales sign hangs from a tree limb. Digger is digging beneath it. Tyg is just looking at us. Pammy is waving at us and emerging from a hollow place near the roots of the tree. Bogey is swinging from two tree limbs, and Rick is waving from a hole in the tree's trunk. "© 1980, 1981, 1982 Hallmark Cards, Inc." appears at the bottom of the tree. There is also a $5\frac{1}{2}$" version **[HA11]** of this glass. **[HA12]** Value: $1–$3.

9" Decanter. Decanter has a wraparound design with two identical panels. On each panel we have the Shirt Tales playing in and around a tree. Tyg is swinging from a limb, Pammy and Rick are holding a Shirt Tales sign, and Digger is half buried in the ground. Below Tyg are the small black words: "© 1980, 1981, 1982 Hallmark Cards, Inc." If you like small animals that fool around in trees, this is the set for you. **[HA13]** Value: $3–$5.

Hardee's

The Chipmunks (1985). A set of four $5\frac{7}{8}''$ glasses featuring the three original Chipmunks—Alvin, Theodore, and Simon—and the more recent Chipettes. These musical creatures are represented in ovals on the fronts of the glasses, and their names appear underlined in black. On the reverse, these harmonious rodents are pictured in musical action scene roles with the title "The Chipmunks" below. Black musical notes link the two panels, and toward the bottom of the Alvin, Simon, and Theodore glasses are the words "© 1985 Bagdasarian Productions." On the Chipettes glass appear the words "© 1985 Karman/Ross Productions Inc." These glasses are not as easy to find as one might think. Distributed by Hardee's, though they do not have the Hardee's logo. Value: $2–$4.

Alvin (vocals) **[HR1]**
Simon (synthesizer) **[HR2]**
Theodore (drums) **[HR3]**
The Chipettes (backup: guitar, vocal, tambourine) **[HR4]**

Smurfs (1982). A set of eight round-bottom 5⅞" glasses featuring the popular Smurf cartoon characters. Although these glasses do not carry the Hardee's logo, they were distributed by Hardee's. The scenes on these glasses are essentially action scenes with the Smurfs engaged in various characteristic activities. Below these scenes appear the character's name in white, a blue and white Smurfs logo, and these words in black: "© Peyo 1982 Lic. By Wallace Berrie & Co., Inc. S.E.P.P. D.M. Intl." Generally easy to find. *Note:* the colors on these glasses are very susceptible to fading. Bright copies are relatively rare. Value: $1–$3.

Gargamel/Azrael **[HR10]**
Papa **[HR11]**
Brainy **[HR12]**
Hefty **[HR13]**
Grouchy **[HR14]**
Smurfette **[HR15]**
Jokey **[HR16]**
Lazy **[HR17]**

Smurfs (1983). A same-shape-and-size followup set to the 1982 issue, but this time there are six glasses. This set seems more colorful and the action more complex. Easily recognized by the fact that the word "Smurf" appears after each character's name (with the exception of Smurfette). Near the bottom of each glass appear the words "© Peyo 1983 Licensed by Wallace Berrie & Co. Van Nuys, Ca. S.E.P.P. D.M. Intl." Value: $1–$3.

Papa Smurf [HR18]
Handy Smurf [HR19]
Clumsy Smurf [HR20]
Smurfette [HR21]
Baker Smurf [HR22]
Harmony Smurf [HR23]

Ziggy (1979). Cheery 6" glasses featuring Ziggy in cartoon situations with upbeat sayings like "Try to Have a Nice Day." The cartoon and caption are on the front. Each glass has a dominant color theme, and on the back there are the words "ZIGGY Tom Wilson © Universal Press Syndicate 1979 HARDEE'S ®" Also available without any restaurant logo and with a Pizza inn logo. Value: $2–$4.

Be Nice to Little Things [HR30]
Try To Have A Nice Day [HR31]
Time for a Food Break [HR32]
Smile . . . It's Good For Your Complexion
   [HR33]

Johnny Hart

B.C. Glassware. Johnny Hart's B.C. characters are available on a set of non-Arby's-sponsored glassware with a wide variety of sizes and designs. There are plates, cookie jars, glasses, and other serving pieces. The glasses are scrunched, as if made by a primitive potter. Perhaps they were! No dates or characters' names appear. Familiarity with the B.C. family is assumed. These pieces are not very plentiful, and they are unusual enough to command rather high prices. (See also Arby's)

3¼" Anteater $5–$7 **[JH1]**
3¾" Thor (riding wheel), $4–$6 **[JH2]**

5¼" Thor (riding wheel on frosted panel, 2¼" mouth diameter), $4–$6 **[JH3]**

7⅝" Frosted Pitcher (Anteater capturing ant), $10–$12 **[JH4]** (There is also a larger clear glass pitcher with various B.C. characters on it.)

8¼" Cookie Jar (All of the B.C. characters appear in black in their characteristic poses and activities on this white cookie jar.) Value: $8–$10. **[JH5]**

"Grog" Milk Glass Mug. A 3⅛" white milk glass mug which features an embossed image of Johnny Hart's Grog character on one side and the embossed name "Grog" on the other with "hart" embossed to its lower right. The mug, like its related glassware, has a sort of primitive, bumpy surface. Even at a fairly close distance, one might not notice the embossed figure on this mug; it becomes very clear when the cup is held

up to the light. There are probably other B.C. characters available on mugs like this. **[JH20]** Value: $3–$5.

H. Salt

Historic Ships Series. A set of six 6¼" rather plain but interesting glasses commemorating some of the world's most successful ship designs. The front of each glass features a vessel in color, and the reverse has a brief description of the ship type, as well as reference to a specific significant example of it. Below this description is the H. Salt logo. These glasses are undated, and they are fairly uncommon. Value: $5–$7.

Chinese Lorcha **[HS1]**
The Frigate **[HS2]**
James Watt **[HS3]**
The Prince Royal—1610 **[HS4]**
The Caravel "Nina" **[HS5]**
The Flying Cloud **[HS6]**

Hershey's

Hershey's Chocolate World. A $5\frac{9}{16}''$ stained glass/filigree design glass in brown, white, and lime green and with the same design on both sides. "Hershey's" appears in large white letters on a brown background sign, and "Chocolate World" appears below this in small white capitals. Below this are a white cocoa plant blossom and a brown-outlined lime green cocoa pod with the brown words "Cocoa Pod" below it. Between the panels on each side of the glass are green, white, and brown cocoa plants. There is no date or other information. This glass is beautiful when it is held up to the light. **[HE1]** Value: $3–$5.

Hershey's Milk Chocolate Kisses. An undated $5\frac{5}{8}''$ glass promoting Hershey's Kisses. The focus of the glass is a young lady putting a Hershey's Kiss into the mouth of a young man. Between these young people in white letters appear

these words: "A Kiss for You." A dark blue band with red-lined borders encircles the bottom of the glass. On it in red and white are the words: "Hershey's Milk Chocolate Kisses/ Reg.U.S.PAT.OFF." On the back of the glass in vertical white letters appear the words: "Trademark Of Hershey Foods Corporation/Libbey Glass Co., Licensee." A cute glass with an air of nostalgia. **[HE5]** Value: $2–$4.

Hickory Farms

Hickory Farms Country Scene. A $4\frac{1}{8}''$ glass featuring a red barn, silo, cattle, chickens, fences, trees, and rolling hills with white clouds above them. The name "Hickory Farms" appears on a mailbox in the foreground. The colors are brown, green, white, and red. There is no date and, while the glass is not particularly fascinating, it is not common. **[HF1]** Value: $1–$3.

Hickoryville Collection Mug (1987).
This is a $3\frac{11}{16}''$ mug with a red, white, and blue wraparound panel. "Hickoryville" and "Hickory Farms" alternate in white print on a blue band at the top and bottom of the panel. The major center panel is red and has on it a repeated pattern of paired capital "Bs" which no doubt refer to the red, white, and blue teddy bear which appears on opposite sides of the mug. On a piece of tape securely stuck to the bottom of this mug are the following words: "© Hickory Farms Of Ohio/Maumee, OH 43537/Hickoryville Collection 1987/ Made In Taiwan." **[HF2]** Value: $2–$4.

Hires Root Beer

Genuine Hires Root Beer. A $5\frac{3}{16}''$ small-bottomed modern glass with identical panels on each side. "Genuine/HIRES/ Root Beer" appears in white letters on the traditional orange and brown Hires label. **[HI1]** Value: $1–$3.

Hot Dog Castle

1977 Hot Dog Castle Collector Series. A set of three 6″ tumblers featuring the past, present and future of Abilene, Texas. Each glass shows buildings and modes of transportation typical of the era featured. The glasses are black and white with the words "Copyright—Hot Dog Castle Collector Series" in black lettering around the bottom. Value $3–$5.

1977 Collector Edition: Abilene Past **[HO1]**
1977 Collector Edition: Abilene Present **[HO2]**
1977 Collector Edition: Abilene Future **[HO3]**

Hulk Hogan

Hulkamania (1985). One of several efforts to promote "the single biggest superstar of wrestling" who, we are informed on the reverse of this glass, possesses "ultra-charismatic charm" and a "highly animated personality." This 5″ glass features "The Hulkster" flexing his muscles on the front, and on the reverse at the top is red monster script touting the word "HULKAMANIA." Below that is a nine-line paragraph of nonsense (from which we have already quoted) which likens the "Hulkster" to legimate heroes such as Superman. It is even claimed here that he "never cheats, and fights the bad guys in the name of good." Yeah! Is there anyone out there who wants to buy the Brooklyn Bridge? Below this rubbish is a large "WF" logo, and below that in small black letters are the words "© 1985 Titan Sports, Inc." Flea market tables are clogged with these things. **[HH1]** Value: $0.25–$0.75— unless, of course, his "deep but friendly voice" has already made you a "Hulkamania" fan.

WWF Heroes. A 7″ pedestal glass with WWF heroes on the front. The reverse of the Hulk Hogan glass reads "HULK-AMANIA" in red letters with a paragraph in white lettering below. A yellow World Wrestling Federation logo completes the reverse. These glasses can also be found with several WWF "heroes." The only redeeming quality of these is their ability to hold large quantities of liquid. Value $0.50–$1.00.

Hulk Hogan **[HH5]**
Andre the Giant **[HH6]**

K-Mart

K-Mart 20th Anniversary (1982). A $5\frac{1}{2}″$ flared glass commemorating K-Mart's 20th anniversary in business. A red and blue design on one side says "20/Grand Years/Of Saving/Kmart," and on the other (also in red and blue) there is a drawing of a modern K-Mart store, below which are the words: "First Kmart Opened At/Garden City, Michigan/ March 1, 1962/Limited Edition." Not a terribly exciting glass, but offbeat enough to deserve a place on the shelf. **[KM1]** Value: $1–$3.

Keebler

Keebler Soft Batch Cookies (1984). A set of four colorful $5\frac{9}{16}''$ glasses promoting the bakery products of the Keebler Company and the ovenly abilities of the Keebler elves. A nicely detailed and very colorful front panel features Ernest and his mom in the kitchen of their treehouse. Soft Batch cookies and the Keebler brand name are visible on each panel, and there is a humorous exchange between the characters at the bottom of the panel. On the reverse of each glass, there is a forest scene showing the elves' treehouse with a Keebler

sign hanging from one of the limbs and Ernest standing at an open window with open arms. Near the bottom in small black letters appear the words: "© 1984 Keebler Company." These glasses were mail-order premiums. Value: $4–$6.

Ernest, Soft Batch Reminds/Me Of Cookies I Baked When/You Were Little . . . Mom, I'm An/Elf! I've Always Been Little! **[KE1]**

Mom, You'd Swear These/Soft Batch Cookies Are/Home Made . . ./Ernest, This Is Home! **[KE2]**

Mom, Soft Batch Tastes Like/Cookies Fresh From The Oven . . ./Soft And Chewy! **[KE3]**

Ernest, You Don't Bite Into/Soft Batch Cookies . . ./You Sorta Sink Into 'Em! **[KE4]**

Keebler 135th Birthday Glass (1988). A gaily colored $5\frac{5}{16}''$ glass issued during the summer of 1988 to commemorate Keebler's 135th birthday. The front of the glass features a multicolored cartoon type panel with two Keebler elves sitting at a table in front of a birthday cake which has the numbers 135 on top of it. Naturally, the elves are eating cookies. The elf on the left says (in a black-outlined white balloon): "Hey Ernie, What Are/You Celebrating?!"

Ernie replies: "It's Keebler's 135th/ Birthday!!" Below this panel in small black print appear the words: "© 1988 Keebler Company." On the reverse, the Keebler elves' tree is pictured with colored balloons and a red banner with "135th/Birthday" in gold on it. The price for a set of four of these glasses was $4.99, and people who ordered the "set" thinking they would get four different glasses were certainly surprised. We suspect that there will be a plentiful supply of this glass. **[KE5]**, Value: $2–$4.

Kellogg's

Kellogg's Collector Series (1977). A set of six 4¼" glasses featuring Kellogg's cereal characters. Front and back are identical, and on one side between these representations are the words "Kellogg's/Collector/Series/© 1977 Kellogg Company." The characters' names do not appear on the glasses. The order form which comes with the glasses informs us that each of these glasses could be obtained "FREE for 3 Sugar Corn Pops and/or Sugar Smacks box tops." The offer expired April 30, 1978, and most collectors would now agree that it was a good one. These glasses are getting hard to find, but they are sometimes encountered in their original individual boxes or in a six-glass carton. Value: $4–$6.

Tony the Tiger **[KL1]**
Tony Jr. **[KL2]**
Toucan Sam **[KL3]**
Snap! Crackle! Pop! **[KL4]**
Dig 'Em **[KL5]**
Big Yella **[KL6]**

John F. Kennedy

JFK, 1917–1963 [1963–1964]. A heavy 5⅝″ blue and white glass issued to commemorate the presidency of John F. Kennedy. On the front in an oval frame is the President's picture with the dates 1917–1963 above, and the initials "JFK" below. On the reverse in a white panel there is the Presidential Seal and the famous "Ask Not What Your/Country Can Do For/You . . . Ask What You/Can Do For Your Country" quotation. To the left of Kennedy on the bottom of the glass is "PT 109," and to his right is his famous rocking chair. The top of the glass is encircled by a ring of white stars. These glasses seem to be omnipresent, but they serve to remind us of a great American President. **[JF1]** Value: $1–$3.

Kentucky Derby

Kentucky Derby. A series of interesting and colorful 5¼″ glasses celebrating the yearly run for the roses at Churchill Downs. The Derby goes back to 1875, and the glasses go back to 1949. It is impossible to generalize regarding the colors or scenic representations on these glasses because each is unique. The

"Official Harry M. Stevens Inc." copyright characterizes this series of glasses, and one thing they do have in common is a complete list of Derby winners from 1875 to the most recent issue. Pre-1970s glasses command significantly higher prices than more recent ones. [*Note:* Identification for these glasses consists of the letters KD followed by the last two digits of the year of issue. 1949 = **KD49**, 1950 = **KD50**, etc.]

1949–1955, $20–$25
1956–1960, $15–$20
1961–1965, $10–$15
1966–1969, $8–$12
1970–1976, $5–$7
1977–1980, $4–$6
1981–1988, $3–$5

Kraft

Currier & Ives Cheese Spread Glass (1979). A 4⅝" cheese spread glass with a brown, gold, and white Currier and Ives "Winter In The Country" print on the front. Surrounding the print and extending toward the back of the glass on both sides is fancy filigree decoration. Below the print in brown letters on a gold background appear the words: "Winter In The Country/Currier & Ives." To the left of the print near the bottom of the glass appear the words: "© 1979 Kraft, Inc." Not a particularly beautiful glass, mostly because of drab colors and fuzzy artwork, but typical of the type. There are, no doubt, other Kraft series and other glasses in this series. **[KR1]** Value: $1–$2.

Walter Lantz

Walter Lantz Double Character Action Series. A set of six glasses featuring two Walter Lantz characters per glass in action scenes. There are two sizes and styles for these glasses: a tall 6⅛" version, with a full-sized button base, and a 5⅝" slightly wider and heavier version, with a receding button base. It's possible that Andy Panda/Miranda and maybe other glasses in the set just come in the smaller, wider size and that the set consists of two different sized glasses. Or perhaps there are two separate sets. At any rate, the names of the characters appear below them in white, and on the side near the bottom in white is the Walter Lantz logo which consists of Woody Woodpecker's head and Walter Lantz's signature. There is no date and no food or drink sponsor. The color shades on these glasses are unusual, the character interaction is particularly effective, and the facial expressions of the characters are amusing. These glasses are difficult to find, and a complete set is therefore a challenge to assemble. Value: $4–$6.

(See also Pepsi)

Woody/Knothead and Splinter **[WL1]**
Chilly Willy/Smedly **[WL2]**
Space Mouse/Buzz Buzzard **[WL3]**
Andy Panda/Miranda **[WL4]**
Cuddles/Oswald **[WL5]**
Wally Walrus/Homer Pigeon **[WL6]**

LaRosa's Pizza

LaRosa's (1983). A 5⅞" round-bottom glass featuring Hanna-Barbera characters eating LaRosa's food products on a red and white checked tablecloth. On the top front of the glass (and on the reverse directly opposite), "LaRosa's" appears in black and white on a red banner. Under the front banner, and continuing on around the glass from left to right are Scooby Doo, Luigi [LaRosa], Yogi Bear, Park Ranger, Fred Flintstone, and Wilma. In black print below Luigi and Yogi are the words "Luigi and Friends." At the bottom of the tablecloth on the reverse are the words "© 1983 Hanna-Barbera Productions, Inc." Because the Park Ranger is holding a glass with a Pepsi logo on it, this glass is sometimes classified as a Pepsi glass, but this claim is questionable since the Pepsi logo is practically the last thing

one notices on this quite busy and colorful glass. **[LR1]** Value: $4–$6.

LK's Pierre The Bear

LK's Pierre The Bear Series (1977). A set of four 5" glasses, one for each season, featuring Pierre the Bear involved in appropriate seasonal activities. On the reverse of each glass there is a limerick which illustrates the scene on the front of the glass. These small glasses with lovable Pierre are obviously meant to appeal to children. Pierre may well be French, since he is pictured wearing a beret. Below each front panel appear the words: "[SEASON] LK's Pierre The Bear Series 1977." These glasses are not easy to find, and you have to hunt to put together a set. Value: $2–$4.

Winter (Pierre and child building a snowman) **[LK1]**

Verse on back: "When the snow falls heavy and deep/Pierre rolls it up in a heap,/And while many small hands/Build a giant snowman/He yawns, and goes back to sleep."

Spring **[LK2]**

Summer (Pierre at beach, building sandcastles with child) **[LK3]**

Verse on back: "Every year Pierre saves and saves/For a long holiday by the waves./While the children build forts/And castles with courts,/Pierre builds seven-room caves."

Fall (Pierre carrying kids to school) **[LK4]**

Verse on back: "Every autumn Pierre will help pack/Childrens' school lunches in sacks,/And each day at 8:30/(So their shoes won't get dirty,)/He takes them to school on his back."

LK's Pierre The Bear Series (1978–79).

A set of four 5" glasses basically the same in design and content to the 1977 set above, except in this set there are no verses on the reverse, and the colors are noticeably different (the colors on this set are softer and pastel, as well as being more numerous; the figures on the 1977 set are larger, the detail is better, and the color contrast is more effective). Below the front panels appear the words: "[SEASON] LK's Pierre The Bear Series 1978–79." Like the earlier set, not easy to find. Value: $2–$4.

Winter **[LK5]**

Spring (Pierre picking flowers with children) **[LK6]**

Summer (Pierre netting a fish, children watching) **[LK7]**

Fall (Children raking leaves, Pierre sitting under tree with his lap full of leaves) **[LK8]**

Love Is . . .

Love Is . . . (1975). This set of six 5⅞" glasses shares the same captions as the Centsible Place set of "Love Is . . ." glasses, but on these glasses there is no sponsor. The "Love Is . . ." title appears in various colors at the top of the

Love Is . . . (1976). This is a set of four unnumbered, small flat-bottomed glasses with black captions. "Love Is . . ." appears at the top in a circular border, and "Los Angeles Times 1976" appears vertically on the side of the glass. Value: $2–$4.

. . . bringing her breakfast in bed./. . . taking a turn in the kitchen occasionally. **[LI7]**

. . . letting him eat onions on his hamburger./ . . . eating garlic bread only when he does. **[LI8]**

. . . sharing a bag of roasted chestnuts./. . . drinking hot chocolate by firelight. **[LI9]**

. . . letting her try out new dishes on you./. . . when her cooking experiments are delicious. **[LI10]**

Love Is . . . . This is a set of four unnumbered "Love Is . . ." glasses shaped like the Burger Chef "Presidents/Patriots" series. Value: $2–$4.

. . . adjusting the bindings on her skis./. . . helping her up the tow rope. **[LI11]**

. . . telling him he plays tennis better than Rod Laver./. . . when he does what he wants and you do what he wants. **[LI12]**

. . . helping him paint his boat./. . . letting her crew your yacht. **[LI13]**

. . . listening again how he made the hole in one./. . . telling him how much his golf game has improved. **[LI14]**

Love Is . . . Brandy Snifter (1976). There are five captions and pictures on this brandy snifter. "Los Angeles Times 1976" appears on the side. **[LI15]** Value: $3–$5.

(See also Centsible Place and Pizza Hut)

. . . bringing her some daisies for her kitchen.
. . . whatever you make it.
. . . sending her some roses when she's sick.
. . . giving her a red rose.
. . . when he says it with flowers.

glass along with variously colored flowers, and the captions at the bottom appear in red, blue, or green. The number of the glass and the copyright information appear on the side of the glass vertically: "[number] Copyright Los Angeles Times 1975." Value: $2–$4.

#1 . . . whatever you make it.
. . . sharing even the hard times. **[LI1]**

#2 . . . an autumn walk through the woods.
. . . tickling his nose with a long piece of grass. **[LI2]**

#3 . . . telling her she's as lovely as the day you were married.
. . . making marriage last 75 years. **[LI3]**

#4 . . . that first kiss in the morning.
. . . watching the sun sink into the sea. **[LI4]**

#5 . . . telling him how much his golf game has improved.
. . . listening again how he made the hole in one. **[LI5]**

#6 . . . telling him his paint job is marvelous when it isn't.
. . . holding the ladder while he paints the ceiling. **[LI6]**

Mattel

Masters of the Universe (1983). A set of four 5⅝″ glasses featuring four of Mattel's futuristic sword and sorcery characters. Each of these characters is posed on the front of a glass against a black-bordered colored circle, and with the exception of Teela, each is wielding a weapon and attempting to look as threatening as possible. The reverse design is the same on all four glasses: each character's name appears in black within a banner which matches the color of the background circle on the front. Below this name/banner appears a brief description of each character in black, and near the bottom is a forboding castle with a center section looking very much like a skull (apparently this is where some of these steroid users live!). To the right of this castle are the words: "© Mattel, Inc. 1983 All Rights Reserved/ Masters Of The Universe, And Associated/Characters, Are Trade-Marks Owned By/And Used Under License From Mattel, Inc." On the opposite side of the glass near the bottom appears the "Masters Of The Universe" logo in black. A colorful set which is not frequently encountered, and a must for extraterrestrial buffs. Value: $3–$5.

He-Man. (White circle and banner) "Defender of Right. Hero of Good./The most powerful man in the/Universe. Equipped by the sorceress/of Eternia with weapons of unearthly/ power." **[MA1]**

Man-At-Arms. (Blue circle and banner) "Trusted companion of He-Man./A hero in his own right. A warrior/ against evil." **[MA2]**

Skeletor. (Yellow circle and banner) "A devious and cunning foe for/the true and forthright He-Man." **[MA3]**

Teela. (Orange circle and banner) "The beautiful. Pure of heart and/gentle of touch. But will she be the/happy bride of He-Man or the un-/willing prize of the evil Skeletor?" **[MA4]**

Masters Of The Universe (1986).

Masters Of The Universe (1986). A set of four colorful 4¼" glasses featuring Masters Of The Universe characters in various action poses. The characters are nicely detailed. Below each character there is a two-colored band which encircles the glass. The character's name appears in black in the middle of the glass to the left or to the right of the character. The reverses of all four glasses are the same: various planets and small celestial bodies in yellow, red, and blue. Below this reverse panel, interrupting the two-colored bands, are the "Masters/Of The Universe" logo and "© Mattel, Inc. 1986." Though there is no prose commentary on these glasses, this set is interesting because there is at least one new character (Orko), and on two glasses there is mild action (He-Man, Skeletor). If you are into these characters, you have to have this set. Value: $2–$4.

He-Man/Battle Cat (Red/Blue) **[MA5]**
Man-At-Arms (Green/Blue) **[MA6]**
Orko (Orange/Blue) **[MA7]**
Skeletor/Panthor (Yellow/Blue) **[MA8]**

McDonald's

Cartoon Characters and Movies

Camp Snoopy Collection [1983]. A set of five—yes, five—round-bottom 6" glasses featuring Charles Schulz's popular cartoon characters in wraparound action and generous color. The title of each glass appears in a bubble spoken by Schulz's characters. On the reverse in white are the words "Camp Snoopy Collection," and below those in black the words "© 1950, 1952, 1958, 1965, United Feature Syndicate, Inc." There is also a yellow McDonald's logo near the bottom to the right of these words. These are charming glasses which were heavily bought by McDonaldites. As a result, they are plentiful and inexpensive. *Note:* Do not waste your time arguing with fleamarket vendors who insist these glasses were issued in 1965! It isn't worth the effort, and you won't win because they want to believe these glasses are worth $7 each. Take our word

for it: they were summer 1983 issues.
Value: $1–$2.

Rats! Why Is Having Fun Always So Much
  Work? (Charlie Brown) **[MC1]**
Civilization Is Overrated! (Snoopy) **[MC2]**

There's No Excuse For Not Being Properly Pre-
  pared (Lucy) **[MC3]**
Morning People Are Hard To Love (Snoopy)
  [MC4]
The Struggle For Security Is No Picnic! (Linus)
  [MC5]

Disney Movie Series. A set of four 5⅝″ glasses commemorating four of Disney's finest films. This particular set was issued in Canada and bears a white Coca-Cola logo with French wording, and there is a small gold maple leaf centered below the McDonald's logo near the bottom of the glass. These glasses are very colorful, and there is wraparound action. At the top of each glass, the name "Walt Disney" appears in red (Cinder-ella and Snow White) or blue (Fantasia and Peter Pan). The red Disney name glasses have blue movie titles, and the blue Disney name glasses have red movie titles. There is no date, and the small words "© Walt Disney Productions" appear at the bottom of each glass. On two glasses, the title of the movie appears in both French and English. A beautiful set which is popular with both Disney and McDonald's collectors.

Value: $6–$8.

Garfield Mugs (1987). A set of four 3½″ mugs featuring Jim Davis' Garfield characters. On each mug Garfield is depicted in an action scene with one or more other characters, and there is a white bubble containing one of his philosophical sayings. The copyright dates of the various Garfield characters appear near the bottom of each mug, along with a black McDonald's logo. These are nicely designed mugs with appealing color. The mugs are unnumbered, so we list them below in the order they were released. Value: $1–$3.

"I'm Easy To Get Along With When Things Go
    My Way" **[MC10]**
"Use Your Friends Wisely" **[MC11]**
"I'm Not One Who Rises To The Occasion" \
    [MC12]
"It's Not A Pretty Life But Somebody Has To |
    Live It" **[MC13]**

The Great Muppet Caper! (1981). *The Great Muppet Caper* movie provided the inspiration for this set of four 5⅝″ glasses featuring the lovable Muppet characters. Complex wraparound action characterizes each glass, and there is a rainbow of color to engage the eyes. The characters' names appear above them, and at the bottom of each glass appear the words "© Henson Associates, Inc. 1981." To the right of this is a small yellow McDonald's logo. These glasses are plentiful due to extensive distribution. A Canadian version of this set exists; a small yellow maple leaf below the McDonald arches distinguishes it from the U. S. version. Value: $1-3; Canadian: $2–$4.

<table>
<tr><td></td><td>[U.S.]</td><td>(Canadian)</td></tr>
<tr><td>Kermit the Frog</td><td>[MC14]</td><td>(MC18)</td></tr>
<tr><td>Kermit the Frog, Fozzie Bear, the Great Gonzo</td><td></td><td></td></tr>
<tr><td>[MC15]</td><td>(MC19)</td><td></td></tr>
<tr><td>Happiness Hotel</td><td>[MC16]</td><td>(MC20)</td></tr>
<tr><td>Miss Piggy</td><td>[MC17]</td><td>(MC21)</td></tr>
</table>

Events, Places, Unusual Motifs

Big Mac Multi-Language Glass. A 5" glass promoting the Big Mac sandwich. There are six bands of words encircling the glass from top to bottom. The topmost band is yellow, and in it the name "Big Mac" appears in five languages, alternating with golden arches. The languages are English, German, Italian, Spanish, and Greek. The next band down is red (English), and it is a list of the Big Mac's ingredients in English, without any spacing between words. It looks like this: "Twoallbeefpattiesspecialsauce-lettucecheesepicklesonionsona-sesameseedbun." This list is then re-peated below in various languages in two black bands (Italian and German), a yellow band (Spanish), and a red band (Greek). There is no date and no other information. This glass is very interesting. It should provide hours of entertainment for the student of foreign languages. **[MC21]** Value: $4–$6.

Denim Collection. A 6⅛" glass with an overall design featuring the rear pockets of a pair of blue denim jeans. A red and white bandana hangs out of one pocket on one side of the glass, and there are red, white, and yellow wildflowers on the other panel's pocket. Above each pocket there is a brownish red-tooled leather panel with "Enjoy Coca-Cola" on it. Red stitching appears where it normally would on a pair of jeans. "The Denim Collection From McDonald's" appears in small white letters below the red bandana. There is no date. The word "Collection" suggests that other glasses accompany this one. This particular issue is not widely known and was probably a limited regional promotion. **[MC25]** Value: $5–$7.

McDonald's Hawaii. A set of four heavy 4" smoke-tinted glasses celebrating Hawaii's culture, occupations, and attractions. A frosted wraparound band contains the theme of each glass. On the reverse of each glass is a frosted McDonald's logo with the word "Hawaii" after "McDonald's." There is no other writing and no date on these unusual glasses. Difficult to find, even on the West Coast, and not generally known anywhere else. These glasses are still available at Hawaiian McDonalds' in a gift box with a mailing label on the top. The top of this gift box says "Hawaiians And Their Sea Glassware/A Souvenir From Hawaii," and each side of the box has one of the designs from the glasses on it. Value: $3–$5.

Fishermen Bringing In Their Nets At Sunset **[MC30]**
Surfing **[MC31]**
Outrigger Racers (two boats with five people in each) **[MC32]**
Sunset with Catamaran and Outrigger, island background, people on the shore waving **[MC33]**

The 1982 Knoxville World's Fair. This classic 5½" flare is co-sponsored by Coca-Cola, and it vividly commemorates the 1982 World's Fair in Knoxville, Tennessee. The colorful front panel shows a family against the fair background and the red energy logo, and the back panel has this explanation beneath the "Energy Turns The World" heading: "This exciting celebration of/energy brings together the/culture, cuisine and colors of/the world through national/and international pavilions/and major industrial exhibits./A once-in-a-lifetime/experience set in the rolling/foothills of

East Tennessee." After a space appear these words: "This Commemorative Glass/Was Developed By McDonald's [logo]/The Coca-Cola Company." A ¼" white band with red-lined borders encircles the glass below both panels. In it on the front in black are the words: "May–October, 1982 Knoxville, Tennessee USA," and on the reverse the words: "The 1982 World's Fair." **[MC35]** Value: $4–$6.

1984 Olympic Mugs. A set of four 3½" glass mugs commemorating the 1984 Olympic Games. With the handle on the right, the glasses are identical from the front which shows, from top to bottom, the following: red, white, and blue Olympic stars logo below which are the words "© 1980 L. A. Olympic Committee℠"; the International Olympic five-linked-circles logo; a yellow McDonald's logo; and the words "Games of the XXIIIrd Olympiad Los Angeles 1984." On the reverse of each glass are four cubes depicting individual Olympic sports in four colors: red, blue, white, and yellow. On each glass, all four sports are outlined in one color (red, blue, white, or yellow), and it is these colors which "define" the four issues. Below the cubes appear the words "1984 Olympics," and vertically along the right edge of the cubes appear the words "© 1981 L. A. Olympic Committee." A very desirable set which is not easy to complete. Value: $3–$5.

Yellow: Weightlifting, Wrestling, Track, Archery **[MC40]**

Red: Steeplechase, Fencing, Ice Skating, Cycling **[MC41]**

White: Baseball, Volleyball, Basketball, Soccer **[MC42]**

Blue: Sailing, Kayaking, Sculling, Swimming **[MC43]**

McDonaldland Characters

Collector Series. It's difficult to know what name to give this set of six 5⅛" glasses with the familiar McDonald Collector Series characters on them. These glasses are thick and heavy, and they resemble jelly glasses. They were probably issued in the early 1970s. Front and reverse are the same: a single character appears with its title below. There is no other writing. These glasses are appealing because of their straightforward simplicity of design and vivid colors. Quite difficult to find, and a must

for every McDonald's collector. Value: $5–$8.

Captain Crook [MC50]
Grimace [MC51]
Ronald McDonald [MC52]
Mayor McCheese [MC53]
Hamburglar [MC54]
Big Mac [MC55]

Collector Series. A set of six 5⅝" glasses featuring the same popular McDonald's promotional characters as the earlier set above. These are probably mid-seventies issues and are more fragile. There are slight design differences in the characters, but the most apparent difference is in the colors. Collectors will note that the earlier Grimace is a dark purple, while the one in this set is lavender. Captain Crook in the earlier set is predominantly purple and lavender, while in this set he is predominantly black and red. Again, identical images on front and back; below them, the character's name followed by the words "Collector Series." This set is readily available. But wait! There is yet another set of these glasses with the same characters and in the same size, but with obvious design differences. For instance, Ronald McDonald in this set has red lettering instead of black and his hands are in a slightly different position. Grimace's

body in this set is dark blue with black dots all over it, and he has white eyes and mouth as opposed to the more commonly encountered version where he is a light purple color with a red mouth. Furthermore, the dark blue Grimace has a "textured" surface, whereas the light purple version is smooth. Finally, the dark blue Grimace has a Libbey Glass Company imprint on its bottom; the light purple Grimace has no glass company identification. Collectors who assemble both versions of this set will immediately notice the differences between them. Until further information is available, this is all we can report. Values: well-known Collector Series, $2–$4; lesser-known—and perhaps earlier—series, $4–$6.

Big Mac [MC60]
Captain Crook [MC61]
Grimace [MC62]
Hamburglar [MC63]
Mayor McCheese [MC64]
Ronald McDonald [MC65]

McDonaldland Action Series (1977).

In this set of six 5⅝" glasses, McDonald's once again gives us its well-known cast of six characters, but this time they are involved in dynamic action on the fronts of each glass. This action is continued in white line drawings on the reverse side, and here children are represented in a variety of physical activities. Clearly superior to the two previous sets, excellent color, and interesting facial expressions on the characters. At the bottom of each glass are the name of the character and the words "1977 McDonaldland Action Series." Plentiful in some areas of the country and scarce in others. Value: $3–$5.

5⅝" Glasses

Big Mac on roller skates directing traffic, kids on scooter, pogo stick, and tricycle **[MC70]**
Captain Crook in leaking boat, kids in inner tube pulling plug **[MC71]**
Grimace on pogo stick racing fries, kids holding finish flag **[MC72]**
Hamburglar on flatcar, kids driving locomotive **[MC73]**
Mayor McCheese taking picture of kids and fries and holding sign which says "Say Cheeseburger" **[MC74]**
Ronald McDonald leapfrogging over fries creature and about to land in "Filet O' Fish Lake," kids playing leapfrog **[MC75]**

Note: There is another set of 1977 McDonaldland Action glasses with scenes identical to those above, but this time they are on a stately 6³⁄₁₆" footed-base glass which is ⅛" larger in diameter at the rim. These unusual glasses have an immediate appeal because of their design, and they are much rarer than their shorter kin. Value: $6–$8.

6³⁄₁₆" Glasses

Big Mac **[MC80]**
Captain Crook **[MC81]**
Grimace **[MC82]**
Hamburglar **[MC83]**
Mayor McCheese **[MC84]**
Ronald McDonald **[MC85]**

McDonaldland Adventure Series (1980).

A set of six glasses, identical in shape and size to the tall 1977 Action Series (above) and with the same six successful McDonald's characters involved in various realistically detailed and imaginative actions. This is a very desirable series, and because of uneven regional distribution, these glasses are extremely difficult to obtain. Title of glass appears immediately above the main character. Below the character are the words "McDonaldland Adventure Series." On the reverse near the bottom are the words "© 1980 McDonald's Corporation." Value: $6–$8.

Ronald McDonald Saves The Falling Stars **[MC90]**

Grimace Climbs A Mountain [MC91]
Big Mac Nets The Hamburglar [MC92]
Mayor McCheese Rides A Runaway Train
   [MC93]
Hamburglar Hooks The Hamburgers [MC94]
Captain Crook Sails The Bounding Main
   [MC95]

McVote '86 (1986). A set of three $5\frac{7}{8}''$ glasses which have as their theme a mock election, urging McDonald's patrons to vote for the finest McDonald hamburger. These barrel-shaped glasses are colorful and have wraparound campaign-related action. Near the top, over each hamburger candidate, there is a red, white, and blue banner with the words "McVote '86" on it. From this point on, the glasses are very individual. Apparently, this series was distributed only in the Northeast; as a result, it is quite scarce and almost unheard of in other regions. Near the bottom of each glass appear the words "© 1986 McDonald's Corporation," followed by McDonald's golden arches. Very interesting and beautiful glasses. Value: $6–$8.

McD.L.T. (McD.L.T. riding in open convertible, sign on door saying "All The Makings Of A Winner," campaigners holding sign saying "McD.L.T. For Burger Of The Year," another sign saying "Vote For Me McD.L.T.")
   [MC100]
Quarter Pounder With Cheese (Quarter Pounder campaigning from rear of train, sign below saying "He's The Big Cheese in Burgers," campaigners holding signs saying "Count On Him" and "Quarter Pounder With Cheese in '86.") [MC101]
Big Mac (Big Mac standing at the bottom of a flight of steps after getting off an airliner and being welcomed by crowd. Three people hold a sign which says "BIG MAC—No One Else Stacks Up.") [MC102]

Mugs

Ceramic Mug. A heavy $4\frac{15}{16}''$ white ceramic mug with golden arches and red lettering. Below the arches appear the words: "McDonald's Corporation/ Washington, D. C. Region/703-698-4000." Obviously an in-house item not intended for public distribution. **[MC110]** Value: $6–$8.

Ceramic Mug, Black. A $3\frac{5}{8}''$ black mug with "McDonald's" in beautiful gold script which is underlined and at an angle. In the same family as the blue ceramic mug above and no doubt another in-house item. **[MC115]** Value: $6–$8.

Ceramic Mug, Blue. A heavy $4\frac{7}{16}''$ blue ceramic mug with "McDonald's" written across the front in gold script. Probably available only within the company and therefore rare. **[MC130]** Value: $6–$8.

Coffee Mug Set. This is a set of four $3\frac{5}{8}''$ ceramic mugs with office motifs and the standard jokes about how tough it is to function on the job early in the morning, especially before that first cup of coffee. These came out in the mid-eighties and, because people actually use them, they are not that easy to find. Value: $2–$4.

"It's much too/early to start/talking . . . /LEAVE A/NOTE!" (black and white tack, yellow notepaper, black writing) **[MC135]**

"Gone For The/Morning!" (red and white "While You Were Out" memo form, black writing) **[MC136]**

"Warning:/FIRST CUP/Talk to me at your/own risk!" (black and yellow caution sign) **[MC137]**

"I'd like mornings better/if they started LATER!" ("a. m." in black, red sign, black script below) **[MC138]**

"Good Morning" Mug. A 3½" milk glass mug with golden arches, black Mc-Donald's name, and a smiling orange sun saying "Good Morning." The Canadian version of this mug [MC124] is exactly the same, except it says "Good Morning Canada." **[MC125]** Value: $1–$2.

My Morning Mug. A 3¾" white ceramic mug with a smiling yellow sun rising above and to the right of a red square, which contains golden arches and a white McDonald's name. Below appear the words, "My Morning Mug." Very unusual and probably available only to McDonald's employees. **[MC120]** Value: $5–$7.

Philippines Collector Series Ceramic Mugs. A set of six 2⅞" ceramic mugs issued in the Phillipines and featuring the six McDonald's Collector Series characters. The name of the character appears in black opposite the handle. The gold and black McDonald's logo appears below this in the middle of the mug. A continuous band of golden arches encircles the bottom of the mug. To the left of the [centered] logo the character appears in a small action scene, and to the right of the logo the character's head is depicted. On the bottom of the mug, the familiar Mc-Donald's arches appear in black with "Phillipines" below them. These mugs are bright and colorful and, as one might expect, not common in the United States. Value: $8–$10.

Big Mac **[MC145]**
Captain Crook **[MC146]**
Grimace **[MC147]**
Hamburglar **[MC148]**
Mayor McCheese **[MC149]**
Ronald McDonald **[MC150]**

Smoked Glass Mugs. $4\frac{7}{16}''$ smoked glass mugs with embossings of the Collector Series characters in action. These mugs are undated, but they were most likely issued in the mid-seventies, perhaps as a transition between the rather static Collector Series and the later, more dynamic, 1977 and 1980 Action Series. The character's name is embossed at the bottom of the mug; front and back are identical. A large embossed McDonald's logo appears on the bottom of each mug. Unusual and quite difficult to find. There may be as many as eight mugs in this set, since we have reliable information that Ronald is available in two different poses. We have also received reports that there is a McDonald's smoked glass mug with a white McDonald's logo on the front and a white date (1979) on the back. We assume that both varieties of mugs were issued regionally, since they are not available everywhere. Value: $5–$7.

Captain Crook Hitting A Baseball With His
    Sword **[MC155]**
Grimace Shooting A Basket **[MC156]**
Ronald McDonald Throwing A Football
    [MC157]
Hamburglar As Hockey Goalie **[MC158]**
Mayor McCheese **[MC159]**
Big Mac **[MC160]**

Sports

Atlanta Falcons [1980 or 1981]. This set of four $5\frac{5}{8}''$ glasses honoring players of the Atlanta Falcons football team was sponsored by Dr Pepper and Mc-

Donald's. On each glass, three players appear in a pyramid above a border of white McDonald arches. On the reverse, behind the players' pictures, is an action illustration with an NFL Players Association logo below it. To the right of these are an Atlanta Falcons logo in black and a small Dr Pepper logo in white below it. Above the players, a red and white band with stars encircles the glass. Colors: red, white, and black. Very appealing design. Value: $3–$5.

William Andrews, Jeff Van Note, Mike Kenn **[MC170]**
R. C. Thielemann, Bobby Butler, Lynn Cain **[MC171]**
Steve Bartkowski, Alfred Jackson, Al Jenkins **[MC172]**
Fulton Kuykendall, Joel Williams, Buddy Curry **[MC173]**

Houston Livestock Show and Rodeo (1983). A set of four heavy $4\frac{3}{4}''$ glasses commemorating the 1983 Houston Livestock Show and Rodeo. Colors, size, and shape are the same as the 1982 All-Time Greatest Steelers (below). Glasses feature rodeo and livestock themes. "Houston Livestock Show/And Rodeo 1983" appears near the top of each glass. The name of the rodeo event appears near the bottom of each glass, and each glass pictures two such events. At the bottom of one of the other "quarters" of the glass appears a small square "Coke" logo with the word "Houston" above it; between the logo and the word "Houston" are, from left to right, a small likeness of a steer's head, a city skyline,

and an oil derrick. On the opposite side in the same relative location is a McDonald's logo which has the following words under it: "McDonald's Collector Series 1983/[First, Second, Third, Fourth] In A Series of Four/© 1983 McDonald's Corporation." Though only five years old, these are elusive glasses. Value: $6–$8.

First In A Series of Four (Bareback Bronc Riding/Saddle Bronc Riding) **[MC180]**
Second In A Series of Four (Women's Barrel Racing/Chuckwagon Races) **[MC181]**
Third In A Series of Four (Cutting Horse/Calf Scramble) **[MC182]**
Fourth In A Series Of Four (Steer Wrestling/Bull Riding) **[MC183]**

Houston Livestock Show and Rodeo (1984). In size, shape and color, virtually the same as the 1983 set, except the title is now "Houston Livestock Show And Rodeo 1984," and, above the McDonald's logo, $\frac{1}{8}''$ letters tell us that this is the "Second Edition Series." The Coke logo which appears on the 1983 glasses appears on these unchanged. Again, rodeo events are depicted with appropriate captions. Like their 1983 brethren, quite difficult to round up! Value: $6–$8.

First In A Series Of Four (Bareback Bronc Riding/Saddle Bronc Riding) **[MC184]**
Second In A Series Of Four (Women's Barrel Racing/Chuckwagon Races) **[MC185]**
Third In A Series Of Four (Cutting Horse/Calf Scramble) **[MC186]**
Fourth In A Series Of Four (Steer Wrestling/Bull Riding) **[MC187]**

Milwaukee Brewers (1982). A set of four 5⅝" glasses spotlighting members of the 1982 Milwaukee Brewers baseball team. There are two players per glass. On the reverse is the Major League Baseball Players Association logo and a representation of a pitcher-batter confrontation. The top border consists of a yellow and blue Brewer's logo and the words "milwaukee brewers 1982" in blue. The bottom border consists of yellow golden arches with black McDonald's lettering. An attractive set. Value: $3–$5.

Paul Molitor and Pete Vuckovich **[MC195]**
Robin Yount and Ben Ogilvie **[MC196]**
Gorman Thomas and Cecil Cooper **[MC197]**
Rollie Fingers and Ted Simmons **[MC198]**

Philadelphia Eagles (1980). A set of five 6" glasses celebrating members of the Philadelphia Eagles in action scenes. Each glass spotlights two players. Each player's face appears within a football frame beside a representation of the player in action. A black McDonald's logo and a black NFL Players Associa- tion logo appear opposite each other between the action scenes. The colors are distinctive: green, white, black, and burnt orange. At the bottom of each glass appear the words "© 1980 McDonald's Corporation." An unusual feature of these glasses is that, beneath each play- er's signature the abbreviation for the player's position appears. Value: $3–$5.

Ron Jaworski, QB and Keith Krepfle, TE [MC205]

Harold Carmichael, WR and Randy Logan, S [MC206]

Tony Franklin, K and Stan Walters, T [MC207]

Wilbert Montgomery, RB and Billy Campfield, RB [MC208]

John Bunting, LB and Bill Bergey, LB [MC209]

Pittsburgh Steelers—The All-Time Greatest Steelers Team (1982).

A set of four heavy 4¾" glasses honoring twenty-four of the all-time greatest Steeler football players. The front of each glass pictures six players who are recognizable either by their well-known faces or by the numbers of their uniforms. Below this front collage of players appear the words "McDonald's Corporation 1982." The name of the artist, Mahoney, appears in small black letters close to the design. On the reverse near the top is a "Steelers 50 Seasons" logo, below which are the words "The All-Time Greatest Steelers Team" in white, followed by the names of six players and the years they played. Below the names is a McDonald's logo and the words "McDonald's Collector Series 1982," followed by the numbering sequence, for example: "First In A Series Of Four." Colors: black, gold, beige, brown, and white. A beautiful set which contains a veritable storehouse of Steelers information. Value: $4–$6.

First In A Series Of Four: Mullins, Brown, Lambert, Harris, Brady, and White [MC215]

Second In A Series Of Four: Greene, Nickel, Kolb, Bleier, Shell, Ham [MC216]

Third In A Series Of Four: Gerela, Davis, Wagner, Greenwood, Webster, Swann [MC217]

Fourth In A Series Of Four: Blount, Stoutner, Bradshaw, Russell, Stallworth, and Butler [MC218]

Pittsburgh Steelers—Superbowl XIII: Pittsburgh 35, Dallas 31 [1978].

A set of four 6" glasses in black, white, and yellow celebrating Superbowl 13 and members of the Pittsburgh Steelers. The major focus on each glass is a group of three players; behind each group is a different scene from the actual game and an NFL Players Association logo. Encircling each glass at the bottom is a white-bordered band of golden arches. The "Superbowl XIII" title is in white lettering. Plentiful in Western Pennsylvania and wanted everywhere else. Value: $3–$5.

John Stallworth, Joe Greene, Mike Wagner [MC219]

Mike Webster, Terry Bradshaw, L. C. Greenwood [MC220]

Sam Davis, Jack Lambert, John Banaszak [MC221]

Donnie Shell, Rocky Bleier, Jack Ham [MC222]

Pittsburgh Steelers—Superbowl XIV: Pittsburgh 31, Los Angeles 19 [1979].

A set of four 5⅝″ glasses commemorating Superbowl 14 and members of the Pittsburgh Steelers football team. Again the colors are black, white, and yellow; general design is the same as the Superbowl 13 glass (above); however, this glass has a few small differences: the "Superbowl XIV" title with the score is in yellow, and the action scenes from the game behind the player groups are specifically described in white lettering. Bottom border decoration is same as 1978 glass. Like its predecessor, a prized set. Value: $3–$5.

Rocky Bleier, John Stallworth, Dirt Winston
  [MC223]
Jon Kolb, Jack Lambert, Mel Blount **[MC224]**
Sam Davis, Terry Bradshaw, Jack Ham
  [MC225]
Sidney Thornton, Joe Greene, Matt Bahr
  [MC226]

Seattle Seahawks [1978 or 1979]. A set of four 6" glasses commemorating twelve Seattle Seahawks football players. There are three players arranged in a pyramid on the front of each glass. Just below them, a blue and green band which encircles the glass culminates in two opposing beaked seabird heads. On the reverse in large white letters appear the words "Seattle Seahawks" and at the same height to the right is a large McDonald's logo in white. The NFL Players Association logo appears in black below the Seahawks team name. A simply designed glass, but attractive because of its excellent color. Probably issued in 1978 or 1979 because at least nine of these players were starters during those years. Value: $3–$5.

Terry Beeson, Carl Eller, Autry Beamon
  [MC230]
Dennis Boyd, Bill Gregory, Manu Tuiasosopo
  [MC231]
Steve Raible, Jim Zorn, Sam McCullum
  [MC232]
Sherman Smith, Steve Largent, David Sims
  [MC233]

Mobil

Mobil NBA Logo Glasses. These are 5⅝" Libbey glasses with wraparound frosted panels which feature the logos of National Basketball Association teams. The frosted panel has colored bands at top and bottom; the colors vary from team to team, giving the glasses a pleasing variety. On the reverse near the bottom, "Mobil" appears in black. There is no other writing on the glasses. Presumably, there is a glass for each NBA team. Value: $1–$3.

Los Angeles Lakers **[MB1]**

Mobil NFL Helmet Glasses. These 4" glasses, distributed by Mobil gasoline stations, feature National Football League helmets, team logos, and team names on a frosted background. On the reverse there is a NFL shield logo in the

center and the "Mobil" name in black. The 1¾" high helmets are nicely colored and detailed. Presumably there is a glass for each team and a number of different universities. Value: $1–$3.

New England Patriots **[MB31]**
Pittsburgh Steelers **[MB32]**
Philadelphia Eagles **[MB33]**
New York Giants **[MB34]**
New York Jets **[MB35]**
Seattle Seahawks **[MB36]**
Syracuse University—Carrier Dome **[MB7]**
University of Washington Huskies **[MB8]**

(*CAUTION:* These glasses reportedly contain lead paint on the outside design. It is not recommended that they be used as drinking glasses.)

Monarch Foods

Lucy and Luke. 5¼" food glasses which come in a variety of colors and feature Luke the Lion and Lucy, a little Alice-in-Wonderland-looking girl. Each of these glasses comes in at least four colors: blue, green, red, and maroon. There are probably six or more glasses in the set. They probably date from the fifties. The single-color line drawings on each glass are quite involved. A complete set is a challenge to assemble. There is no date or brand name on these glasses.

Because each design comes in at least four colors, a complete set of these glasses will be hard to assemble. Value: $4–$6.

Lucy sitting beneath tree by edge of pond taking shoe off, Luke the Lion sipping lemonade at a makeshift lemonade stand and fanning himself, rabbits jumping into the pond (the name "Luke" appears on the lion's crown) **[MF1]**

Luke and Lucy having a picnic, blanket on ground, rabbits serving food and playing in tree, horse and wagon with rabbits in it waiting at right (the name "Lucy" appears on little girl's dress) **[MF2]**

Mother's Pizza-Pasta Restaurant

Mother's Pizza Collector's Series. A set of six 5½" flare glasses in the old-time brown Coca-Cola colors. The front of each glass has an oval panel with a Coke lady in it and a smaller illustration below, featuring scenes from the 20s. On the reverse there is a panel full of information about the series, which we quote here: "To/remember/an era gone by,/the famous 20's./We have recreated/a series of/the then popular soda/fountain flare glass." Next, in the center of this panel, appears the name "MOTHER'S/Pizza Parlour & Spaghetti House" followed by a "Drink Coca-Cola" logo. At the bottom of the panel appears the series information: "Collector's Series/No. [1, 2, 3, 4, 5, or 6] of 6." Small brown print below the panel reads as follows: "Mother's and Mother's Pizza Parlour are registered trade marks of Mother's Restaurants Inc./Coca-Cola is a registered trade mark which identifies only the product of Coca-Cola Ltd./Made in Canada." This is an interesting series that is difficult to find. Value: $4–$6.

Couple with Motorcycle (#1 of 6) **[MP6]**
Airplane and Train (#2 of 6) **[MP7]**
Flapper Girl (#3 of 6) **[MP8]**
Delivery Truck (#4 of 6) **[MP9]**
Baseball Player, Cars (#5 of 6) **[MP10]**
Trumpet Player and Keystone Cops (#6 of 6) **[MP11]**

Mother's Pizza-Pasta Flare (1986). A standard 5½" flare in brown and beige with a thirties-type lady holding an identical flare with the words "Coca-Cola" on it on one side in an oval, and a Mother's Pizza logo on the other side which reads: "This re-creation of a circa/ 1920 soda-fountain flare glass/is presented in the spirit of the times by/Pizza-Pasta [above]/Mother's/Restaurant [below]/Pizza Pasta Made Perfect/© 1986 Mother's Restaurants Limited." Very similar to the Coca-Cola 16 oz. archives re-creation. **[MP1]** Value: $2–$4.

Mountain Dew

Mountain Dew Badger Hockey Collector Series. These are 6" round-bottom glasses in red and white featuring Bucky Badger in the same pose as on the Pepsi/ Wisconsin Badger Collector Series. "Badger Hockey/[dates]/Home Games" appears near the top on the reverse, and then there is a list of these games in red. Near the bottom of the glass there is a white Mountain Dew logo with "Collector/Series" below it. Like their Pepsi counterparts, these are interesting and fairly unusual regional issues, and they should be of interest to sports collectors. We are not sure how many glasses there are in the series. Value: $6–$8.

Muppets

Muppets. A $5\frac{1}{16}$" glass featuring Big Bird pouring orange juice for Ernie, Oscar, Cookie Monster, and a little girl. Near Cookie's legs appear the words "© Muppets Inc.," and right in front of Big Bird's toes appear the letters "Doc." There is no date, but this is a modern glass. There is also a mug. Glass, **[MP1]**; Mug, **[MP2]**. Value: $1–$2.

National Flag Foundation

Bicentennial 200 Collection (1974– 1976). Eighteen $6\frac{7}{16}$" pedestal-base glasses featuring historic flag scenes on the front and historical background information on the reverse. Also referred to in Anchor Hocking's promotional lit- erature as "Americana '74," these glasses actually consist of six sets of three glasses each. Nationally known artist Don Hewitt, under commission from the National Flag Foundation in Pittsburgh, did the artwork for these beautiful glasses,

which have also received praise for their educational value. On the reverse near the bottom appear the series number in Roman numerals and these words: "This illustration portrays one of a series of/ works depicting America's history for the/exclusive heritage collection at Flag Plaza,/Pittsburgh, Pa. © [date, sometimes '1973' alone and sometimes '1968, 1973'] National Flag Foundation." (Each three-glass set was packaged by Anchor Hocking in a red, white, and blue cardboard case that was labeled "Bicentennial 200 Collection," and there were two of each glass in this package for a total of six glasses.) At least 16 of these flag design glasses were distributed on the West Coast by Herfy's in 1975 and 1976 in a round-bottom version with Coca-Cola sponsorship. Eight of these pedestal glasses ("Americana '74") were sponsored by the Pittsburgh Press and came out with the words "The Pittsburgh Press/Bicentennial Collection" just below the historical information. One of these designs, the Confederate Battle Flag, appears for the first time in this set (see listing below). These glasses are fairly difficult to find in good condition, and a complete set of eighteen lined up on a shelf would be a beautiful sight indeed. Value: $4–$6. The headings for each set of three glasses are taken from Anchor Hocking promotional material.

Americana '74

Flags for Freedom
  Bennington [NF1]
  Guilford Courthouse [NF2]
  Serapis [NF3]
Early Flags of Our Nation
  Grand Union [NF4]
  First Stars and Stripes [NF5]
  Star Spangled Banner [NF6]
Discovering A Continent
  Royal Standard of Spain [NF7]
  British Union [NF8]
  French Fleur de Lis [NF9]
The Revolution
  Bunker Hill [NF10]
  Green Mountains [NF11]
  Taunton [NF12]
From Yorktown West
  The Alamo [NF13]
  General Fremont [NF14]
  Commodore Perry 1813 [NF15]
Revolution at Sea
  Rattlesnake [NF16]
  Washington's Cruisers [NF17]
  Gadsden [NF18]

Pittsburgh Press Issue (1974)

Bunker Hill Flag [NF19]
Commodore Perry [NF20]
Confederate Battle Flag [NF21]
First Stars and Stripes [NF22]
Gadsden [NF23]
Iwo Jima [NF24]
Star Spangled Banner [NF25]
Washington's Cruisers [NF26]

9-Lives

Morris [the cat] Series. These $5\frac{1}{16}''$ glasses feature Morris the 9-Lives cat in various poses plugging 9-Lives Cat Food. On the front panel Morris imperturbably stares at the beholder, and there is a balloon with one of his catty thoughts inside it. These were probably mail-order premiums, and it's hard to believe that many people would have gone to the trouble of ordering them. Clearly, these glasses are for cat lovers. On the reverse of the glasses "9-Lives" appears in large red letters. There is no date or other information, and there are two glasses in the set. Value: $3–$5.

Morris On Glass/Is Like/Sterling On Silver. (Morris lying down with catfood bowl be-

tween his paws, name "Morris" on bowl) **[NL1]**

There's Something Irresistible/About This Glass. (Morris' head is shown with his name below it) **[NL2]**

Nursery Rhymes

Two-Color Wraparound Action Set. These $4\frac{1}{2}''$ Hazel Atlas glasses feature the namesakes of a number of popular nursery rhymes in characteristic action. The name of the rhyme/character appears near the top, the character appears in the center, and the nursery rhyme appears on the back, usually in four or five lines. At the bottom of the glasses there is a wraparound floral border. Unknown number of glasses in this set. Value: $6–$8.

Peter Piper (white name and illustration, blue border) **[NR1]**

Vertical Name Single-Color Set. These glasses, which come in 4⅛″, 4⅝″, and 5″ sizes, are single-color glasses which show the name of the rhyme/character vertically to the right of the character. The nursery rhyme appears on the reverse in print. The illustrations on this set are rather one-dimensional, static, and uncomplex; the glasses are light and fragile. The glasses come in yellow, red, blue, and white, and they date from the 30s and 40s. Made by Libbey. Un-

known number in set. Value: $6–$8.

Little Bo-Peep **[NR15)**
Little Miss Muffet **[NR16]**
Mary **[NR17]**
Red Riding Hood **[NR18]**
Tom, Tom, The Piper's Son **[NR19]**
Jack Horner **[NR20]**
Old King Cole **[NR21)**

Ohio Indians

Famous Ohio Indians. A set of iced tea glasses resembling the Famous Oklahoma Indians and probably sponsored and distributed by Bonded Oil Company. Date and number of glasses in set are uncertain. Value: $4–$6; pitcher **[OH1]**, $10–$15.

Blue Jacket/Shawnee **[OH2]**
Chief Logan/Mingo **[OH3]**
Cornstalk/Shawnee **[OH4]**
Little Turtle/Miami **[OH5]**
Pontiac/Ottawa **[OH6]**
The Prophet/Shawnee **[OH7]**
Tecumseh/Shawnee **[OH8]**
White Eyes/Delaware **[OH9]**

Oklahoma Indians

Famous Oklahoma Indians. Frosted $6\frac{9}{16}''$ iced tea glasses featuring, as the top of each glass informs us in white, "Famous Oklahoma Indians." On the front center of each glass an Oklahoma Indian is posed against thematic and historically important background details. Below the feet of each Indian appears his name and tribe's name. Near the bottom of each glass appears the artist's name: Blue Eagle. There is also an $8\frac{7}{8}''$ pitcher with the title: "Oklahoma/Home of the Red Man" near the bottom. All of these pieces are very colorful, and they are undated, though collectors we know say that they came out in the years 1959–1962. They were probably meant to appeal to tourists passing through the state of Oklahoma, and there is reason to believe they may have been available at gas stations. Worthy subject matter, to be sure, and collectible; not exactly plentiful either. Number of glasses in set unknown. Value: $4–$6; pitcher, $10–$15.

Geronimo/Apache. (Background material includes warriors on horses, a burning wagon, and buzzards in sky; we are to associate Geronimo with war.) **[OK1]**

Sequoyah/Cherokee. (Background material includes a log cabin, leaves blowing in the wind, and a plow; Sequoyah is reading a paper with letters on it and smoking a pipe, so the idea here is civilization of the Indian.) **[OK2]**

Bacon Rind/Osage. (Background material includes grazing horses and an oil derrick, so the idea here is the co-existence of commerce and the Indian lifestyle.) **[OK3]**

Hen-Toh/Wyandot **[OK4]**

Pitcher: On the front of the pitcher below the spout is a teepee, the center of the design. The designs to the right and left of the teepee are identical: an Indian chief in war bonnet playing a flute-like musical instrument, a full red sun behind a tree, a fawn, and swallows flying in the sky. **[OK10]**

Olympic Games

Games of the XXIIIrd Olympiad Los Angeles (1984). A 5⅝" red, white, and blue glass celebrating the 1984 Olympic Games in Los Angeles. On the front appear the blue, clear, and red Olympic stars. Below them are these words in blue: "Games of the XXIIIrd Olympiad Los Angeles 1984." Then there are the five interlocked rings in blue, beneath which are these words in blue: "© 1980 L. A. Olympic Committee." Three colored bands (red, white, blue) encircle the glass at the bottom. On the reverse in blue, Sam the Olympic eagle appears wearing a striped top hat with the five interlocked ring logo, and he is shown jumping a hurdle, performing on the pommel horse, and dribbling a basketball. Just above the red ring are the

following words in blue: "© 1981 L. A. Olympic Committee." **[OG1]** Value: $2–$4.

Pancho's

Pancho's Restaurant. A 5¹⁵⁄₁₆" round-bottom glass featuring jolly, full-bellied Pancho in sombrero and serape. The colors are black, red, orange, and white. There is no writing on this glass, but it is the non-Pepsi version of the Pancho's Pepsi glass, **[PP73]**. *See Pancho's Restaurant* under Pepsi. **[PN1]** Value: $2–$4.

Papa Gino's Pizza

Papa Gino's Collectors Series 1976.
These 6¼" glasses, which were made by
Libbey, feature nicely detailed black and
white portraits of major league baseball
players. The player's signature appears
in black below his portrait. On the reverse, near the bottom, there is an "MLB"
Major League Baseball Players logo in
black and a Papa Gino's logo with these
words around it: "The Papa Gino's Collectors Series 1976." "© Major League
Baseball Players Assn." appears in black
at the base of the glass. Unknown number of glasses in set. Value: $5–$7.

Bill Lee [**PG1**]
Fred Lynn [**PG2**]

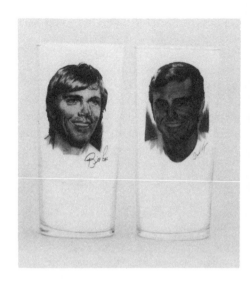

Pappan's

Toofy Tiger Milk Glass Mug. This 4¹¹⁄₁₆"
pedestal-base milk glass mug features
"Toofy Tiger" on each of its sides. Opposite the mug's handle near the top
are the words "Toofy Tiger," and below
that the tigers' tails meet. Below the tails
is the "pappan's" logo in orange. Near
the bottom of the mug, the Pappan's
slogan appears in black: "All we want
to do is make you happy." The colors
are orange, black, and white. There is
no date, but this mug goes back to the
seventies. [**PA1**] Value: $3–$5.

Gary Patterson

a miniature three-wheeled cart. Our "Pro" has a flask on his hip and a frog on his cap. Wonder what he shoots? "© Thought Factory" appears between the panels, and Gary Patterson's name appears underneath the caddy's cart. **[PT10]** Value: $2–$4.

The Dentist. A 4⁷⁄₁₆" glass in brown and pale yellow with identical opposing panels. What we have on this glass is Gary Patterson's interpretation of dentistry. It is not reassuring: the small victim crouching in the dentist's chair, a hypodermic sticking in the chair above his/her? head, and a smiling dentist who looks like Groucho Marx holding a pair of pliers behind his back. Between the panels "© Thought Factory" appears in white print. Gary Patterson's name appears in small print beneath the dentist's chair, right next to the dentist's wooden tool box. **[PT1]** Value: $2–$4.

The Pro. A large brown and yellow 6¾" glass with a 3⅜" diameter mouth and identical design on both sides: a ridiculous-looking, laughter-provoking turn of the century golfer wearing a sweater with the word "PRO" on it and posing with a miniature caddy who is sitting in

The Secretary. A 4¾" white milk glass pedestal mug with a yellow and brown panel containing a cartoon of a secretary sitting at a desk surrounded by stacks of paper and general office clutter. This cartoon appears on each side of the mug, and "The Secretary" appears in brown capitals opposite the handle at the bottom of the panel. "© Thought Factory" appears vertically in small brown letters on the edge of the panel. **[PT20]** Value: $2–$4.

Peanuts

Charlie Brown Flying Kite. A 5¼″ glass featuring Charlie Brown running with a kite. Woodstock, Snoopy, and Lucy are watching him, and the sun is coming out from behind a cloud. The following information appears in clear glass letters on the green grass border which encircles the glass: "PEANUTS Char- acters: Copr. © 1950, 1958, 1965, 1966 United Feature Syndicate, Inc." **[PE1]** Value: $1–$3.

"It never fails . . . " Mug. A 5⅝″ handle mug featuring Snoopy and Woodstock. Woodstock is flat on his back with a "Z" in a balloon coming out of his mouth, and Snoopy is wearing his usual expression. The text, in black, is as follows: "It never fails . . . /three root beers/ and Woodstock/falls sound asleep!" Three empty black-outlined mugs appear below the text, along with the following information: "© 1958, 1965 United Feature Syndicate, Inc." **[PE20]** Value: $1–$3.

Lucy Jumping Rope. 1950, 1952, 1958, 1960, 1965 United Feature Syndicate, Inc. **[PE10]** Value: $1–$3.

Lucy's Lemonade Stand. A brown, yellow, green, and white glass featuring the Peanuts characters patronizing Lucy's Lemonade Stand. At least two sizes are available: a large 5¼″ version and a small, identically shaped and colored 4″ version. On the front of this wraparound design glass, Lucy is selling lemonade to Charlie Brown. The sign above her says "Lucy's Lemonade Stand," and the one below her says "Now Serving 5¢ Please." The other Peanuts characters are sitting on the grass sipping lemonade. Below the design in green appear the words "Copr. © 1950, 1952, 1958, 1965, 1966, United Feature Syndicate, Inc." Value: 4" **[PE30]**, $2–$4; 5¼" **[PE31]**, $2–$4.

"Never Underestimate ... Pretty Face!". A 5$\frac{15}{16}$" glass featuring the Peanuts characters in dating situations. Woodstock hovers above Sally and Linus with a bow and arrow, playing Cupid. Charley Brown and Peppermint Patti are dancing. Schroeder is playing the piano, and Lucy is kneeling on it and looking at him saying "Never/Underestimate/the Effects Of A/Pretty Face!" Snoopy, looking disgusted, expresses his opinion with the word "BLAAH!" At the bottom in black letters is the copyright information: "© 1950, 1951, 1952, 1958, 1960, 1965, 1966 United Feature Syndicate, Inc." This colorful glass is similar in color and design to the McDonald's "Camp Snoopy" set, but its shape, particularly the bottom, is different and unique. **[PE45]** Value: $2–$4.

Snoopy/Candy/Sundae. A small 3$\frac{7}{8}$" glass featuring Snoopy daydreaming about candy on one side and preparing to eat a huge sundae on the other. Two orange bands encircle the glass at the middle. The name "Schulz" appears in the lower one just to the right of Snoopy and the sundae. On the other side just below and to the right of Snoopy and the candy appear the words: "© 1958, 1965/ United Feature Syndicate, Inc." Unusual size and subject matter. **[PE40]** Value: $2–$4.

Snoopy Eating Spaghetti. A 5$\frac{7}{8}$" barrel-shaped glass featuring Snoopy eating spaghetti on one side and carrying a submarine sandwich on the other. A very colorful glass. On the red and white checkered tablecloth appear these words: "© 1958, 1965 United Features Syndicate, Inc." **[PE15]** Value: $1–$3.

Snoopy and Large Apple. A 4$\frac{1}{16}$" juice glass featuring Snoopy drinking apple juice and sitting with his back against a large red apple. On the reverse in small brown print are the words: "SNOOPY: Copr. © 1958 United Feature Syndicate, Inc." **[PE5]** Value: $1–$3.

Snoopy Mugs

Expert/Skateboard. A 4″ white mug with a colorful front panel depicting Snoopy in a helmet riding a skateboard. On the reverse in green is the caption: "It's Great To/Be An Expert." Toward the bottom in black are these words: "© 1958, United Feature Syndicate, Inc." **[PE50]** Value: $3–$5.

"M". A 3½″ ceramic mug featuring Snoopy standing beside a large green "M." The only other writing on the mug is on its bottom: "SNOOPY/Copr. © 1958/United Feature Syndicate, Inc./ Another Determined Production." **[PE75]** Value: $2–$4.

Morning Allergy. A 4″ white mug which shows Snoopy lying on the roof of his doghouse. Beneath this scene are the words: "SNOOPY: © 1958 United Feature Syndicate, Inc." "I Think/I'm Allergic/To Morning" appears in large red letters on the reverse. **[PE65]** Value: $3–$5.

Pure Joy. A 4$\frac{1}{16}$" white mug showing Snoopy and Woodstock dancing. Below them are the words: "Peanuts Characters: Copr. © 1958, 1965 United Feature Syndicate, Inc." "At Times/Life Is Pure/Joy!" appears in black letters on the reverse. **[PE70]** Value: $3–$5.

"Snoopy, Come Home." A 4" white mug in red and yellow. On the front we have Snoopy walking with a hobo sack on a stick over his shoulder. Woodstock is following him. Beneath them are these words in red: "Copr. © 1958, 1965 United Feature Syndicate, Inc." On the reverse, "Snoopy,/Come Home" appears in large red letters. **[PE60]** Value: $3–$5.

Snowflakes/French Toast. A 4" white mug with green and yellow colors featuring Snoopy sitting on the ground in a yellow stocking cap. A stack of French toast is in front of him, and it is snowing green snowflakes. Beneath this scene are the following words in green: "Snoopy: Copr. © 1958 United Feature Syndicate, Inc." On the reverse in green capital letters are Snoopy's thoughts: "I HATE/IT WHEN/IT SNOWS ON/MY FRENCH/TOAST!" **[PE55]** Value: $3–$5.

Snoopy's Kitchen. A 4" glass and 9$\frac{1}{2}$" juice decanter featuring the Peanuts characters running towards Snoopy, who appears in a chef's hat sounding a dinner triangle. "Snoopy's/Kitchen" appears in black on the red tablecloth, and below the characters is the copyright information: "© 1950, 1952, 1958, 1960, 1965, 1966 United Feature Syndicate Inc." Value: glass **[PE80]** $1–$2; decanter **[PE81]** $2–$4.

Snoopy Sitting On Lemon. A small 4" glass very simply designed: Snoopy is pictured sitting on a large lemon drinking lemonade. The name "Schulz" appears just to the right of the lemon. On the reverse of the glass are these words: "SNOOPY: Copr. © 1958 United Features Syndicate, Inc." There aren't a lot of these floating around. **[PE35]** Value: $2–$4.

"This has been a good day!" A 3$\frac{3}{8}$" highball glass in blue and white. The front features Snoopy and Woodstock lying on the doghouse roof, and "This/has/been/a good day!" appears in blue and white letters on the reverse. Near the base of the glass in small blue letters appear these words: "Copr. © 1958, 1965, United Feature Syndicate, Inc. Made In U.S.A." **[PE47]** Value: $2–$4.

"To You My Special Friend!" A 6$\frac{3}{4}$" glass featuring Snoopy and Woodstock. **[PE25]** Value: $1–$3.

Pepsi

Cartoon Characters

(See separate listings for *Disney* and *Warner Bros.* cartoon characters.)

Al Capp (1975). A set of six glasses featuring Al Capp's famous characters. Value: $10–$12.

Lil Abner **[PP240]**
Daisy Mae **[PP241]**
Snuffy Smith **[PP242]**
Hairless Joe **[PP243]**
Mammy and Pappy Yokum **[PP244]**
Marryin Sam **[PP245]**

Hanna-Barbera Collector Series (1977). A set of six 6$\frac{5}{16}$" glasses featuring popular Hanna-Barbera cartoon characters in colorful wraparound action. The character's name appears near the top of the glass in one of the lighter colors used elsewhere on the glass, and the Pepsi logo and other lettering is also in this color. Below the Pepsi logo, appear the words "Collector/Series." "© 1977 Hanna-Barbera Productions, Inc." appears below the logo on some glasses and below and to the right, under the main design, on others. These glasses are quite colorful and easy to grow fond of. They are also getting quite difficult to find. (Three other Hanna-Barbera characters—Space Ghost, Muttley, and Frankenstein Jr.—exist only as prototypes which were not released to the public.) Value: $8–$10.

Dynomutt **[PP110]**
The Flintstones **[PP111]**
Huck & Yogi **[PP112]**
Josie & The Pussycats **[PP113]**
Mumbly **[PP114]**
Scooby Doo **[PP115]**

Harvey Cartoons Collector Series.

A set of six 6¼" glasses featuring Harvey Cartoon series characters. The same design appears on both sides of the 6¼" glasses. The white Pepsi logo appears near the bottom of the glass between the panels, and directly beneath it are the words "Collector Series," followed by "© Harvey Cartoons" in white (except for the Hot Stuff glass where those words appear in black). The characters' names, which appear below the characters, are white except for Casper, which is blue. Hot Stuff also comes with black lettering. All the characters except Richie Rich and Sad Sack come in 5" versions and 5" action versions. Like other Pepsi cartoon character glasses, these are quite desirable. Values: $7–$9*; $8–$10†; $9–$11‡.

Big Baby Huey† [PP120]
Casper* [PP121]
Hot Stuff* [PP122]
Richie Rich† [PP123]
Sad Sack† [PP124]
Wendy* [PP125]

Note on Casper: There is a 6⅛" creased-bottom, straight-sided Casper with white lettering, but it does not have a Pepsi logo. It does have "© Harvey Cartoons" in white. Casper is smaller on this glass, only 3½" high, while he is 4¼" high on the Pepsi glass. We cannot "ex-

plain" this glass, and we don't know if there are others like it which form a set of six Harvey Cartoon characters to parallel the Pepsi Harvey Cartoon set. We picture it with the Pepsi Casper to illustrate the similarities and differences.

*5" Versions**

Big Baby Huey [PP126]
Casper [PP127]
Hot Stuff [PP128]
Wendy [PP129]

5" Action Versions‡

Big Baby Huey (lifting weights/circus poster) [PP130]
Casper (Casper flying/haunted house/bats) [PP131]
Hot Stuff (walking through fence) [PP132]
Wendy (stirring pot) [PP133]

Walter Lantz. A set of six $6\frac{1}{4}''$ glasses featuring popular Walter Lantz characters in the same pose on both sides of the glass. The character's name appears below the character in white letters, and Woody Woodpecker comes in either black or white lettering. Near the bottom between the opposed characters there is the Walter Lantz logo in white (on the Woody Woodpecker black-lettered glass this logo is black), a Pepsi logo in white, and the words "Collector Series" directly below it. Woody Woodpecker and Chilly Willy also come in a $5\frac{1}{8}''$ version and in $5\frac{1}{8}''$ action versions. Space Mouse is particularly difficult to find and therefore more costly than the others; because of this, putting a set of these glasses together is a definite challenge. Values: $6\frac{1}{4}''$, $5–$7; Space Mouse, [rare]; $5\frac{1}{8}''$ Chilly Willy, Woody Woodpecker, $5–$7; $5\frac{1}{8}''$ Chilly Willy, Woody Woodpecker—Action, $6–$8.

$6\frac{1}{4}''$

Andy Panda **[PP540]**
Chilly Willy **[PP541]**
Cuddles **[PP542]**
Space Mouse **[PP543]**
Wally Walrus **[PP544]**
Woody Woodpecker **[PP545]**

$5\frac{1}{8}''$

Chilly Willy **[PP546]**
Woody Woodpecker **[PP547]**

$5\frac{1}{8}''$ Action

Chilly Willy (painting picture of snowman on easel) **[PP548]**
Woody Woodpecker (chasing butterfly with net) **[PP549]**

Leonardo-TTV Collector Series. A set of four 6¼" glasses featuring characters from the popular Underdog cartoon series. These glasses come in several variations. The basic set of four glasses comes with the characters' names in white. All but Go-Go Gophers come in black. There are 5" versions of all but Go-Go Gophers. The 6¼" Underdog comes with blue lettering and Underdog in a different pose. Finally, there is a 5" Underdog action glass with Underdog breaking out of a phone booth in his costume, ready to fight crime. Minor variations, such as no "© Leonardo-TTV" have been reported on the white-letter Sweet Polly and Simon Bar Sinister glasses. Except for the action glass, the same design appears on both sides. A white Pepsi logo appears near the bottom between the panels. Beneath it the words "Collector Series" appear in white, followed by "© Leonardo-TTV" in black or white. The white Pepsi logo on the blue-lettered Underdog is larger than the other logos and 2" from the bottom of the glass. On this glass, "© Leonardo-TTV" appears in blue at the bottom. (For the curious: "Leonardo" refers to a production company; "TTV" stands for "Total Television Production.") For Pepsi collectors, this is a "must have" set, and some of the glasses, especially the blue lettered Underdog, are getting hard to find. Values: $6–$8*; $8–$10†; $15–$20‡.

Underdog (blue lettering)‡ [[PP225]
Underdog (action)† [PP226]
Underdog (white, black)† [PP227]
Sweet Polly (white, black)* [PP228]
Simon Bar Sinister (white, black)† [PP229]
Go-Go Gophers (white)† [PP230]
5" Underdog, Sweet Polly, Simon† [PP231]

M-G-M Collector Series (1975). A set of six 6¼" glasses featuring popular M-G-M characters in poses which seem to emphasize each character's arms and hands. The same design appears on both sides of the glass. The character's name appears below his picture in black or in white. Near the bottom between the designs appears a white Pepsi logo. Be-

neath it in white are the words "Collector Series," and below that the name of the character appears. Then, at the bottom, we have "© 1975 M-G-M Inc." One slight oddity is that on both the Tom and Jerry glasses, the names "Tom & Jerry" both appear beneath the Pepsi logo and "Collector Series" information. Tom has been reported with a gray-green body color variation instead of the more usual gray color. Tom and Jerry also come in $5\frac{1}{8}$" action glasses; Jerry is brown and white on this smaller glass, not blue and white as he is on the larger. On the small action glasses, the Pepsi logo and "Collector Series" are in white,

and "Tom & Jerry © 1975 M-G-M Inc." appears in black on the opposite side of the glass. The action glasses are more difficult to find than the larger ones. Values: $6\frac{1}{4}$", $5–$7; action, $7–$9.

$6\frac{1}{4}$" Glasses

Barney [PP275]
Droopy [PP276]
Jerry [PP277]
Spike [PP278]
Tom [PP279]
Tuffy [PP280]

Action Glasses

Jerry (catching Tom's tail in mousetrap) [PP281]
Tom (chasing Jerry into mousehole) [PP282]

P.A.T. Ward Productions Collector Series. A set of six $6\frac{1}{4}$" glasses featuring P.A.T. Ward Productions cartoon characters. The basic set consists of six characters with white lettering, the same design on both sides. All the characters except Snidely Whiplash come with black lettering. On four of the glasses (Bullwinkle, Dudley, Mr. Peabody, Rocky) near the bottom between the

panels there is a white Pepsi logo followed by "Collector Series," and beneath that in black appears "© P.A.T.-Ward." On the Boris and Natasha and Snidely Whiplash glasses, the white Pepsi logos are larger, and they appear near the center of the glass with "Collector Series" in white just below them. On these two glasses, instead of "© P.A.T.-Ward," we have "© P.A.T.-Ward/Productions, Inc." and this information is green on the Snidely Whiplash glasses. There are a few other lettering color variations. Bullwinkle also comes with brown lettering, Rocky comes with gray, and Dudley comes with red. There is also a set of seven 5" glasses featuring the characters singly. The characters' names are black on these glasses, the Pepsi logos are white followed by "Collector Series" in white, and the "© P.A.T.-Ward" information is black. Finally, there are three 5" action glasses. On these glasses, the white Pepsi logo with "Collector Series" beneath it is on one side of the glass, and "© P.A.T.-Ward" in black is on the other. As far as variations go, in the white $6\frac{1}{4}$" set, Snidely and Bullwinkle have been reported without the "© P.A.T.-Ward," and sometimes Dudley can be found with his hat rather oddly

tipped. It takes some persistence and luck to find all these desirable glasses, but assembling the basic set of six is relatively easy. Values: $6–$8*; $8–$10†; $10–$12‡.

$6\frac{1}{4}$":

Boris and Natasha (black, white)† **[PP300]**
Bullwinkle (black, white)† **[PP301]**
Dudley Do-Right (black, white)† **[PP302]**
Mr. Peabody (black, white)† **[PP303]**
Rocky (black, white)† **[PP304]**
Snidely Whiplash (white, green)† **[PP305]**

$6\frac{1}{4}$" lettering variations

Bullwinkle (brown)‡ **[PP306]**
Dudley Do-Right (red)‡ **[PP307]**
Rocky (gray)‡ **[PP308]**

5" single-character, black lettering

Boris Badenov‡ **[PP309]**

Bullwinkle* **[PP310]**
Dudley Do-Right* **[PP311]**
Mr. Peabody† **[PP312]**
Natasha‡ **[PP313]**
Rocky* **[PP314]**
Snidely Whiplash* **[PP315]**

5" action designs

Bullwinkle—running, holding balloons/ amusement park background† **[PP316]**
Dudley Do-Right—happily paddling canoe, unaware of waterfall/trees and mountains in background† **[PP317]**
Rocky—preparing to jump off of platform/circus tents in background† **[PP318]**

Popeye's Famous Fried Chicken (1982). A set of four 5⅝" glasses featuring four of the Popeye cartoon characters "Thru The Years." These are very colorful and busy glasses with cartoon scenes and oval frames focusing on the specific characters. One side of the glass shows the character in 1982, and the other side shows the same character at an earlier date. A blue, white, and yellow band encircles the bottom of the glass and has "10th Anniversary Collectors' Series" inside it in black. Also in the band are a white Pepsi logo and a black, orange, and red Popeye's Famous Fried Chicken sign. At the bottom of the band in small black letters are these words: "© 1982 King Features Syndicate, Inc."

and "© 1982 Popeye's Famous Fried Chicken, Inc." These beautiful glasses are difficult to describe; they have to be seen to be fully appreciated. They are also quite difficult to find. Value: $9–$11.

Brutus (1933, 1982) **[PP250]**
Olive Oyl (1919, 1982) **[PP251]**
Popeye (1929, 1982) **[PP252]**
Swee' Pea (1933, 1982) **[PP253]**

Terry Tunes (1977). Mighty Mouse is the only one of seven 16-ounce glasses that made it to the distribution stage. The rest are prototypes and, as a result, this one is extremely rare! **[PP260]** Value: [rare].

Christmas

Christmas Collection (1982). A set of four $5\frac{7}{8}$" barrel shaped glasses with a crease just above the button base featuring four verses from "The Night Before Christmas" on the reverses, and four verse-related scenes on the fronts. The front scenes are enclosed in a red and green striped frame, and the verses from the story begin with a large red capital letter and are then continued in white. Between the panels to the right of the front design there is a white Pepsi logo and below it the words: "1982/Christmas/Collection." This is a festive set. Value: $4–$6.

Mouse in Bed **[PP1]**
Fireplace with Stockings **[PP2]**
Santa Claus **[PP3]**
Reindeer over Houses **[PP4]**

Christmas Collection (1983). This is the same set as the one listed above, but it bears a 1983 date and the glass shape is different. Here we have $5\frac{7}{8}$" round-bottom glasses instead of the bottom crease and button base. Otherwise the glasses are identical. Value: $3–$5.

Mouse in Bed **[PP5]**
Fireplace with Stockings **[PP6]**
Santa Claus **[PP7]**
Reindeer over Houses **[PP8]**

Visual Creations Collector Series. A set of six $6\frac{1}{4}$" glasses featuring animals designed by the artist Szeghy whose name appears on each glass. The same design appears on both sides, and there is a caption in black below each animal representation. Between panels near the bottom of the glass in white is a Pepsi logo with "Collector/Series" directly below it. At the bottom in black is the copyright information: "© Visual Creations." These glasses are cute, unusual and quite difficult to find. Value: $10–$12.

Camel (You're too nice to forget!) **[PP265]**
Giraffe (You Give Me A Lift!) **[PP266]**
Monkey (Friends Like You Are Very Few!) **[PP267]**
Ostrich (I'm Glad We're Friends!) **[PP268]**
Owl (I only have eyes for you!) **[PP269]**
Tiger (Knowing You Makes Me Feel Good All Over!) **[PP270]**

Christmas Collection (1983). A set of four 5⅞" round-bottom glasses featuring verses from traditional Christmas carols on the reverses and illustrative related scenes on the front panels. Below the front panel scene, the title of the Christmas song appears in white in quotation marks. On the reverse, the verse from the song appears in white lettering with decorative motifs which vary from glass to glass above and below it. On the "Toyland" glass, the verse appears within a toy drum frame. To the right of the front panel near the bottom of the glass there is a white Pepsi logo beneath which are the words: "1983/Christmas/Collection." The general format of these glasses is more pleasing than the 1982–1983 "Night Before Christmas" set. It may be due to the enhanced color and complexity of design. Value: $3–$5.

"O Christmas Tree" (decorated tree in front of fireplace, presents) **[PP9]**
"Toyland" (teddy bear sitting on rocking horse, doll, ball, presents) **[PP10]**
"We Wish You A Merry Christmas" (group of carolers) **[PP11]**
"Jingle Bells" (couple in one-horse open sleigh) **[PP12]**

Christmas Collection (1984). This set is identical to the 1983 Christmas song set listed directly above, but "1984" appears below the Pepsi logo instead of 1983. Value: $3–$5.

"O Christmas Tree" **[PP13]**
"Toyland" **[PP14]**
"We Wish You A Merry Christmas" **[PP15]**
"Jingle Bells" **[PP16]**

Twelve Days of Christmas. A set of twelve 6¼" glasses, each of which features a design which relates to one of the verses in the Christmas carol, "The Twelve Days of Christmas." The design on each glass is essentially the same: a pear tree in a pot with a banner just above the pot designating the day, and an illustration in the tree corresponding to the verse in the song. On the reverse in a holly/berry frame, the verse from the song appears. Toward the bottom of the glass to the left of the pot and banner is a black Pepsi logo. There is no other information. The colors on these glasses are vivid and varied, and when the glasses are lined up they are an impressive sight. There is also a 5⅞" round-bottom version with Pepsi logo. Col-

lectors are no doubt aware that the 6¼″ glasses also come without the Pepsi logo, and that there are two other non-Pepsi logo sets: a 5″ round-bottom version and a 5½″ thick-bottom version (see "Christmas"). Values: 6¼″, $1–$3; 5⅞″, $2–$4.

[6¼″] (5⅞″)

1st Day (A Partridge In A Pear Tree) [PP20] (PP32)
2nd Day (Two Turtle Doves) [PP21] (PP33)
3rd Day (Three French Hens) [PP22] (PP34)
4th Day (Four Colly Birds) [PP23] (PP35)
5th Day (Five Gold Rings) [PP24] (PP36)
6th Day (Six Geese A-Laying) [PP25] (PP37)
7th Day (Seven Swans A-Swimming) [PP26] (PP38)
8th Day (Eight Maids A-Milking) [PP27] (PP39)
9th Day (Nine Drummers Drumming) [PP28] (PP40)
10th Day (Ten Pipers Piping) [PP29] (PP41)
11th Day (Eleven Ladies Dancing) [PP30] (PP42)
12th Day (Twelve Lords A-Leaping) [PP31] (PP43)

Co-sponsored

Bakersfield College (1976). A 12-ounce glass celebrating the 1976 Junior Rose Bowl Champions. [PP44] Value: $7–$9.

Caterpillar Tractor Series. A set of two 5⅞″ round-bottom glasses showing the evolution in design of Caterpillar Tractors. On the "old" sides of the glasses, early Caterpillar Tractors are pictured in gray and black with extremely fine detail, and older fancy Pepsi-Cola tradenames are featured in white. On the reverses, modern Caterpillar equipment is pictured in yellow, and there are modern block-type Pepsi logos. Names of tractor models are printed below them in gray lettering, and there are dates for the older models. Between the tractors on one side of each glass, there is black vertical lettering which provides the title and number of the glass. These are very unusual and interesting glasses, and—for machinery appreciators—we therefore picture all four sides. Value: $3–$5.

Caterpillar Track-Type Tractor/first in a series (vertical black, side lettering) [PP46]
Holt "Caterpillar" 40 Tractor/1908 (red, gray, and black tractor; gray lettering)/Pepsi-Cola (white script logo)
Caterpillar D8L Tractor (yellow and gray tractor; gray lettering)/Pepsi (white block-type logo)

Caterpillar Motor Grader-Auto Patrol/second in a series (vertical black, side lettering) [PP47]
"Caterpillar" Auto Patrol/1931 (gray and black tractor; gray lettering)/white script "Drink Pepsi-Cola" logo
Caterpillar 16-G Motor Grader (yellow, gray, and black tractor; gray lettering)/white block-type Pepsi logo

Clemson University Tigers. A set of two round-bottom glasses celebrating the Clemson Tigers football team. One glass features the team's record, and the other pictures its helmet. Value: $8–$10.

"Go Tigers!" Team record through 1974 **[PP50]**
"Go Tigers!" Helmet over Clemson **[PP51]**

Country Kitchen. A Pepsi glass featuring a country boy and girl. This is another regional issue. **[PP55]** Value: $8–$10.

KYYX Radio. This Seattle radio station combined radio call numbers and a Pepsi logo to produce another single issue collectible. **[PP60]** Value: $8–$10.

La Rosa's Pizzeria (1983). Another regional glass promoting local pasta. The characters on this one are Luigi and his Hanna-Barbera friends: Scooby Doo, Yogi Bear, Park Ranger, Fred Flintstone, and Wilma. *See LaRosa's Pizza* for full listing and picture and for commentary regarding this glass's right to be called a Pepsi glass.

Michigan 150th Anniversary (1987). A $5\frac{9}{16}$" glass celebrating the 150th anni-

versary of Michigan statehood. On one side there is a red and blue rectangular Pepsi logo, framed by a thin blue line. On the other side, "Michigan Sesquicentennial 1837–1987" appears in white in a circle around red "150" numerals with a wavy blue underline beneath them. **[PP65]** Value: $4–$6.

Ohio Bicentennial (1976). A set of three 5$\frac{1}{16}$" red, white, and blue glasses issued during the Bicentennial year to commemorate Ohio historical events and history. The front of each glass has a rectangular panel with "1776*1976" at the top, an oval historical scene in the middle, and the words "Ohio Bicentennial" at the bottom. On the lower edge of the oval appear the names that relate to the historical illustration. Below the panel in white are the words "Pepsi-Cola Bottling Company—Lima–Findlay, Ohio 45804." The reverses of these three glasses share the same design: a white map of the state of Ohio with blue county lines, dates, and place-names, and red county names. The state flag and miscellaneous historical facts also appear on this map/panel. At the bottom of the glasses in white letters appear these words: "Quality Bever-

ages continuously/from 1862 to 1976 Pepsi-Cola Lima–Findlay, Ohio 45804." These glasses, which were accompanied by similarly designed Pepsi bottles, are desirable and fairly difficult to find. Value: $8–$10.

Fort Amanda/Fort Findlay (man plowing behind horse, fort in right background) **[PP70]**
Miami-Eire Canal And The Railroad (donkeys pulling boat on the left, steam locomotive on right) **[PP71]**
Tecumseh/Johnny Appleseed **[PP72]**

Pancho's Restaurant. This is a 16-ounce Brockway 6$\frac{1}{4}$" glass featuring a Mexican character in sombrero and serape. A white Pepsi logo appears near the base of the glass. Difficult to obtain, due to small regional distribution, it therefore commands a high price. There is also a 5$\frac{15}{16}$" round-bottom version of this glass without the Pepsi logo. *See Pancho's Restaurant.* **[PP73]** Value: $8–$10.

Ringling Brothers and Barnum & Bailey Collector Series (1975). A set of six $6\frac{1}{4}''$ glasses featuring colorful Ringling Brothers and Barnum and Bailey circus posters. The same poster appears on both sides of the glass. Below each poster in white lettering are the words: "© Ringling Bros. And Barnum & Bailey 1975." Between the posters near the bottom of the glass is a white Pepsi logo with "Collector Series" below it. These glasses were made by both Federal and Brockway; the Federal glasses are lighter and seem to be "thin;" the Brockway glasses are heavier and "thick." In either version, these glasses are extremely beautiful, and it is difficult to assemble a set. Collectors who complete both sets and compare them carefully will notice small design differences between the two versions. Value: $10–$12.

[Brockway] (Federal)

Combined Circus (chariot race) **[PP75] (PP81)**

100th Anniversary (leaping tiger and circus wagon) **[PP76] (PP82)**

Greatest Show On Earth (tiger growling) **[PP77] (PP83)**

"Felix" and 99 Other Famous Clowns ("Felix" holding umbrella) **[PP78] (PP84)**

Bears That Dance (bears on roller skates) **[PP79] (PP85)**

World's Biggest Menagerie (elephant with other animals in background) **[PP80] (PP86)**

1962 Seattle World's Fair Twentieth Anniversary (1982). This little blue and yellow $5\frac{1}{16}''$ glass was distributed by Herfy's. At the top of the front yellow and blue panel there are the blue words: "1962 Seattle/Worlds/Fair," on a yellow background, and in the middle there is a picture of the fairgrounds, the Space Needle, and Mt. Rainier. Below this the words "Twentieth/Anniversary" appear in yellow on a blue background. On the reverse, from top to bottom, there are the following: "The New/Original/Herfy's/Established 1962"/[large blue Pepsi logo]. This lettering is all in blue, and "Herfy's" appears on a yellow background. This rare glass is nicely designed. **[PP90]** Value: $10–$12.

Shakey's Pizza Restaurant. This red, black, yellow, and white leaded glass window diamond design tumbler features a Shakey's crest within a circle on the front (see "Shakey's") and "Pepsi-Cola" in black-bordered red script on the reverse. This round-bottom glass was made by Anchor Hocking. **[PP95]** Value: $3–$5.

Sonic [Drive-in]. A colorful 6¼" glass in red, white, light blue, dark blue, and yellow. The wraparound panel depicts a mid-fifties drive-in with two waitresses on roller skates and four vintage automobiles parked under the drive-in roof. Just above the roof, the word "Sonic" appears in bold red capitals, and to its right is a large red, white, and blue Pepsi logo. The top of the glass has

a white cloud and baby blue sky motif. This is a funky glass which accurately captures the ambiance of the 50s. It is not often encountered because of limited regional distribution. **[PP96]** Value: $6–$8.

Taco Time. A 6" round-bottom glass with three equally spaced orange cactus trademarks around the center portion and three "TacoTime" names in black encircling the bottom of the glass. Between two of the cacti there is a tiny black Pepsi logo which you might not notice unless you were looking for it. This is a rather Spartan glass, but it is quite hard to find since it was distributed only on the West Coast. There is also a non-Pepsi version of this glass, identical except for the absence of the small black Pepsi logo. Value: with Pepsi logo **[PP100]** $5–$7; without Pepsi logo **(PP101)** $1–$3.

University of Arkansas Razorbacks. A single issue celebrating the famous Arkansas football team. **[PP105]** Value: $8–$10.

Disney Cartoon Characters

Disney Character [Milk Glass Mugs] Collector Series. A set of four 4" white milk glass mugs featuring single Disney characters in conventional poses and vivid colors. The same design appears on both sides of the cup. The character's name is in black beside the character. Near the bottom of the mug there is a black Pepsi logo with "Collector/ Series" immediately below it. Just to the right of those words appears the copyright information in black: "© Walt Disney/Productions." The embossings on the cups' bottoms tells us that they are made by Anchor Hocking and that they are ovenproof. These cups are hard to find; there just don't seem to be enough to go around. Value: $7–$9.

Mickey **[PP450]**
Minnie **[PP451]**
Donald **[PP452]**
Daisey **[PP453]**

Happy Birthday Mickey (1977, 1978). A set of eight 6⅜" glasses issued to commemorate the 50th anniversary of Mickey Mouse's creation by Walt Disney. On the front of each glass the major Disney characters appear alone or in combination (Daisey & Donald, Horace & Clarabelle); on the reverse, there are action scenes with combinations of characters, both major and minor. The names of the characters appear in white below them, and on the side near the bottom in white appears the "Happy Birthday Mickey" logo followed by "© [1977 or 1978] Walt Disney/Productions." This is a nice, colorful set. Horace & Clarabelle was produced in limited quantities and distributed only in a few states, so it is a tough glass to find, and a relatively expensive one. Collectors who are fortunate enough to complete both sets will notice minor design differences between them. Values: 1977 issue, $10–$12; 1977 Horace & Clarabelle, $12–$15; 1978 issue, $5–$7; 1978 Horace & Clarabelle, $11–$13.

[1977] (1978)

Daisey & Donald (dancing)/Daisey and Donald dancing **[PP460] (PP468)**
Donald (playing violin)/Huey, Dewey, Louie, plugging their ears **[PP461] (PP469)**
Goofy (standing with pitchfork)/Goofy cooking hot dogs on pitchfork, Pluto anticipating **[PP462] (PP470)**
Horace & Clarabelle (Horace twirling lasso/ Horace lassoing Clarabelle) **[PP463] (PP471)**
Mickey (holding roses, tipping his hat)/Mickey presenting roses to Daisey **[PP464] (PP472)**

Minnie (in apron, mixing batter)/Morty and Ferdie running away with gingerbread man **[PP465] (PP473)**
Pluto (newspaper in mouth)/Mickey holding chewed-up newspaper, Pluto looking chagrined **[PP466] (PP474)**
Uncle Scrooge (about to pick up paper money with spiked cane)/Scrooge dumping money out of hat for nephews **[PP467] (PP475)**

Jungle Book (1977). This beautifully colored set of eight $6\frac{1}{4}$" glasses is every collector's candidate for most favored set. For some reason, this set was not produced in large numbers or widely distributed; it is therefore extremely difficult to find the individual glasses, not to mention completing the set. Value: $15–$20.

Bagheera (Leopard) **[PP480]**
Baloo (Bear) **[PP481]**
Colonel Hathi (Elephant) **[PP482]**
Kaa (Snake) **[PP483]**
King Looie (Gorilla) **[PP484]**
Rama (Boy) **[PP485]**
Shere Khan (Tiger) **[PP486]**
Mowgli (Fire) **[PP487]**

Mickey Mouse [Milk Glass Mugs] Collector Series (1980). A set of four 4" white milk glass mugs focusing on the career of Mickey Mouse from 1928 to 1980. The same design appears on both sides, and titles and dates appear in black capital letters. While the representations on these cups are not exactly action scenes, they do appear to have life and variety, partly because Mickey appears in different costumes and engaging color. The Pepsi logo which appears near the bottom of each cup is blue with the words "Collector/Series" below it in blue. The date of the set is the date of the last cup: 1980. These cups were made by Anchor Hocking and are oven-proof. This is a key set for Disney collectors, and it is hard to find. The Steamboat Willie mug is, like the original movie, in black and white. Value: $8–$10.

Steamboat Willie (1928) **[PP490]**
Mickey Mouse/In/Fantasia (1940) **[PP491]**
The/Mickey Mouse/Club (1955) **[PP492]**
Mickey Mouse/Today (1980) **[PP493]**

"Picnic" Collector Series [1979]. A set of six $5\frac{15}{16}$" glasses identical in size and shape to the single-character set below, but in this set we have multicharacter wraparound action and lots of vivid color. Referred to by collectors as the "Picnic Set," or the "Texas Set" because it was distributed only in Texas, this Disney set is very difficult to find, the Goofy and Pluto glasses especially so due to the fact that in some areas they were never distributed. Near the bottom of the glass there is a white Pepsi logo with the words "Walt Disney/Collector/Series" below it. The names of the characters appear in white also, as does the small print near the bottom which says "© Walt Disney Productions." Values: $8–$10*; $14–$16†.

Daisey (holding pie)/Huey, Dewey, Louie playing baseball/ Donald getting hit on head by pie **[PP500]***

Donald (wielding butterfly net)/Scrooge throwing paper airplanes made of dollar bills/ Huey, Dewey, Louie trying to catch airplanes **[PP501]***

Goofy (digging hole for plant)/Pluto digging hole for bone/ Morty with plant in wheelbarrow **[PP502]**†

Mickey (carrying picnic basket full of food)/ Goofy tending the barbeque/Pluto pilfering sausage links **[PP503]***

Minnie (with overturned laundry basket)/Mickey as cowboy/ Morty and Ferdie as Indians **[PP504]***

Pluto (wearing Donald's cap)/Donald expressing anger/Morty with sailboat in small pool **[PP505]**†

"The Rescuers" Collector Series (1977).
A set of eight 6¼" glasses featuring characters from the popular "Rescuers" cartoon feature. The characters are depicted in mild action and nice color on the front of the glasses, and their names appear below them in one of the lighter colors used elsewhere on the glass. (The

Pepsi logo, as well as the series and copyright information, is in the same color as the character's name.) On the reverse of the glasses appear character combinations or the title character in another pose. On the side near the bottom appears the Pepsi logo. Beneath it are the words " 'The Rescuers'/Collector/Series" and after a space the words "© 1977 Walt Disney/Productions." This set is a must for Disney collectors. Some of the glasses are getting hard to find, however. Values: $3–$5*; $6–$8†; $8–$10‡.

Bernard (holding lantern)/Bernard and Bianca looking at Penny's note (gray name, logo, etc.)† [PP510]

Bianca (displaying Penny's "HELP!/I am in/terrible/ trouble!" note)/Bianca kissing Bernard (gray name, logo, etc.) [PP511]

Brutus and Nero (looking threatening)/Madame Medusa hugging a friendly Brutus—or is it Nero? (yellow name, logo, etc.)‡ [PP512]

Evinrude (propelling leaf in water)/Evinrude lifting leaf out of water (white name, logo, etc.)† [PP513]

Madame Medusa (gesturing and sitting on cushion)/Madame Medusa in rain outfit holding wand and teddy bear (flesh-colored name, logo, etc.)‡ [PP514]

Orville (flapping wings, trying to fly)/Orville crashing (white name, logo, etc.)‡ [PP515]

Penny (holding teddy bear)/Penny sitting in bucket holding rope (flesh-colored name, logo, etc.)* [PP516]

Rufus (sitting upright)/Rufus on all fours (white name, logo, etc.)‡ [PP517]

Single Character Collector Series [1979].

A set of six 5$\frac{15}{16}$" round-bottom glasses featuring six of the major Walt Disney cartoon characters. The same design appears on each side of the glass. The character's name appears in white below the character. On the side near the bottom there is a white Pepsi logo with "Collector/Series" immediately below it and then, after a space, the words "© Walt Disney/Productions." Compared to other sets, this one is rather unexciting, but if you collect Disney, it is desirable and not that easy to find. There is no date on the glasses, but it is thought among collectors that it was issued in 1979. Value: $7–$9.

Daisey [PP520]
Donald [PP521]
Goofy [PP522]
Mickey [PP523]
Minnie [PP524]
Pluto [PP525]

Wonderful World of Disney Collector Series. A set of six 5$\frac{15}{16}$" glasses identical in size and shape to the "Picnic" and "Single Character" Disney sets. These glasses celebrate six of Walt Disney's most famous and successful films from 1937 to 1961. There is wraparound action and inviting color on these beautiful glasses. The name of the film appears near the top of the glass in white, and near the bottom in white are the words "Wonderful/World Of Disney/[Pepsi logo]/Collector Series." "© Walt Disney Productions" appears in white on all glasses except Alice In Wonderland and Pinocchio, where it appears in black. This series, which is not dated, is another "must" for Disney lovers. We include the dates of the films for informational purposes. Value: $5–$7.

101 Dalmations (1961) **[PP530]**
Bambi (1942) **[PP531]**
Lady & The Tramp (1955) **[PP532]**
Snow White (1937) **[PP533]**
Alice In Wonderland (1951) **[PP534]**
Pinocchio (1940) **[PP535]**

Fountain Glasses

Bottle Cap Logo. A simply designed 4$\frac{5}{8}$" glass with white line drawings of a "PEPSI" bottlecap logo on one side and a "PEPSI-COLA" bottlecap logo on the other. **[PP140]** Value: $2–$4. There is also a 5½" version **[PP139]**.

Bottle Cap Logo. A 5$\frac{3}{8}$" glass similar in design to the bottlecap logo glass above. This glass features a white split circle "PEPSI-COLA" logo on one side and a split circle "PEPSI" logo on the other. **[PP145]** Value: $2–$4.

Bulbous Fountain Glass and Pitcher. A 6" fountain glass with a narrow base and bulbous top. Around the top of the glass there are three equally spaced fancy white "Pepsi-Cola" script designs. **[PP150]** Value: $1–$3. The 8" pitcher is the companion piece. Three fancy white "Pepsi-Cola" logo designs are positioned on the middle of this pitcher, one underneath the spout, and one on each side. Like most pitchers that accompany glasses, this one, though it is fairly modern, is not clogging up flea market tables! **[PP151]** Value: $10–$12.

Diet Pepsi. A uniquely styled $6\frac{7}{8}$" glass in red, white, and blue promoting the virtues of Diet Pepsi. This glass is only $2\frac{1}{4}$" wide at its mouth, and presumably people who drink Diet Pepsi will be this wide at the waist. "One Calorie/DIET/PEPSI" appears in white at the top of the glass, and the red, white, and blue Diet Pepsi design encircles the bottom. **[PP170]** Value: $1–$3.

Goblet. This 6″ goblet has "Pepsi-Cola" on each side and it comes with either red or blue lettering. Value: $1–$3.

Red Lettered Goblet **[PP175]**
Blue Lettered Goblet **[PP176]**

Historic Pepsi-Cola Posters. This 5⅞″ barrel-shaped glass has a brown bordered wraparound frosted floral/filigree

design with two brown-bordered ovals which feature historic Pepsi-Cola posters. One poster shows a lady in a hat and frilly gown holding a glass of Pepsi. Near the bottom of the oval there is a small, old-fashioned "Drink Pepsi-Cola" logo with a small "5 cents" enclosed within the "C" on "Cola." On the other side, a girl in street clothes is depicted at a drugstore counter sipping Pepsi through a straw from a fountain glass. Near her arms on the counter are the words "I Love Its Flavor," and just below that there is the same "Drink Pepsi-Cola [5 cents]" logo. This glass has a button base with a crease just above it. **[PP180]** Value: $3–$5.

Pedestal Glass (small). A 6½″ red, white, and blue pedestal glass with three panels. Two of the panels feature "Pepsi" logos, and the other one shows a "Pepsi-Cola" logo with "12 Fluid Ounces" printed near the bottom in dark blue on a light blue background. **[PP185]** Value: $2–$4.

Pedestal Glass (large). A 7" pedestal glass with a Pepsi logo on each side. One side has the word "Pepsi" in blue with a predominantly red logo. The reverse reads "Pepsi-Cola" with a predominantly blue logo. **[PP187]** Value: $2–$3.

Pepsi Circa [date] Series. A set of four 5$\frac{11}{16}$" glasses with two opposing round "windows" in a wraparound gray "frosted" panel which covers almost all of the glass. Blue lines encircle the glass at the top and bottom of the large gray panel, and they also define the windows. In one of the windows a date appears in blue with "Circa" (*about* or *approximately*) above it, and on the other there is a Pepsi logo which was in use and current at that approximate time. Although these glasses are rather simply designed, they effectively convey the evolution of the Pepsi trademark from 1906 to 1973. Value: $3–$5.

Circa 1906 **[PP155]**
Circa 1950 **[PP156]**
Circa 1962 **[PP157]**
Circa 1973 **[PP158]**

Pepsi-Cola Red Diamond Leaded Design. A 5$\frac{15}{16}$" round-bottom glass with a red, blue, and black leaded glass window design. The same design appears on both sides. "Pepsi-Cola" appears at the bottom of the glass in black outlined red script. Black outlined red diamonds encircle the top of the glass, and there are two black outlined blue bands that encircle the glass at its middle. The

Red, White, and Blue Pepsi Logo. This small bottom 5¼" Pepsi glass has three equally spaced red, white, and blue round Pepsi logos with red bases on a white background panel. Two of the round logos say "PEPSI," and the other says "PEPSI-COLA." **[PP190]** Value: $1–$3.

overall pattern is held together by a network of black lines. This glass can be found with various sponsors on the reverse. In such cases, the sponsor's name replaces the Pepsi-Cola script on the reverse. For instance, we have one which says "Union/Station/Indianapolis" and has a picture of Union Station. There is also a carafe. Value: with sponsor **[PP165]** $5–$7; without sponsor **[PP166]** $4–$6; carafe **[PP167]** $3–$5.

32-Ounce Glass. A modern 6¾" glass identical in shape to the 32-ounce Coca-Cola glass listed under "Coca-Cola." On this Pepsi glass, "Pepsi-Cola" appears vertically in red script three times. **[PP195]** Value: $2–$3.

Tiffany Style Pepsi-Cola. These red, blue, and black glasses were made by Continental Can Company in the early seventies. The same design appears on both sides: "Pepsi-Cola" in red script with black outlines with a blue and black leaded glass design in the background. The $3\frac{5}{16}''$ glass has baked-on leaded lines and designs which seem to have been applied to the surface. These are very desirable glasses. A matching pitcher completes the set. Value: $6–$8.

$3\frac{5}{16}''$ Tiffany Style **[PP200]**
$5\frac{1}{8}''$ Tiffany Style **[PP201]**
$6\frac{1}{4}''$ Tiffany Style **[PP202]**
$9''$ Pitcher **[PP203]**

Norman Rockwell

Norman Rockwell Spring Scenes. A set of four tall glasses featuring nostalgic Rockwell spring domestic scenes. There are U. S. and Canadian versions of this set and, since they were not widely distributed, they are difficult to find. Value: $10–$12.

[U.S.] (Canadian)
A Scholarly Pace **[PP290]** (PP294)
Beguiling Buttercups **[PP291]** (PP295)
Pride Of Parenthood **[PP292]** (PP296)
A Young Man's Fancy **[PP293]** (PP297)

Norman Rockwell Winter Scenes (1979). This set of four 4″ glasses is listed and pictured under "Arby's" since that restaurant was the primary distributor of this set.

Sports

Sport Collector Series (1979). A set of ten $5\frac{3}{8}$"-thick glasses featuring the satiric sports cartoons of Gary Patterson. The same cartoon appears on both sides of the glass, and the title of each cartoon is near the bottom of the panel. Gary Patterson's name appears on the lower part of each cartoon. Between the panels a white Pepsi logo appears, followed by "Sport/Collector/Series/[space]/© 1979 Thought/Factory." Gary Patterson's strangely twisted humor is beautifully conveyed in these colorful cartoons, and it is impossible not to laugh when looking at them! This is an interesting set, especially popular with Patterson and sports collectors. Some of the glasses are quite difficult to find. (Six of the titles were reissued in 1980 for a collectors' convention in Las Vegas. These glasses command substantially higher prices than the 1979 set.) Values: $5–$7*; $8–$10†.

[1979 set] (1980 Las Vegas)
Birdie (Golf) **[PP325]*** **(PP335)†**
Leader Of The Pack (Bicycling) **[PP326]*** **(PP336)†**
Line Drive (Baseball) **[PP327]*** **(PP337)†**
Psyche Out (Skiing) **[PP328]*** **(PP338)†**
Nice Try (Racquetball) **[PP329]*** **(PP339)†**
Panic (Tennis) **[PP330]*** **(PP340)†**
The Split (Bowling) **[PP331]†**
Heads Up **[PP332]†**
Sportsmanship **[PP333]†**
Backlash (Fishing) **[PP334]†**

Super Action (1981). A set of $5\frac{5}{8}$" glasses featuring major league baseball superstars in action. Each glass shows a remarkable likeness of the player in the act of doing what he is best at and, on most of these glasses, that is hitting the ball. Each player's name appears in large letters, and on some of the glasses there is an additional saying relating to the player. The player's number appears in large numerals on the reverse. Below the number there is a white Pepsi logo, and under that is the "MSA" copyright. Below that are the words: "© 1981 Super Action, Inc." These glasses are fairly difficult to find, probably because sports/baseball collectors have to have them for their collections. We know of six glasses in this set, but occasionally we hear rumors that additional glasses may exist. Time will tell. Value: $6–$8.

Park-er (Dave Parker) "Dave Out Of The Park-er" **[PP340]**
Brett (George Brett) **[PP341]**
Reggie (Reggie Jackson) **[PP342]**
Seaver (Tom Seaver) **[PP343]**

Rice (Jim Rice) "Pitchers Pay The Price/When They Face Jim Rice" **[PP344]**
Schmidt (Mike Schmidt) "Long ball/or/base hit/ Count on/ Schmidt" **[PP345]**

Wisconsin Collector Series. A set of six red and white 6¼" glasses celebrating six University of Wisconsin varsity sports. The focus of each glass is the Wisconsin Badger mascot performing one of these sports. Below him the name "WIS-CONSIN" appears in large red-outlined white letters. On the reverse of each glass near the bottom is a white Pepsi logo with the words "Collector/Series" beneath it. This is a hard-to-find set and a "must" for sports collectors. (There is quite a variety of these Badgers glasses, including a round-bottom non-Pepsi version which is slightly less valuable, 16-oz. Pepsi/Badger Hockey glasses with season records, and 16-oz. Badger Hockey Home Game Schedules without Pepsi logos [Bucky Badger is shown with hockey stick held above his head]. See listing below.) Value: $9–$11.

Baseball **[PP360]**
Basketball **[PP361]**
Football **[PP362]**
Hockey **[PP363]**
Track **[PP364]**
Wrestling **[PP365]**

Wisconsin Hockey Record. Heavy 6¼", 16-oz. glasses share the same colors and general designs as the Wisconsin Badger

Collector Series (above). Bucky Badger is in the same pose as he is on the hockey glass in the set above. "Wisconsin Badgers/[date] Hockey Record" appears on the reverse in red near the top of the glass, and below in white the season's honors and scores are listed. There is a white Pepsi logo near the bottom with "Collector/Series" beneath it. We do not know how many glasses there might be in this series, but they strike us as quite desirable companions to the Wisconsin Badgers Series. Value: $8–$10.

Wisconsin Badgers 1976–77 Hockey Record **[PP370]**

Super Heroes

DC Comics Inc. Double Character Super Heroes. A set of four $5\frac{1}{2}''$ thick-based glasses with Superman on one side of each glass and Batman, Robin, Superman, or Wonder Woman on the other. Superman on each glass is pictured in a static pose with his hands on his hips and his cape flying. On the reverse side, the characters are depicted in mild action. Between the panels on one side beginning at the bottom is a Pepsi logo with these vertical words: "TM and © DC Comics Inc" and on the other side a Pepsi logo with these vertical words above it: "Pepsi and Pepsi Cola Are Registered/Trade Marks Of Pepsico Inc, Purchase, NY." There is no date and no character name. These unusual and nicely detailed glasses are hard to find. Value: $7–$9.

Superman/Batman swinging on rope (blue logos and lettering) **[PP380]**
Superman/Robin riding motorcycle (white logos and lettering) **[PP381]**
Superman/Superman running with fists extended, cape flying **[PP382]**
Superman/Wonderwoman twirling rope (white logos and lettering) **[PP383]**

DC and NPP Super Series (1976). A set of fourteen $6\frac{1}{4}''$ glasses featuring D. C. Comics and National Periodical Publications superheroes. Frequently re-

ferred to as the "moon" set because each superhero appears in front of a $2\frac{15}{16}''$ colored circle, the designs on both sides of the glass are identical. Near the bottom between the designs appear in black the following: a Pepsi logo, beneath which are the words "SUPER/Series" followed, a few spaces below, by either "© D C Comics Inc. 1976" or "© 1976 National Periodical/Publications Inc." These two copyrights in effect create two different sets for a total of twenty-eight different glasses. These glasses are colorful and attractively designed, though the characters are generally depicted in a static manner. Complete sets

are very desirable, and some of the characters are getting rather difficult to find. Values: $3–$5*; $6–$8†; $9–$11‡.

[DCC] (NPP)
Aquaman† **[PP390]** (PP404)
Batgirl‡ **[PP391]** (PP405)
Batman* **[PP392]** (PP406)
Green Arrow‡ **[PP393]** (PP407)
Flash† **[PP394]** (PP408)
Green Lantern‡ **[PP395]** (PP409)
Joker‡ **[PP396]** (PP410)
Penguin‡ **[PP397]** (PP411)
Riddler‡ **[PP398]** (PP412)
Robin-The Boy Wonder* **[PP399]** (PP413)
Shazam!* **[PP400]** (PP414)
Supergirl‡ **[PP401]** (PP415)
Superman‡ **[PP402]** (PP416)
Wonder Woman‡ **[PP403]** (PP417)

Super Heroes Collector Series (1978).

A set of seven 6¼" glasses featuring super heroes in action scenes on the front and the name and logo of the super hero on the reverse. These dynamically designed and colorful glasses were issued in 1978, but some of them bear other copyright dates (see individual listings below), which tend to confuse collectors. The Pepsi logos, which appear near the bottom of each glass, have "Collector/Series" below them and after a space the words "© [date] DC Comics Inc." (Rumor has it that there is a 1978 Supergirl prototype and a 1978 Wonder Woman front-logo prototype that were never distributed and an Aquaman, which is missing the date, but for most collectors this information is irrelevant.) The Pepsi logos and the small print below them are flesh colored on all the glasses except The Flash, where this information is in white. This set of seven glasses is quite appealing and relatively challenging to find. Value: $6–$8.

Aquaman (1978) **[PP419]**
Batman (1966) **[PP420]**
Shazam! (1978) **[PP421]**
The Flash (1971) **[PP422]**
Wonder Woman (1978) **[PP423]**
Robin (1978) **[PP424]**
Superman (1975) **[PP425]**

Super Heroes Collector Series (1978).

A set of six 5⅞" round-bottom glasses featuring all the super heroes in the 1978 6¼" set except Aquaman. The super hero designs are identical to those on the larger set. The Pepsi logo followed by "Collector/Series" [space] "© [date] DC Comics Inc." appears at the lower right of each superhero. The Pepsi logos and other lettering on all the glasses except The Flash (where this information is printed in white) are flesh colored. Like the larger set of seven, this is an extremely nice set which is difficult to assemble. Value: $7–$9.

Batman (1966) **[PP426]**

The Flash (1978) **[PP427]**
Robin (1978) **[PP428]**
Shazam! (1978) **[PP429]**
Superman (1975) **[PP430]**
Wonder Woman (1978) **[PP431]**

Superman The Movie (1978). A set of six $5\frac{5}{8}''$ glasses featuring themes and scenes from "Superman The Movie" in brightly colored front panels. On the reverse, there is a large white panel topped by a large blue Superman "S" symbol. Below this appears the title of the glass's front panel action, followed by a brief passage of descriptive information. Near the bottom of the panel, "SUPERMAN/The Movie" appears in blue letters, beneath which appears "™ and © DC Comics Inc. 1978," also in blue letters. A white Pepsi logo appears below the panel. The likenesses on these glasses are quite accurate, and the colors are bold, making this set a desirable one. Value: $6–$8.

The Caped Wonder to the Rescue. **[PP435]**
The Characters **[PP436]**
From Kal-el the Child to the Man of Steel.
  [PP437]
Kal-el comes to Earth. **[PP438]**
Lois Lane is saved by her hero. **[PP439]**
Superman saves the day. **[PP440]**

Warner Brothers

Canadian Warner Brothers (1975, 1977, 1978). A set of six $4\frac{3}{4}''$ glasses featuring a selection of Warner Brothers cartoon characters. The same design appears on both sides, and the character's name appears in black in quotation marks below the character. On the side, near the middle of the glass, are the following in white: "Serie De/Collectioneur/[Pepsi logo]/Collector Series"; then, ¾" below, these words: "© Warner Bros./Inc. [1975, 1977, or 1978]." Infrequently encountered in the U. S. and a bit out of the mainstream for most collectors, but worthwhile for the variety. Value: $9–$11.

[1975] (1977) {1978}
Bugs Bunny [**PP560**] (**PP566**) {**PP572**}
Daffy Duck [**PP561**] (**PP567**) {**PP573**}
Porky Pig [**PP562**] (**PP568**) {**PP574**}

Road Runner [**PP563**] (**PP569**) {**PP575**}
Sylvester [**PP564**] (**PP570**) {**PP576**}
Tweety [**PP565**] (**PP571**) {**PP577**}

Canadian Warner Brothers/Tim Horton, 1978.
A set of six glasses featuring a selection of Warner Brothers cartoon characters. Value: $9–$11.

Elmer Fudd [**PP580**]
Foghorn Leghorn [**PP581**]
Pepe Le Pew [**PP582**]
Speedy Gonzales [**PP583**]
Wile E. Coyote [**PP584**]
Yosemite Sam [**PP585**]

Collector Series (1973).
A set of eighteen 6¼" single-character glasses featuring popular Warner Brothers cartoon characters. The subject of each glass appears in the same pose on the front and back of the glass, and the name of the character appears below the character in quotation marks. On the side near the bottom of the glass, there is a white Pepsi logo beneath which in white are the words "Collector Series/© Warner Bros./Inc. 1973." Glasses belonging to this set are frequently encountered, and it is safe to say that the initial

glass-collecting interests of many collectors have been stimulated by them. Most of these glasses are relatively easy to acquire, so assembling a complete set of eighteen characters is possible. However, there are a number of variations which push the total number of different glasses to over one hundred. We assume that the average collector is interested mainly in obtaining the basic eighteen-character set, so we will briefly mention variations without dwelling on them.

"Beaky Buzzard" **[PP700]**
"Bugs Bunny" **[PP701]**
"Cool Cat" **[PP702]**
"Daffy Duck"**[PP703]**
"Elmer Fudd" **[PP704]**
"Foghorn Leghorn" **[PP705]**
"Henry Hawk" **[PP706]**
"Pepe Le Pew" **[PP707]**
"Petunia Pig" **[PP708]**
"Porky Pig" **[PP709]**
"Road Runner" **[PP710]**
"Slow Poke Rodriguez" **[PP711]**
"Speedy Gonzales" **[PP712]**
"Sylvester" **[PP713]**
"Tasmanian Devil" **[PP714]**
"Tweety" **[PP715]**
"Wile E. Coyote" **[PP716]**
"Yosemite Sam" **[PP717]**

Variations and Values. (1) The basic eighteen-character set comes in a thick $6\frac{1}{4}$" 16-ounce Brockway glass or a thin, lighter Federal glass. Both of these sets come with the characters' names in both black and white lettering. So far, then,

we have 72 "different" glasses. (2) Six of the glasses come with the Pepsi logo under the characters' names (therefore referred to as "logo under name" or "double logo" or "front logo" glasses); this variation applies to the black-lettered 16-ounce Federal and Brockway glasses, and to smaller $11\frac{1}{2}$-ounce Brockway and Federal versions. The six front logo glasses include Bugs Bunny, Daffy Duck, Porky Pig, Road Runner, Sylvester, and Tweety. So add 24 more "different" glasses for a subtotal of 96. In addition, there are eighteen 15-ounce thin Federal black-lettered logo-under-name glasses, which brings our subtotal to 114. (3) Five of the Brockway $6\frac{1}{4}$" black-lettered glasses have been known to come without the "Warner Bros." designation. These glasses include Elmer Fudd, Foghorn Leghorn, Road Runner, Sylvester, and Tweety. Our total is now 119. (4) Pepe Le Pew can be found in the 16-ounce Brockway black-lettered version and the 16-ounce Federal white- lettered version with clear, unpainted eyes; Petunia Pig can be found with clear eyes in the 16-ounce white Federal version. Add 3 more for a subtotal of 122. (5) In the 16-ounce black Brockway, Road Runner can sometimes be found without the "Beep Beep" coming out of his mouth, and he can sometimes be found with his feet from one side of the glass touching his feet on the other. Add two more for a subtotal of 124. (6) Sylvester can sometimes be found in the 16-ounce black Brockway with a small red nose, instead of the more common large one. We are now up to 125. (7) Cool Cat can sometimes be found in the white 16-ounce Brockway version with eyes that are squinting instead of open. Our total is 126. Other variations and production errors are possible, and they will come to light as collectors look more closely at these glasses. Glasses may be identified with the following codes for a catalogue system: PP#; B or F (Brockway or Federal); BL or WH (black or white lettering); T, M, or S (16-oz. = tall, 15-oz. = medium, 11½-oz. = short); CL (center logo, if applicable). A Bugs Bunny Federal glass with black lettering in the 16-oz. size with a center logo would be identified as a [PP701-F-BL-T-CL]. Values: Brockway 16-oz. black and white, $2–$4; Federal 16 oz. black and white, $4–$6; Federal 15-oz. black "front logo," $10–$12; Brockway 16-oz. black "front logo," $5–$7; Federal 16-oz. black "front logo," $7–$9; Brockway 11½-oz. black "front logo," $8–$10; Federal 11½-oz. black "front logo," $10–$12; Variations (3) through (7), [caveat emptor!].

Collector Series (1976). This set of twenty-four 6¼" glasses features characters from the 1973 Warner Brothers set in interaction with one another. There doesn't seem to be too much logic to the character combinations, but the interaction is creative and amusing, the detail is nice, and the colors are attractive. Assembling a complete set of these glasses is difficult because some were

available to distributors on a minimum order basis, and many distributors therefore chose to pass at that point in the promotion. This set, referred to as the "action" or "interaction" set, has no character names on it, and the action is such that the viewer is invited to become an interpreter, and perhaps even a contributor, to the depicted interaction. Near the bottom of each glass there is a white Pepsi logo, beneath which are the words "Collector/Series" and then a bit further down, "© Warner Bros./Inc. 1976." This is a very desirable set, not easy to complete. Value: $3–$5*; $6–$8†; $9–$11‡.

Elmer Fudd/shotgun/Bugs/carrots* **[PP750]**
Henry Hawk/tennis/Foghorn Leghorn/bomb* **[PP751]**
Pepe Le Pew/kinked hose/Daffy Duck† **[PP752]**
Petunia Pig/paint/Porky Pig/lawnmower* **[PP753]**

Daffy Duck/Elmer Fudd/marching band‡ **[PP754]**
Road Runner/catapult/Wile E. Coyote* **[PP755]**
Slow Poke Rodriguez/Sylvester/Speedy Gonzales/hammer‡ **[PP756]**
Tweety/birdbath/Sylvester/Granny‡ **[PP757]**
Sylvester/limb/Tweety/saw† **[PP758]**
Daffy Duck/firecracker/Tasmanian Devil‡ **[PP759]**
Porky Pig/fishing/Tasmanian Devil/fish‡ **[PP760]**
Sylvester/net/Tweety/Marc Antony† **[PP761]**
Wile E. Coyote/Ralph/sheep/rope‡ **[PP762]**
Yosemite Sam/gold pan/Speedy Gonzales/gold nuggets† **[PP763]**
Yosemite Sam/cannon/Bugs Bunny/match‡ **[PP764]**
Beaky Buzzard/Cool Cat/kite* **[PP765]**
Bugs Bunny/Ray Gun/Martian† **[PP766]**
Cool Cat/coconut/hunter‡ **[PP767]**
Daffy Duck/Elmer Fudd/Bugs Bunny/hunting‡ **[PP768]**
Foghorn Leghorn/Marc Antony/dog house/dynamite‡ **[PP769]**
Pepe Le Pew/girlfriend/perfume‡ **[PP770]**
Porky Pig/Daffy Duck/pot/ladle‡ **[PP771]**

Sylvester/Hippity Hop/Sylvester Jr./boxing‡ **[PP772]**

Wile E. Coyote/Road Runner/skateboard with sail and fan‡ **[PP773]**

Variations. This set is simple and straightforward compared to the 1973 Collectors Series, but a few minor variations have been noted. (1) Elmer Fudd/ shotgun/ Bugs/carrots has been reported with large red dots on Elmer's face. (2) Pepe Le Pew/kinked hose/Daffy Duck and Sylvester/limb/Tweety/saw have been reported with no "Warner Bros. 1976" inscriptions. (3) Beaky Buzzard/ Cool Cat/kite has been reported with black dots on Cool Cat's chest. (4) On Petunia Pig/paint/Porky Pig/lawn- mower, it sometimes occurs that the last note Porky is whistling comes out clear instead of having a white center. We judge these variations to be fairly minor and inconsequential manufacturing de- fects. They should not unduly preoc- cupy collectors. It is not surprising, however, that some departures from the norm have occurred, considering the size of this set.

Warner Brothers Looney Tunes [ac- tion] Collector Series (1979). A set of six 5⅞" round-bottom glasses, featuring Warner Brothers Looney Tunes char- acters in interaction scenes. On each glass, three characters are involved in wraparound action which reminds us of the 1976 Warner Brothers interaction series. The main character's name ap- pears near the bottom of the glass, ex- cept Tweety's name, which appears to- ward the top, and all character names are in white, except Bugs Bunny's, which is in black. Pepsi logos and copyright information are white on all glasses, ex- cept on the Bugs Bunny glass where they are in black. The configuration is as follows: "Looney Tunes TM/[Pepsi logo]/Collector Series." Appearing at various locations near the bottom of the glass and sometimes directly below the logo are the words: "TMs and © War- ner Bros. Inc.1979." Except for the Tweety glass, which has vivid color, these glasses are somewhat drab, but the amusing action scenes more than make up for this deficiency. This is a very desirable set, but it is not unduly difficult to find. Value: $5–$7.

Bugs Bunny: Bugs Bunny running with suitcases full of carrots/Elmer Fudd chasing him with shotgun/Daffy Duck in porter's cap wheeling baggage cart **[PP780]**

Daffy Duck: Daffy Duck in Indian warbonnet/ Yosemite Sam shooting at him/Bugs Bunny sitting in director's chair near camera, direct- ing action **[PP781]**

Porky Pig: Porky plugging his ears/Daffy playing bass drum/ Bugs dressed as drum major **[PP782]**

Road Runner: Wile E. Coyote with rocket on his back pursuing Road Runner/Bugs Bunny opening trap door in front of oncoming Wile E. Coyote/Road Runner looking back at imminent collision **[PP783]**

Sylvester: Sylvester snorkeling underwater/

Tweety water-skiing putting cork in end of Sylvester's snorkel/ Granny driving boat **[PP784]**

Tweety: Tweety flying/Granny hitting Sylvester on head with broom/Sylvester Jr. looking on in horror **[PP785]**

Warner Brothers Looney Tunes Collector Series [1980].

A set of seven round-bottom $5\frac{7}{8}''$ glasses featuring popular Looney Tunes characters. Sometimes referred to as the "banner" series, since each character's name appears in a colored banner on one side of the glass, and sometimes referred to as the "head in star" series since each character's head appears in a star just below the banner. The design of these glasses is fairly simple but quite appealing because of the vivid colors and the unusual detail of the character depictions. Each character is represented in a characteristic pose on one side of the glass, and in a balloon the character's best-known expression or saying appears. Near the bottom of each glass in white appears the following information: "Looney Tunes T.M./[Pepsi logo]/Collector/Series/[space]TMs and © Warner Bros. [1966 on all glasses but Daffy Duck, which is dated 1980]." In some respects, this set is confusing to collectors, partly because of the number of glasses in it and partly because of the copyright dates. Without Daffy Duck, we have a neat set of 1966 copyright glasses. The 1980 Daffy Duck forces us to the conclusion that all seven glasses were issued in 1980 and that the "© 1966" glasses just carry an earlier copyright date than the Daffy Duck design does. 1966 as an issue date for the © 1966 glasses does not seem likely. (Collectors will note that this set is identical to the 1980 Arby's Looney Tunes set.) Road Runner, Yosemite Sam, and Daffy Duck are more difficult to find than the other four characters and therefore command premium prices. Values: $5–$7*; $8–$10†.

Bugs Bunny (What's Up/Doc?)* **[PP790]**
Daffy Duck ("You're Disspicable!!")† **[PP791]**
Porky Pig (That's All Folks)* **[PP792]**
Road Runner (Beep/Beep!!)† **[PP793]**
Sylvester (Sufferin'/Succotash!)* **[PP794]**
Tweety (I Tawt I Taw A/Puddy Tat!)* **[PP795]**
Yosemite Sam (I'll Gets That/Varmint!!!)† **[PP796]**

Pizza Hut

All-Time Bronco Greats 25th Anniversary (1984).

A set of four $4\frac{1}{8}''$ glasses in brown, beige, orange, black, blue, and white celebrating the Denver Broncos' silver anniversary. (This set is very similar to the McDonald's 1984 All-Time Greatest Steelers set.) On the front of each glass there are six players represented in various poses or actions. Beneath this scene, "© 1984 Pizza Hut, Inc." appears. On the reverse at the top is a round black "Original American Football League Team—1960–1984—Silver Anniversary" seal. Below this in white are the words: "25th Anniversary/All-Time Bronco Greats" followed by the names, positions, and career dates of six Bronco players. Beneath the names are a black Pizza Hut logo and black KCNC [TV] 4 logo. Near the bottom of the glass in white are the words: "Pizza Hut Collector Series 1984. [Number] In A Series Of Four." Just to the right of the front panel, near the bottom of the glass in white, are a NFL Players Association logo and an "MSA" copyright. These are very pretty, "busy" glasses. Value: $4–$6.

First In A Series Of Four: Odoms, Wright, Smith, Gradishar, Turner, Chavous **[PH1]**
Second In A Series Of Four: Johnson, Taylor, Jackson, Swenson, Minor, Little **[PH2]**

Third In A Series Of Four: Van Heusen, Morton, Upchurch, Thompson, Bryan, Moses **[PH3]**
Fourth In A Series Of Four: Glassic, Watson, Tripucka, Alzado, Jackson, Gonsoulin **[PH4]**

Beer/Soft Drink Glasses.

$5\frac{5}{8}''$ glasses, one with a red roof over the words "Pizza Hut" in black and the other, all in red, showing a pizza chef standing beside a drawing of a Pizza Hut Restaurant with the words "Pizza Hut" above it. Value: $1–$2.

Red roof/"Pizza Hut" in black **[PH10]**
Pizza chef/"Pizza Hut"/restaurant **[PH11]**

Care Bears Collector's Series (1983). A set of four glasses identical in shape and size to the E.T. set (following), featuring four different pastel Care Bears. A bear appears on the front of each glass with a symbol on his/her stomach illustrating his/her personality. On the reverse there is a lot of writing: first the Care Bears logo, then the name of the bear with that bear's "message," then the Pizza Hut logo in red and white with the words "Limited Edition" on the left and "Collector's Series" on the right. Below appear the words "Trademark of American Greetings Corp., Pizza Hut/ Authorized User © 1983 American Greetings." The motif which appears on the stomach of each bear is elaborated on the reverse bottom of each glass. A cute set, but extremely plentiful. Value: $1–$2.

Cheer Bear (Stomach motif: rainbow; message: "Enjoy!"; color: pink) **[PH15]**
Funshine Bear (Stomach motif: sun with happy smile; message: "Feeling funtastic!"; color: yellow) **[PH16]**
Grumpy Bear (Stomach motif: cloud; message: "Hugs welcome"; color: blue) **[PH17]**
Tenderheart Bear (Stomach motif: heart; message: "Share some love"; color: ginger) **[PH18]**

E.T. Collector's Series (1982). Issued by Pizza Hut to coincide with public enthusiasm for the successful film, this set of four slightly flared 6″ glasses features E.T. in memorable scenes from the film. Captions referring to key scenes appear in white letters above ("Home") or below (other three glasses) the characters. Identical material appears on the backs of all four glasses: a blue space capsule at the top, "E.T./The Extra-Terrestrial/© 1982 Universal City Studios, Inc. All Rights Reserved./A Trademark of and licensed by Universal City Studios, Inc." and, near the bottom of the glass, a black Pizza Hut logo with "Limited Edition" on the left and "Collector's Series" on the right. The colors of these glasses are rather subdued and unattractive, and the subject matter seems to have lost its appeal, judging by the plentiful numbers of these glasses on flea market tables. Value: $1–$3.

"Be Good" (Girl and E.T. Rubbing Noses) **[PH25]**

"Home" (E.T. and stuffed animals) **[PH26]**

"I'll be right here" (E.T. touching boy's forehead) **[PH27]**

"Phone Home" (E.T., small figure of boy riding bicycle into sky, moon in background) **[PH28]**

The Flintstone Kids (1986). In this set, Pizza Hut/Hanna-Barbera turn the clock back to capture the Flintstones as youngsters. Same shape and size as the Pizza Hut "Popples" glasses. On the front of each glass each child-Flintstone appears portrait-style within an oval with his/her name below. The reverse features the character in action. Between the panels near the bottom appear the words in black: "The Flintstone Kids/© 1986 Hanna-Barbera Productions, Inc." and, on the other side near the bottom, a black Pizza Hut logo. The color combinations on these glasses might be considered slightly irritating to adult collectors. Value: $1–$2.

Barney/Barney riding alligator skateboard **[PH35]**

Betty/Betty dancing to music of birds-radio **[PH36]**

Freddy/Freddy wearing earphones, dancing, and listening to birds singing **[PH37]**

Wilma/Wilma playing with hula hoop **[PH38]**

Green Bay Packers National Football League Players. Handsome 6³⁄₁₆" glasses honoring, one to a glass, a selection of the all-time greatest Green Bay Packers players. On the front of each glass the individual player's picture appears with his name printed underneath; below that is the name "Green Bay Packers," underneath which is the player's signature. On the reverse at the top appear the player's name and position and other personal information, followed by a full paragraph summarizing the player's career and accomplishments. Below this is the MSA copyright. On one side near the bottom appears the NFL Players logo, and on the other there is a similarly sized black Pizza Hut logo. These glasses are not dated, but we estimate that they were issued in the mid-seventies. They are hard to find in good condition. Number in set not known at this time. Value: $4–$6.

Willie Davis–Defensive End **[PH45]**
Paul Hornung–Halfback-Kicker **[PH46]**
Jerry Kramer–Guard **[PH47]**
Ray Nitschke–Linebacker **[PH48]**
Vince Lombardi **[PH49]**

Harvard, Illinois: Milk Center of the World. A 5⅛" glass in red, white, and black promoting Harvard, Illinois, and

Harmilda, the Holstein. There are two panels on this glass, and each is bordered at top and bottom by a white bar which contains red four-sided designs. On one side of the glass, the world is pictured with a red drawing of North America. A black arrow points to a black star which marks the location of Harvard, Illinois, and "milk center of the world" appears in white print on a black banner just below the black star. Above this representation in red is the word "Harvard," and below it "Illinois." Below all this near the bottom of the glass is a red and black Pizza Hut logo. On the other side of the glass, a black and white Holstein on a stone base appears. There are two plaques on the statue's base. One contains the cow's name, "Harmilda," and the other says "Welcome To/Harvard/Milk/Center/Of The/World." A very unusual regional issue. **[PH55]** Value: $4–$6.

Love Is . . . (1977). A set of twelve 14-ounce glasses with the "Love Is . . ." characters in various illustrations of the sayings. On the side of the glass, running from the bottom to the top, is the number of the glass and the copyright information. Glasses one through three say "Copyright Los Angeles Times 1975," and glasses four through twelve say "© 1970 Los Angeles Times." The "Love Is . . ." characters are beige with black outlines, and the "Love Is . . ." lettering at the top of the glass and the definitions of love at the bottoms of the glasses appear in a wide range of colors. There are two different but complementary "Love Is . . ." sayings per glass, for a grand total of twenty-four. This set is difficult to complete due to the sheer number of glasses involved. Value: $2–$4.

#1 . . .whatever you make it.
  . . . sharing even the hard times. **[PH70]**
#2 . . . telling him how much his golf game has improved.
  . . . listening again how he made the hole in one. **[PH71]**
#3 . . . telling her she's as lovely as the day you were married.
  . . . making marriage last 75 years. **[PH72]**
#4 . . . pretending you didn't notice the blonde.
  . . . turning all the other boys away. **[PH73]**
#5 . . . giving her a credit card.
  . . . leaving your credit cards at home when you go window shopping. **[PH74]**

#6 . . . looking the other way when she weighs herself.
  . . . making desserts for him when you're on a diet. **[PH75]**
#7 . . . soothing the expectant father.
  . . . taking turns with the midnight shower. **[PH76]**
#8 . . . counting your blessings.
  . . . making the most of whatever you have. **[PH77]**
#9 . . . a kiss in a summer shower.
  . . . when making up last [sic] longer than the spat. **[PH78]**
#10 . . . selling your motorcycle to marry her.
  . . . protecting her in scary movies. **[PH79]**
#11 . . . not expecting too much of each other.
  . . . forgiving each others' mistakes. **[PH80]**
#12 . . . making memories today to share tomorrow.
  . . . remembering all the happy times. **[PH81]**

P.A.T. Ward/CB Lingo Series. A series of 6¼" glasses featuring P.A.T. Ward and Leonardo-TTV characters in interaction which includes CB radio lingo. The CB expressions appear in white balloons outlined in black, and the action scenes are amusing. A black Pizza Hut logo appears near the bottom of the glass, and beneath it there are these words: "© P.A.T. Ward" or "Leonardo TTV." Since these glasses were distributed in Kansas, Missouri, Indiana, and Arkansas, they do not seem to be widely known. Unknown number of glasses in the set. Value: $3–$5.

Coat Rack To Fat Tail! How's The Tide, Good Buddy?/In! (Bullwinkle with fishing gear/Rocky submerged in water) **[PH35]**

Back Door To Front Door! Watch It, Good Buddy, I Hear There's A Tijuana Taxi Ahead!/That's A Big 10-4! (Bullwinkle driving police van/Collision with Boris) **[PH36]**

Popples (1986). A set of four 5⅞" round-bottom glasses featuring teddy-bear-type creatures called "Popples" engaged in various actions. A posing Popple appears on the front of each glass below a saying which characterizes the Popple. On the reverse we have each Popple in action, usually dancing. The name "Popples" appears between the two panels near the bottom of each glass, and it has these words beneath it: "© 1986 Those Characters From Cleveland, Inc." On the other side, between the two panels near the bottom, appears the name of each Popple. Interesting but strange subject matter and color combinations, no doubt geared to a youthful audience. Pizza Hut's name does not appear on these glasses, but they were definitely distributed by Pizza Hut and possibly other franchises. We suspect this was not a successful promotion since the Popples are not well known, and the glasses surface only occasionally. Value: $2–$4.

Party Popple (saying: "Any time is party time!") **[PH50]**

P.C. Popple (saying: "Smile—it's a snap!") **[PH51]**

Puffball Popple (saying: "Steppin' out for fun!") **[PH52]**

Puzzle Popple (saying: "Fun's a popping!") **[PH53]**

Pizza inn

Ziggy (1979). A set of four 6" glasses featuring Ziggy and his friends and up-beat "Ziggyisms" like "Be Nice to Little Things." See Hardee's for complete listing and values, since this set was also distributed by Hardee's. In this set, the "Time for a Food Break" glass is changed to read "Time for a Pizza Break." (*See also Hardee's*)

Be Nice to Little Things **[PN1]**
Try To Have A Nice Day **[PN2]**
Time for a Pizza Break **[PN3]**
Smile . . . It's Good For Your Complexion **[PN4]**

Pizza Pete

Pizza Pete Series. A set of six 6" glasses featuring personified pizza toppings along with clever names for each. There's no other writing on these glasses, but we understand that a West Coast pizza outfit was responsible for this subtle humor. The shape of this glass is typical of the mid-seventies. Value: $3–$5.

Charlie Cheezerella **[PZ1]**
Olive—Name Me! **[PZ2]**
Rosie Tomato **[PZ3]**
Boom Boom Mushroom **[PZ4]**
Frankie Pepperoni **[PZ5]**
Pizza Pete **[PZ6]**

There's a Pete/behind every Petesa. A heavy 5½" orange decorated glass depicting a whole pizza standing on a pair of legs. Beneath the ground the legs are standing on are the words: "There's a Pete/behind every Petesa." (We figured as much!) This glass tapers to a narrow base, which then flares outward. **[PZ10]** Value: $2–$4.

Popeye's Famous Fried Chicken

Popeye's Famous Fried Chicken (1978). A set of four glasses featuring the Popeye comic strip characters and promoting the fried chicken of "Popeye's Famous Fried Chicken" Restaurants. Value: $6–$8.

Popeye [PO1]
Brutus [PO2]
Olive Oyl [PO3]
Swee' Pea [PO4]

Popeye's Pals (1979). A set of four $5\frac{7}{8}''$ glasses featuring characters from the Popeye comic strip. These Libbey glasses are colorful and easy to like. Each glass has a wraparound comic strip scene with four frames of character interaction promoting the chicken and other food products of Popeye's Restaurants. At the top of the front of each glass, "Popeye's Pals" appears in red, white, and black letters. Just below that, a $\frac{1}{4}''$ black filigree band encircles the glass with these words in it: "Original New Orleans Flavor!" The featured character appears in the center of the glass in a red and yellow star, beneath which is the character's name in black. To the left of the character's name beneath the lower black filigree band are the words "© Popeye's Famous Fried Chicken, 1979," and to the right of the name, also under the band, are these words: "King Features Syndicate, Inc." Between these two groups of words near the bottom of the glass appears the "Popeyes [clear glass on red]/Famous/Fried/Chicken [black on gold]" logo. The color and action combine to make these glasses very desirable. Value: $5–$7.

Popeye [PO10]
Brutus [PO11]
Olive Oyl [PO12]
Swee' Pea [PO13]

Raggedy Ann and Andy

Raggedy Ann and Andy. $6\frac{1}{8}''$ glasses in red, white, black, and blue depicting Raggedy Ann and Andy in various activities on a single wraparound panel. "Raggedy Ann and Andy" appears in blue at the top of the panel on one side of the glass, and the activity's title appears in red on the opposite side of the glass. "The Bobbs-Merrill Company,

Inc." appears in black print at the bottom of each glass. There is no date, and the number of glasses in the set is unknown at the present time. Value: $3–$5.

Doing Chores **[RA1]**
Gone Fishin **[RA2]**
Raggedy Rollers **[RA3]**

RC Cola

Me and my RC. A 5½" thick-bottom glass with the words "Me and my" appearing in blue above a white circle which contains "RC" in large red letters. **[RC1]** Value: $1–$3.

Oregon Kamikaze Basketball. A set of six 5⅝" yellow and green glasses issued by radio station KUGN 590. Each glass has a bright yellow panel with a green caricature of one of KUGN's disc jock-eys playing basketball. Above this panel are the words: "OREGON [green] KAMIKAZE [green and yellow] BASKETBALL [green]." On the reverse, near the top in green, appear these words: "Royal

Crown Cola/RC," and near the bottom in green letters: "Listen To/Oregon Sports On/KUGN/590." Near the top of each panel there is a quotation from the crowd, and at the bottom of the panel the disc jockey's name appears. These glasses are definitely off the beaten track!

Value: $4–$6.

Ernie Kent/"GO! GO! GO" **[RC11]**
Ron Le/"4-3-2-1. . . . 0" **[RC12]**
Greg Ballard/"AW . . . WRITE" **[RC13]**
Stu Jackson/"STU" **[RC14]**
Mike Drummand/"KA-SWISSH-H-H . . ." **[RC15]**
Mark Barwig **[RC16]**

RC Salutes The Champs/Portland Players [1979]. A set of eight 6¼" glasses honoring members of the NBA Portland Trailblazers championship basketball team. The front of each glass features a player's picture; below it are his name, height, position, signature, birthdate, birthplace, weight, alma mater, and year of graduation. Directly behind this picture on the reverse are the words "Me and my RC" in large black letters, and between the front and back are action drawings of basketball players and a black NBA Players Association logo. A blue band encircles the top; within it are the words: "RC Salutes The Champs, Portland Players." The "MSA" copyright appears at the bottom. Not dated, but we know the Trailblazers won the NBA championship in 1979. Value: $5–$7.

Johnny Davis, 6-2 Guard **[RC20]**
Bob Gross, 6-6 Forward **[RC21]**
Lionel Hollins, 6-3 Guard **[RC22]**
Maurice Lucas, 6-9 Forward **[RC23]**
Lloyd Neal, 6-7 Forward **[RC24]**
Larry Steele, 6-5 Guard **[RC25]**
Dave Twardzik, 6-1 Guard **[RC26]**
Bill Walton, 6-11 Center **[RC27]**

Red Steer

Bicentennial Collectors Series (1976). A set of round-bottom $5\frac{7}{8}$" glasses issued by Red Steer during the Bicentennial year to commemorate early Pacific Northwest history. The front of each glass has a drawing related to frontier history, appearing in brown on what appears to be a large piece of irregularly edged beige-colored parchment. There is a line drawing of the state that the historical site is located in, with specific location(s) labeled and marked with small dots or stars. The glass's title appears in brown near the bottom of the parchment. On the reverse, there is an identical parchment section which contains several paragraphs of specific information about the historical site. These explanations are detailed, informative,

and educational. At the bottom of the reverse parchment are the words: "Bicentennial Collectors Series/Red Steer, Inc. 1976." Red Steer apparently folded about 1980, but they left us a nice set of regional glasses to collect—if you can find them! Our guess is that there are a dozen glasses in the set. Value: $4–$6.

Boise **[RS1]**
Cataldo Mission **[RS2]**
Fort Hall **[RS3]**
Fort Okanogan **[RS4]**
Fort Simcoe **[RS5]**
Lewis & Clark **[RS6]**
Massacre Rocks **[RS7]**
Olympia **[RS8]**
Oregon Trail **[RS9]**
Silver City **[RS10]**
Whitman Mission **[RS11]**

Roy Rogers

100th Anniversary of Philadelphia Phillies (1983). A heavy 5½″ glass commemorating the 100th anniversary of the Philadelphia Phillies baseball club. A simply designed glass with a green baseball infield, gold basepaths, and four different red Phillies' "P" logos on the bases. This design is backed by a white circle with red and blue lines on its edge. In the center of the baseball diamond are these numbers: "1883 [in white]/100 [in large gold numerals]/1983 [in white]." A gold rim adds a beautiful finishing touch. On the reverse near the bottom appears the name "Roy Rogers" in red. **[RR1]** Value: $2–$4.

Sam's

Sam's [Nebraska Cornhuskers] Collector Series (1976). A set of ten colorful 5⅞″ round-bottom glasses featuring the helmets of ten of Nebraska's gridiron opponents on the front and a record of their rivalries with all game scores through the year 1975 on the reverse. On each glass, the helmet and the two teams' meetings appear in a colorful frame; on all the glasses, the statistics on the reverse are in white. At the bottom of the reverse frame, "Sam's" shield logo appears in white with "Collector/Series" to the right of it. Near the top of each statistical panel there is a brief account of the teams' rivalry. This set was issued in Nebraska by "Sam's," and it is therefore so regional that it cannot be widely known. It is, quite simply, a beautiful, interesting, and relatively early set. Sports collectors should find it extremely appealing. Value: $5–$7.

University of Colorado Buffaloes **[SM1]**
Oklahoma State University Cowboys **[SM2]**
Iowa State University Cyclones **[SM3]**
Indiana Hoosiers **[SM4]**
Miami University Hurricanes **[SM5]**
Kansas Jayhawks **[SM6]**
Hawaii Rainbows **[SM7]**
Louisiana State University Tigers **[SM8]**
Missouri Tigers **[SM9]**
Kansas State Wildcats **[SM10]**

Sears, Roebuck & Co.

Catalog Pages Circa 1908. A $5\frac{7}{8}''$ round-bottom glass with a variety of advertisements from the 1908 Sears Catalog. A caption near the top reads as follows: "Reproduced From SEARS Catalog Circa 1908," and at the bottom appear these words: "Sears, Roebuck Catalog, Chicago, Illinois." A true glassful of nostalgia, bringing back the days when our dollar had real buying power! Colors: brown and off-white. No date. **[SE1]** Value: $1–$2.

Winnie-The-Pooh Series. A set of four $5\frac{1}{16}''$ round-bottom glasses featuring

Winnie-The-Pooh and his friends. On the reverse near the bottom the name "Sears" appears in a black lined rectangle, and below that are the words: "© Walt Disney Productions." The title of the glass appears in black below the characters on the front of some of the glasses. Value: $3–$5.

Winnie-The-Pooh And Friends (Winnie-The-Pooh with flowers behind his back, Piglet and Tigger with pots of honey) **[SE5]**

Tigger, Piglet, and Pooh (planting tree) **[SE6]**

Winnie-the-Pooh for President (Tigger, Pooh, Piglet beneath campaign banner which says "Winnie-the-Pooh/for President"; map of U.S. on reverse with "Pooh!/Country" written on it) **[SE7]**

7 Eleven

Marvel Comics Group Superheroes (1977). A set of six $5\frac{9}{16}$" glasses that have a right to be described as among the "wildest" glasses in color and design to be issued by anyone to date. Each glass spotlights a Marvel Comics superhero or group of superheroes. There is dynamic, unrestrained wraparound action in bold colors (red, orange, blue, white, and black), and the facial expressions and supporting details are extremely well done. Near the top of each glass is a round 1" 7 Eleven logo in black, beneath which are the words: "A Division Of The/Southland Corporation." At the bottom in small black letters appears the copyright information: "© Marvel Comics Group." This set is quite difficult to complete. It seems that no one wants to part with these glasses, and demand is much higher than the supply. They are quite fragile. There is also a taller, thinner, les often encountered version of this set. Value: $8–$10.

Amazing Spider-Man **[SL1]**
Captain America and the Falcon **[SL2]**
Fantastic Four/Doctor Doom **[SL3]**
Howard The Duck **[SL4]**
The Incredible Hulk **[SL5]**
The Mighty Thor **[SL6]**

Stained Glass Filigree Design. A $5\frac{7}{8}''$ heavy, round-bottom glass with two identical stained glass and filigree panels. Each panel is divided into various sized stained glass pieces by black dividing lines and intricate filigree work. In the center of each panel there is a round 7 Eleven logo, surrounded by an ornate filigree design. This is an unusually colored glass, with green, orange, red, and black appearing on a smoke-colored background. **[SL15]** Value: $3–$5.

7UP

Indiana Jones and the Temple of Doom (1984). A set of four $5\frac{13}{16}''$ glasses featuring dramatic scenes from the popular adventure film starring Harrison Ford. On the center front of each glass, characters in action are pictured in lively color, and above this scene are the words "INDIANA JONES [yellow] and the Temple of Doom [black]." On the reverse, there is a square red 7UP logo, and just to the right of it in yellow appear the Taco Time name and cactus

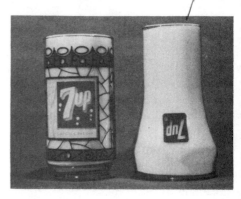

logo. Below that in a black-lined frame are black words explaining the action depicted on the front, as well as these words in small black print: "TM & © 1984 Lucasfilm Ltd. (LFL) All Rights/Reserved. The Seven-Up Co. Authorized User./Seven-Up And 7UP Are Registered/Trademarks Of The Seven-Up Company./Made in U.S.A." These colorful and nicely detailed glasses also appear with the 7UP logo alone, with the In-N-Out Burger logo, and with Brown's Chicken logo. We consider 7UP to be the main sponsor of these glasses and assume that they were distributed with a variety of other company logos on them. Value: $2–$4.

The spiked room/closes in on/Indy and Short/Round . . . time to/think fast! [SU1]
Attempting to/escape, Indiana/Jones turns to/fight pursuing/ Thuggee guards. [SU2]
High Priest Mola/Ram performs/a terrifying/Thuggee ritual. [SU3]
Indy, Willie, and/Short Round are/drenched as/their life raft/hurtles down the/river rapids. [SU4]

7UP Tumbler. A 5$\frac{9}{16}$" glass in orange, green, and white with green and orange filigree designs. There are two square panels on opposite sides of the glass: one with a lady in swimming suit beside older 7UP logo, and another with same lady in swimming suit but this time kicking the 7UP logo into a newer, more modern configuration. [SU25] Value: $1–$3.

7UP The Uncola. A 5$\frac{1}{4}$" green, white, and red glass. "7 UP" appears in large white letters vertically on opposite sides of the glass with a red dot between the "7" and the "U." "The Uncola" appears vertically in white below a red and white 7UP logo, which is near the top of the glass. This design is also repeated on the opposite side. This is a modern glass. [SU10] Value: $1–$3.

The Uncola Glass. Without a doubt, one of the cleverest design concepts yet. A 5$\frac{7}{8}$" glass which is essentially an upside-down Coca-Cola flare glass. This 7UP glass is the design counterpart of its anti-cola [caffeine] marketing philosophy. A memorable glass that fits the hand like no other. Simply designed, but effective. [SU30] Value: $1–$2.

Uncola: Lil' Un. A 3" truncated version of the larger Uncola glass. This unique glass has a right-side-up red 7UP logo on the front. On the reverse, "Lil' Un" appears in red letters with the underlined "un" subtly suggesting the "un-cola" nature of 7UP. "300 Milliliter" appears in small red print on one side of the glass, and "10.14 OZ" appears on the other. The design idea of this clever glass is that less is more. **[SU35]** Value: $2–$4.

7UP Uncola Goblet. A green 6" goblet with "7[dot]UP The Uncola" in white letters on each side. **[SU20]** Value: $1–$3.

7UP Wet & Wild. A 6½" pedestal-based glass in green, white, and red. The panel design and configuration are essentially the same as the smaller glass **[SU10]** with this major difference: on one side there is "The Uncola" below the red and white 7UP logo, and on the other there is "Wet & Wild" below the logo. Another modern glass. **[SU15]** Value: $1–$3.

Ziggy 7up Collector Series (1977). A set of four 5 3/16" glasses featuring Ziggy and his friends. On the front of each glass, Ziggy appears holding an orange umbrella which has "7up Collector Series" on it, and gathered around him are his various animal friends. Below this scene appears the "Ziggy" trademark with the words "By Tom Wilson" below it. Underneath that appear the words "© Universal Press Syndicate 1977." On the reverse, Ziggy is depicted in an action scene with his friends, and there is a caption below. Cute glasses with sympathetic characters. Value: $3–$5.

Here's To Good Friends (Ziggy and cat riding bicycle built for two) **[SU40]**
Here's To Good Friends (Ziggy on swing) **[SU41]**
Here's To Good Friends (Ziggy looking at fish in bowl) **[SU42]**
Here's To Good Friends (Ziggy walking bird on leash) **[SU43]**

Shakey's

Shakey's Filigree. A thick 6¼" yellow, orange, and black glass with identical filigree panels on each side and the name "Shakey's" in the center. There is no date, but this glass has a mid-seventies look about it. **[SH1]** Value: $3–$5.

Shakey's Pizza. A 5⅞" round-bottom glass with a Shakey's crest in a circle, which is in turn part of a leaded glass background. On the front, "Shakey's/Pizza/Restaurant" appears in the crest, and "Pepsi-Cola" appears on the reverse in an identical circle. Four black-bordered yellow bands at the glass's center unite the two circles. The colors on this glass—red, black, white, yellow—are quite vivid. **[SH5]** Value: $3–$5.

Shakey's Pizza Parlor. A 6" small-based glass in red and black with the same design on both sides. On a shieldlike sign outlined in black the name "Shakey's" appears at the top on a red background. Then in black on clear glass appear the words "Pizza/Parlor" followed by the black words "World's greatest pizza." on a red background. In a black-lined balloon directly below the shield are the words "Refill me/free" in black with four small circles "pointing" toward the bottom of the glass. This is a clever glass; it's nice to know that something is free! This glass probably dates from the late seventies. **[SH10]** Value: $3–$5.

Shell Oil Company

Seattle Mariners. A simply designed 5½″ glass with the "Seattle Mariners [logo] Baseball Club" on one side and on the bottom of the other in blue the words: "Shell Oil Company/Collectors Series." No date, unknown number of glasses in set. **[SO1]** Value: $1–$3.

Skipper's Seafood'n Chowder House

Legends of the Sea Series (1979). A set of four 5⅝″ glasses which recount four famous sea legends. Each legend appears in brown script with an illustration (also in brown) on a beige/light brown parchment background which covers three-quarters of the glass. On each glass below the parchment appear these words: " 'Legends of the Sea' from Skipper's Seafood'n Chowder House." The lower right corner of each parchment contains the 1979 copyright date. A nice set from this Seattle-based, rather small franchise. Because the legends are fascinating, we include the full texts. Value: $3–$5.

AS A PUNISHMENT/for selling his soul to the Devil, Van der Straaten,/a 16th century

Dutch sea captain, was condemned by/a spirit to sail forever in the/throes of a violent storm. Rumor has/it that the 'Flying Dutchman' has/been tossed about the seven seas for/over 400 years, battered and beaten/by the ceaseless tempest. (Illustration: threemaster in rough seas) **[SS1]**

HUNDREDS OF SHIPS/and planes have vanished in an area between Cuba,/Bermuda and the Southeast U.S. called The/Bermuda Triangle./Most of the disasters occurred in good weather,/within sight of land. Yet, there have been no survivors and no trace of the ships or/planes. Explanations range from sea/monsters to U.F.O.'s, but The Bermuda/Triangle remains shrouded in mystery. (Illustration: skull and crossbones) **[SS2]**

IN 1849, THE 'MINERVA'/set sail for the Far East from Ely's Harbor, Bermuda./It never reached its destination and was thought to be/lost at sea. But two years later, the 'Minerva' miraculously/reappeared in Ely's Harbor./ There were no crew members/aboard, but somehow the ship/drifted back to its home port/from the Indian Ocean, some/ 11,000 miles away. (Illustration: mariners on dock watching ship drift into harbor) **[SS3]**

OF ALL THE CREATURES/of the deep, none is more famous or feared than the/Loch Ness Monster. It is rumored to be sixty feet long,/ with large humps on its back and a powerful tail./The monster has been sighted dozens of times but has eluded/all attempts to capture it. Recently, a submarine set out in search/of the beast, but the vessel/sank and was never/ recovered. (Illustration: Loch Ness Monster swimming in the loch) **[SS4]**

Sneaky Pete's Hot Dogs

Al Capp (1975). A set of four glasses featuring the popular Al Capp characters. Appearing on each glass are the words"Sneaky/Pete's/Hot Dogs/Birmingham, Alabama." Near the bottom appear these words: "Al/Capp/© 1975 C.E.J." This was a small regional distribution, and the glasses are therefore difficult to find. Value: $8–$10.

Li'l Abner **[SN1]**
Pappy **[SN2]**
Joe Btsfplk **[SN3]**
Daisy-Mae **[SN4]**

Song Series

Song Series Jam Glasses. 5" glasses that come in at least three different series: Nursery Rhymes, Old Time Songs, and State Songs. Each glass comes in a single color with part or all of the lyrics on the reverse and an action scene on the front. Unknown number in each set. Value: $3–$5.

Nursery Rhymes:
  Farmer in the Dell **[SS1]**
  Jack and Jill **[SS2]**
  Row, Row, Row your Boat **[SS3]**
Old-Time Songs:
  After the Ball **[SS50]**
  Auld Lainge Syne **[SS51]**
  The Girl I Left Behind **[SS52]**
  Home Sweet Home **[SS53]**
  Oh, My Clementine **[SS54]**
State Songs: Theoretically there should be 48 different glasses since these date to the 50s.
  Alabama **[SS100]**
  Arizona **[SS101]**

Song Series 215

Space

The Apollo Series. This set consists of four $4\frac{1}{16}$" glasses and a $7\frac{3}{4}$" carafe with a white plastic cap. The colors are red, white, and blue. Each glass commemorates a particular moon mission. Probably issued by various gasoline companies in the early seventies after the Apollo 14 mission. A very interesting and attractive set with significant historical value. Value: glasses, $2–$4; carafe, $8–$10.

Apollo 11: blue band at top with white stars. From left to right on glass: "APOLLO 11" in vertical red bar, Armstrong stepping onto moon, the words "Man On The Moon/July 20, 1969," "USA" in vertical red bar, "Eagle/ Tranquility Base," "Neil A. Armstrong/ Edwin E. Aldrin, Jr./Michael Collins" above moon/eagle/earth logo. **[SC1]**

Apollo 12: red band at top with white stars. From left to right on glass: "APOLLO 12" in vertical blue bar, moonscape with Surveyor 3, Intrepid, and names "Charles Conrad/ Richard F. Gordon/Alan L. Bean," "USA" in vertical blue bar, moonscape with sailing ship and words "Return/To/The/Moon/November 19, 1969." **[SC2]**

Apollo 13: white band, blue borders and blue stars. From left to right: "APOLLO 13" in red on vertical white bar, panel with earth and moon and orbits of spaceship saying "Safe Return April 17, 1970/A Triumph/Of/Cour-

age/Ingenuity/Teamwork," "USA" in red on vertical white panel, and a panel showing the spacecraft docking at Aquarius and the names "James A. Lovell, Jr./Fred W. Haise, Jr./John L. Swigert, Jr." **[SC3]**

Apollo 14: white band, red borders, blue stars. From left to right: "APOLLO 14" in red on white vertical bar, the names "Alan B. Shepard, Jr./Stuart A. Roosa/Edgar D. Mitchell" and the date February 5, 1971 on panel depicting trajectory of Apollo 14, "USA" in red on white vertical bar, and panel showing astronauts playing golf on moon. **[SC4]**

Apollo 11, 12, and 13 Carafe: summarizes accomplishments of Apollo 11, 12, and 13 missions. Red, white, and blue colors. Carafe is shaped like space capsule and has white plastic sombrero type cap. At top is red border with white stars, at the bottom, a red band containing the words "Three Giant Leaps For Mankind." Panel has essentially the same coverage of the space missions as the individual glasses. **[SC5]**

Apollo Series Ceramic Cup. A $2\frac{5}{8}$" heavy ceramic cup made by Sone China. "Apollo/Series" appears on a green and white, gold-fringed tapestry which features an image of the Greek God Apollo. Above the tapestry in a green bar are the Roman numerals "VII-XIII" which refer to the Apollo space missions. The remainder of the cup has a blue panel

which depicts in black and white detail general aspects of space exploration, such as rockets, communication gear, and lunar modules. **[SC10]** Value: $2–$4.

Apollo 11 Moonshot. A 6" glass shaped like a rocket, half serious and half in jest. The top half of the glass holds 8 ounces, and the bottom rocket nozzle holds a shot. The glass is predominantly white with red and blue designs, and hence very official and patriotic looking. The top half, which is essentially a fuel tank, even has a red line near the rim which says "Liquid Fuel Red Line," but there are also realistic and serious pictures of the lunar module "Eagle," Neil Armstrong probing the moon's surface, a Bald Eagle on the moon with the earth in the background, and an American flag with "Man On The Moon July 20, 1969." On opposite sides of the glass in large red letters appear the ver-

tical words "APOLLO 11" and "USA." Gimmicky but likeable. Probably given out by gas stations with a minimum gas purchase shortly after the space mission. **[SC20]** Value: $3–$5.

Friendship 7. A 5⅝" glass honoring John Glenn. The front panel pictures John Glenn in his spacesuit with the earth and its orbit rings in the background. This front panel is a translucent blue with white, and underneath it are the words: "Lt. Col. John H. Glenn Jr., USMC/New Concord, Ohio." On the reverse is a blue and white picture of Friendship 7 with the words "Friendship 7/Feb. 20, 1962" beneath it. **[SC25]** Value: $3–$5.

Harold's Moon Shot. This 6" rocket-shaped beverage container is very similar in design to the Apollo 11 version, but on this glass "Reno" appears in large vertical red letters on one side instead of Apollo 11, and "Harolds Moonshot" appears on the front and reverse instead of the more serious NASA lore. **[SC30]** Value: $3–$5.

Subway Sandwiches & Salads

Christmas Carol Limited Edition. A set of four 5⅞" glasses depicting scenes and characters from Charles Dickens' *A Christmas Carol*. Both sides of the glasses have identical designs except for "Ghost Of Christmas Present" and "Ghost Of Christmas Past," each of which occupies its own separate side of that glass. The characters appear in a white holly leaf frame with decorative bars at the top and bottom, and their names appear in white just above the bottom bar of the frame. Separating the frames on each side of the glass are the words "A Christmas Carol by Charles Dickens" in vertical white letters. The Subway logo and "Limited Edition" appear in white below one of these vertically printed lines. These undated glasses don't look particularly "Christmassy," but they are nice enough and not too easy to find. Value: $4–$6.

Bob Cratchit **[SV1]**
"Tiny Tim" & Bob Cratchit **[SV2]**
Ebenezer Scrooge **[SV3]**
Ghost of Christmas Past/Ghost of Christmas
   Present **[SV4]**

Sunday Funnies

The Sunday Funnies. Without a doubt, one of the prettiest and most colorful series of glasses we have seen. The set consists of eight 5⅝" glasses with wraparound comic strip designs. The color and artwork on these glasses are exceptional, and there is so much content on each glass that it is almost impossible to describe them satisfactorily. This much we can say: the title of each comic strip appears in red near the top of each glass, and the words "The Sunday Funnies" appear in large black capital letters within a white band with black borders which encircles the bottom of each glass. The colorful panels contain the familiar comic strip characters whose names appear in black letters below each. Ap-

pearing vertically on each panel's edge is the copyright information which varies from comic strip to comic strip, but the general copyright date of 1976 is common to all eight glasses. Distributed by various restaurants, including Red Barn. Dick Tracy and Broom Hilda are more difficult to find than the others. A very desirable set. Value: Dick Tracy and Broom Hilda, $15–$20; others, $4–$6.

Brenda Starr, Reporter (New York News Inc.) **[SF1]**
Broom Hilda **[SF2]**
Dick Tracy **[SF3]**
Gasoline Alley (The Chicago Tribune) **[SF4]**
Little Orphan Annie (New York News Inc.) **[SF5]**
Moon Mullins (New York News Inc.) **[SF6]**
Smilin' Jack (New York News Inc.) **[SF7]**
Terry And The Pirates (News Syndicate Co., Inc.) **[SF8]**

Sunshine Pizza Exchange

'83–'84 Portland Trail Blazers. $5\frac{5}{8}$″ glasses, each of which features two players from the 1983–1984 Portland Trail Blazers basketball team. The colors are red, white, and black. On the front of each glass, the players' heads appear in a white circle with a thin black-lined border. The names appear to the left and to the right of the two players. Below the players in red are the words: " '83–'84/portland trail blazers." On the reverse in the center of the glass is the "Sunshine Pizza Exchange" logo, and at the bottom in red are the words "blazers' Favorite Pizza." A red and black band encircles the bottom of the glass, and the words we've just quoted are part of it, as are the small black "MSA ©" letters. There are six glasses and a pitcher in the set. Value: glasses, $4–$6; pitcher, **[SX10]** $8–$10.

Lafayette Lever and Jim Paxson **[SX1]**
Kenny Carr and Audie Norris **[SX2]**
Clyde Drexler and Calvin Natt **[SX3]**
Peter Verhoeven and Mychal Thompson **[SX4]**

Jeff Lamp and Darnell Valentine **[SX5]**
Wayne Cooper and Tom Piotrowski **[SX6]**

Swensen's

"ANNIE" Collector Glass (1982). A heavy 6″ rippled glass with two extruded rings at the base featuring [Little Orphan] "Annie and Sandy" on the front. Issued in conjunction with the re-release of the film "Annie," this is a simple representation with nice color and detail. On the reverse, near the middle, appear these words: "ANNIE/ Swensen's Collector Glass/© 1982 Tribune Company Syndicate, Inc.-/Columbia Pictures Industries, Inc." Made by Libbey. Getting hard to find. **[SW1]** Value: $2–$4.

Taco Bell

Star Trek III (1984). A set of four $5\frac{5}{8}$″ glasses with two extruded rings at the base featuring characters and situations from the film "Star Trek III." The subject of each glass appears on the front with the title in white below. A red ring encircles the glass near the top, and on the reverse in red appears the film's title: "Star Trek III/The Search For Spock." Beneath that, the title of each glass appears in white, followed by a brief paragraph of background information on the character and a small picture of relevant film action. Beneath this appear the words: "® and © 1984 Paramount Pictures Corp." followed by the name "TACO BELL." Wonderful colors (red, white, blue, black, maroon) and excellent design qualities. A set appealing to a wide range of collectors. Value: $3–$5.

Enterprise Destroyed (front)/Scotty, Kirk, McCoy (reverse) **[TB1]**

Fal-Tor-Pan (front)/Spock and Kirk (reverse) **[TB2]**

Lord-Kruge (front)/Kirk and Lord-Kruge (reverse) **[TB3]**

Spock Lives (front)/Genesis Effect Capsule (reverse) **[TB4]**

Taco Time

Cactus Glass. This 5$\frac{3}{16}$" glass features a bright orange wraparound panel with a chartreuse cactus on each side. The Taco Time name appears in orange in the middle of each cactus, and "Any Time Is Taco Time" appears in small chartreuse letters on each side near the bottom between the panels. This most unusually colored glass is undated. **[TT1]** Value: $1–$3.

Taco Villa

Cartoon Characters. A set of eight glasses, each depicting an unusual cartoon character of unknown heritage. These are 6" tumblers with full-figured characters in a variety of colors with the character's name in black below the figure along with the words "Taco Villa Inc." These are available with two dates, 1977 and 1979. Value: $3–$5.

[1977] (1979)
Mortimer **[TV1]** **(TV9)**
Julius **[TV2]** **(TV10)**
Sigmund **[TV3]** **(TV11)**
Lazlo **[TV4]** **(TV12)**
Farley **[TV5]** **(TV13)**
Irving **[TV6]** **(TV14)**
Frawley **[TV7]** **(TV15)**
Beauregard **[TV8]** **(TV16)**

Trivial Pursuit

Trivial Pursuit Game Glasses. A set of six 4⅛" highball glasses, one for each category in the popular Trivial Pursuit board game. Each glass has two black-outlined frosted panels. The front panel of each glass has a black-outlined colored panel within it, and this colored panel has the name "Trivial Pursuit" at its top and a picture illustrating one of the six categories of questions in its center. Below this colored panel in large black letters appears the name of one of the six game question categories. On the reverse panel, there is a game card with five questions and answers from the particular category. Between the panels at the base of the glass appears the following logo: "Culver/for/[logo]/ Horn Abbot." Value: $2–$4.

Art & Literature (Brown) **[TP1]**
Entertainment (Pink) **[TP2]**
Geography (Blue) **[TP3]**
History (Yellow) **[TP4]**
Science & Nature (Green) **[TP5]**
Sports & Leisure (Red) **[TP6]**

Twin Kiss

Twin Kiss Root Beer: A heavy 5⁹⁄₁₆" mug with a similar mug in red depicted in the middle and the word "TWIN" to the left of it and the word "KISS" to the right and the words "ROOT BEER" in red below. **[TK1]** Value: $1–$3.

Ultramart

Chicken EggStraordinary (1986). A 5⅞″ round-bottom Anchor Hocking glass showing a chicken dressed as a chef whipping eggs in a mixing bowl on a small table. Just to the right of the chicken-chef's head on a black-outlined white background are the words "Chicken [yolk colored]/E [red-orange] gg [blue] S [red-orange] traordinary [blue]." These words wrap around nearly three quarters of the glass. On the reverse, a bit below the midway point on the glass, there is a square dark blue logo featuring an eagle and the word "Ultramar." Just below this logo is the word "Ultramart" in black. Finally, near the bottom of the glass, the following words appear in black: "© 1986 Ultramar Petroleum, Inc." This is a very colorful glass. The chicken is yellow, yellow-orange, and white. He is wearing a dark blue apron with "Egg/Chef" written in orange on it, and he is dropping a shelled egg into the bowl. The egg has a little face depicted on it, and that face is apprehensive. All things considered, this is an unusual, puzzling glass. One thing is certain: either eggs or chicken is being promoted. **[UM1]** Value: $2–$4.

Walt Disney Productions

All-Star Parade (1939). A set of ten glasses available in two sizes (4¾″ and 4″) and in a variety of colors, depicting Disney characters in appropriate action. A banner encircling the top of each glass reads: "1939 Walt Disney All Star Parade." "© W.D.Ent." appears on each glass. These glasses are rare and desirable, and it is difficult to complete the set. Value: $15–$18.

[4″] (4¾″)
Donald Duck **[WD1] (WD11)**
The Ugly Duckling **[WD2] (WD12)**
Ferdinand, Senorita, Matador **[WD3] (WD13)**
Snow White and the Seven Dwarfs **[WD4]**
  (WD14)
Mickey, Minnie, and Pluto **[WD5] (WD15)**
Three Little Pigs **[WD6] (WD16)**
Goofy and Wilber **[WD7] (WD17)**
Greedy Pig and Colt **[WD8] (WD18)**

Cinderella. A set of eight numbered glasses that highlight portions of the classic Cinderella story. Each glass features wraparound action in red and yellow. Reportedly available in two sizes. Value: $5–$7.

Prince (1 of 8) **[WD20]**
Mice (2 of 8) **[WD21]**
Clock (3 of 8) **[WD22]**
Dog (4 of 8) **[WD23]**
Sisters (5 of 8) **[WD24]**
Fairy Godmother (6 of 8) **[WD25]**
Wand (7 of 8) **[WD26]**
Rabbit (8 of 8) **[WD27]**

Donald Duck Series [1942]. A series of 4″ glasses featuring Donald Duck and friends. Value: $12–15.

Donald Duck (the reverse reads: "Donald Duck is very gay,/As his guitar he is playing,/He sings a Spanish song as/His burro helps by braying." This glass is pictured in a 1942 Owens-Illinois packaging catalog. **[WD50]**
Donald Duck and Goofy **[WD51]**
Donald Duck with Huey, Louie, and Dewey—
  Boy Scouts **[WD52]**
Donald Duck on Bicycle **[WD53]**
Donald Duck with Huey, Louie, and Dewey—
  Cooking **[WD54]**

Mickey Mouse Filmstrip Series. A more recent 5″ issue with a character's face on the front and an action scene with the characters on the reverse. Unknown number of glasses in the set. Value: $2–$3.

Mickey Mouse/Mickey on roller skates **[WD75]**
Minnie Mouse/Minnie scolding Pluto **[WD76]**
Goofy/Goofy running with Dewey **[WD77]**

Minnie Mouse Canister Set. A 5½″ canister featuring Minnie Mouse on the front. Probably part of a larger set. **[WD100]** Value: $2–$3.

Mug: America on Parade. A 4½″ milk glass mug with the America on Parade logo on the front. Probably issued around the Bicentennial. No other information is printed on the glass. **[WD120]** Value: $2–$4.

Pinocchio [**WD140**]
Coachman [**WD141**]
Geppetto [**WD142**]
Lampwick [**WD143**]
Stromboli [**WD144**]
Jiminy Cricket [**WD145**]
Blue Fairy [**WD146**]
Figaro the Cat [**WD147**]
Cleo the Goldfish [**WD148**]
Monstro the Whale [**WD149**]
Gideon the Cat [**WD150**]

Single Character. A set of glasses similar to the Pinocchio and Snow White glasses, featuring Disney characters in single colors. These are early food containers distributed in the late 30s by the Swift company. Unknown number in the set. Value $12–$15.

Clarabelle Cow [**WD175**]
Donald Duck [**WD176**]
Horace Horsecollar with coin [**WD177**]
Horace Horsecollar with crate [**WD178**]
Elmer Elephant [**WD179**]
Goofy [**WD180**]
Mickey Mouse [**WD181**]
Minnie Mouse [**WD182**]
Pluto [**WD183**]
First Little Pig [**WD184**]
Second Little Pig [**WD185**]
Third Little Pig [**WD186**]

Sleeping Beauty. A set of 5" tumblers celebrating the Disney film "Sleeping Beauty." Unknown number of glasses in the set. Value: $6–$8.

Sleeping Beauty [**WD200**]
Sampson [**WD201**]
Briar Rose [**WD202**]
Good Fairies [**WD203**]
Prince Charming [**WD204**]

Pinocchio. A set of twelve glasses which come in several sizes and colors and feature characters from the Pinocchio feature film. There is no writing on the reverse. Value: $12–$15.

Snow White and the Seven Dwarfs—Bosco Glass. A set of 3″ tumblers with black drawing of Disney Feature movies. The front shows characters from the movie with the title below. The reverse reads "Bosco Glass." Unknown number in the set. **[WD225]** Value: $8–$10.

Snow White and the Seven Dwarfs. A set of eight tumblers showing Snow White and each of the seven dwarfs.

The glasses come in at least four different colors for each character and in at least two different sizes. Value: $8–$10.

[4½″] (5″)
Snow White **[WD250] (WD260)**
Bashful **[WD251] (WD261)**
Doc **[WD252] (WD262)**
Dopey **[WD253] (WD263)**
Grumpy **[WD254] (WD264)**
Happy **[WD255] (WD265)**
Sleepy **[WD256] (WD266)**
Sneezy **[WD257] (WD267)**

Warner Brothers

Porky Pig. A red 5″ glass featuring Porky Pig on the front with the word "Porky" below. Probably part of a larger set similar to the Disney single character glasses and dating from the late 30s. **[WB1]** Value: $8–$10.

Welch's Jam and Jelly Glasses

Archie Comics (1971). A set of six 4¼" glasses featuring characters from Archie Comics. Very colorful glasses with the title near the top, wraparound action scene, and the words "Copyright © 1971 by Archie Comic Publications, Inc." at the bottom. Eight different bottom embossings are possible, so there are 48 different glasses to collect. Value: $2–$4.

Betty and Veronica Fashion Show **[WJ1]**
Reggie Makes The Scene **[WJ2]**
Hot Dog Goes To School **[WJ3]**
Sabrina Cleans Her Room **[WJ4]**
Archie Taking The Gang For A Ride **[WJ5]**
Archies Having A Jam Session **[WJ6]**

Archie Comics (1973). Same design type as the 1971 series above, but with a 1973 copyright at the bottom. There are six glasses with the 1973 date, and with eight different bottom embossings the total number of different glasses is 48.

Value: $2–$4.

Mr. Weatherbee Drops In **[WJ10]**
Archie Gets A Helping Hand **[WJ11]**
Jughead Wins The Pie Eating Contest **[WJ12]**
Friends Are For Sharing **[WJ13]**
Betty and Veronica Give A Party **[WJ14]**
Sabrina Calls The Play **[WJ15]**

Collector Series (1975). A set of two glasses with National Football League Helmets featured on them, one set for the NFC and one for the AFC. Each glass contains the names of all the teams within each division and shows all the teams' helmets. "Welch's" is not present on the glasses themselves; rather, it appeared on the metal lid, where its relationship to the Collector Series is quite specific. These are colorful glasses and difficult to find. Value: $6–$8.

American Football Conference **[WJ50]**
National Football Conference **[WJ51]**

Collector Series (1976). A set of six 5" glasses featuring teams of the National and American Football Conferences and the three divisions within each. NFC team names are blue and white; AFC team names are red and white. Overall colors of both division's glasses are red, white, and blue. Football players in action appear at the top of each glass, along with the name of the conference and division and the NFL logo. Ap-pearing vertically near the top of the glass are the words "1976 Welch's ® Collector Series." Like the 1975 NFL glasses, these are difficult to find. Value: $4–$6.

NFC Eastern Division **[WJ60]**
NFC Central Division **[WJ61]**
NFC Western Division **[WJ62]**
AFC Eastern Division **[WJ63]**
AFC Central Division **[WJ64]**
AFC Western Division **[WJ65]**

Flintstones (1962). A set of six 4¼″ glasses featuring the popular Flintstone characters in wraparound action scenes. The title of each glass appears near the top in white with the words "The Flintstones," followed by a more specific phrase describing the activity depicted on the glass. Eight colors are possible for each glass, and at least an equal number of embossed characters' heads are possible for the bottoms, so a collector wishing to put together a complete set of these glasses has a formidable challenge lying ahead, since there are at least 384 possible combinations. On the bottom of each glass appear the words "© Hanna-Barbera Productions, Inc. 1962." These glasses are becoming more and more difficult to find. Value: $6–$8.

The Flintstones—Having a Ball **[WJ25]**
The Flintstones—Fred In His Sports Car **[WJ26]**
The Flintstones—Fred And His Pal At Work **[WJ27]**
The Flintstones—Fred's Newest Invention **[WJ28]**

The Flintstones—Fred And Barney Play Golf **[WJ29]**
The Flintstones—Fred And Barney Bowl Duckpins **[WJ30]**

Flintstones (1963). Same design, colors, and dimensions of the 1962 set, but with a 1963 copyright date. There are 128 different glasses possible here. Value: $6–$8.

The Flintstones—Pebbles' Baby Sitters **[WJ31]**
The Flintstones—Fred Builds A Doll Cave **[WJ32]**

Flintstones (1964). Same as the 1962 and 1963 copyright glasses above, but having a 1964 copyright date after the "Hanna-Barbera Production, Inc." line near the bottom. There are 384 variations possible. Value: $6–$8.

The Flintstones—Pebbles Lands A Fish **[WJ33]**
The Flintstones—Fred Goes Hunting **[WJ34]**
The Flintstones—Pebbles At The Beach **[WJ35]**
The Flintstones—Bedrock Pet Show **[WJ36]**
The Flintstones—Pebbles' Birthday Party **[WJ37]**
The Flintstones—Fred And Barney Play Baseball **[WJ38]**

Howdy Doody. A set of six 4¼" glasses featuring the Doodyville characters in action related to a circus context. The title encircles the top of the glass and has lines above and below it. The bottom of each glass has a character's head embossed on it. At the bottom of the glass appears the copyright informa-

tion: "© Kagran." There is no date, but these are early fifties glasses, and they are hard to find. Value: $10–$12.

Dilly Dally is Circus Big Shot! **[WJ70]**
Here Comes Music for Doodyville Circus **[WJ71]**
Clarabell Tries Tiger Trick **[WJ72]**
Clarabell Gets a Kick Out of Circus Mule **[WJ73]**
Doodyville Elephant squirts Clarabell! **[WJ74]**
Drinking Grape Juice is Seal's Favorite Act. **[WJ75]**

Howdy Doody (1953). A set of six 4⅛" glasses featuring characters from one of television's earliest and most popular shows for children. Welch's, with keen commercial vision, designed these little glasses to fit comfortably into a child's hands. Now those early Howdy Doody watchers are eagerly seeking these hard to find glasses. Each glass has a Welch's slogan imposed on a musical score running around the top of the glass. The

music notes serve as punctuation for the slogan. There is a wraparound action scene on each glass involving the Doodyville characters, and the bottom of each glass has a character's head embossed on it. The copyright date, 1953, appears on each glass. This is a must set for character glass collectors. Value: $10–$12.

Hey Kids! On Land Or Sea Welch's Tastes Best We All Agree **[WJ80]**

Hey Kids! Hip Hip Hooray Welch's Leads The
  Parade Each Day **[WJ81]**
Hey Kids! What A Shot Just Like Welch's It Hits
  The Spot **[WJ82]**
Hey Kids! Ding Dong Dell Ring For Welch's

You'll Like It Swell **[WJ83]**
Hey Kids! Wherever We Eat Welch's Is Our Fa-
  vorite Treat **[WJ84]**
Hey Kids! Come On Along Your Welch's Sure
  Helps Make You Strong **[WJ85]**

Warner Brothers (1974). A set of eight 4¼" glasses featuring popular Warner Brothers cartoon characters in action scenes. The title of each glass wraps around the top, and the action scene wraps around the remainder of the glass. At the bottom are the words "© 1974 Warner Bros. Inc." There are at least six different bottom embossings, so there are 48 different glasses possible. Value: $2–$4.

I Tawt I Taw A Puddy Tat! **[WJ90]**
TH-TH-TH That's All Folks! **[WJ91]**
Bugs Leads A Merry Chase **[WJ92]**
What's Up, Doc—Fresh Carrots? **[WJ93]**
Speedy Snaps Up The Cheese! **[WJ94]**
Thufferin' Thuccotash!! **[WJ95]**
Wile E. Heads For A Big Finish! **[WJ96]**
Foghorn Switches Henry's Egg **[WJ97]**

Warner Brothers (1976). A set of eight 4¼" individual character glasses with eight different bottom character embossings possible. The Warner Brothers character appears on only one side of the glass with its name in large letters below. To the left of each character running vertically up the center of each glass are the words "© 1976 Warner Bros. Inc."

Value: $3–$5.

Bugs Bunny **[WJ100]**
Daffy Duck **[WJ101]**
Elmer Fudd **[WJ102]**
Foghorn Leghorn **[WJ103]**
Porky Pig **[WJ104]**
Tweety **[WJ105]**
Road Runner **[WJ106]**
Yosemite Sam **[WJ107]**

Wendy's

Antique Advertisements. An undated 5 9/16" glass in brown and beige, similar in concept to the "Do You Know?" glass also shown (see WE10). This glass's surface is covered with antique advertising panels which are reminiscent of the table tops in Wendy's restaurants. The front panel has the Wendy's logo along with "Wendy's Old Fashioned Hamburgers/ Chili & Frosty." Probably issued during the mid-seventies. **[WE1]** Value: $4–$6.

Las Vegas Convention Wine Glass. A 6 5/8" lead crystal wine glass. In four locations on the bowl the following cluster of etched words appears: "WENDY's / We've Got / The Future / 10th Annual/Convention/Las Vegas— 1985." The manufacturer's sticker tell us this glass was made in Italy and contains over 24% lead. Convention giveaways like this are always more difficult to find than mass giveaways. **[WE5]** Value: $7–$9.

Limited Edition Collector Series (1976). A 5" red, white, and blue glass issued by Wendy's to celebrate the Bicenten-

nial. The main front panel contains the Wendy's name and logo followed by "Old Fashioned Hamburgers/Chili & Frosty/Freedom of Choice/Do You Know?/ We fix hamburgers 256 different ways/We start fresh every day with 100% pure beef." At the bottom of this panel are the words: "Limited Edition Collector Series/Copyright © 1976 by/ Wendy's International, Inc./All rights reserved." The remainder of the glass is filled with four "Do You Know?" questions (with answers) relating to American history and two "Do You Know?" panels promoting Wendy's pick-up window and dining room. An attractive, cleverly designed glass that is not encountered often. **[WE10]** Value: $5–$7.

Limited Edition Glasses [1981]. A set of four black and white 4⅛″ glasses celebrating major news stories as reported on the front page of *The New York Times* from 1976 to 1981. The front of each glass features the top half of the front page of the *Times* with a newsprint picture and, of course, the lead story headline. Print quality is excellent, and even the small writing can be read. The back of each glass contains only these words: "Wendy's/Limited Edition Glasses" and near the bottom: "© The New York Times." Beautiful and unusual glasses which are scarce. Probably issued shortly after the successful first flight of the shuttle Columbia. Value: $6–$8.

Men Land On Moon/2 Astronauts Avoid Crater/ Set Craft On A Rocky Plain (July 21, 1969) **[WE15]**

Nation and Millions in City Joyously Hail Bicentennial (July 3, 1976) **[WE16]**

U.S. Defeats Soviet Squad In Olympic Hockey by 4–3 (February 23, 1980) **[WE17]**

Columbia Returns: Shuttle Era Opens (April 15, 1981) **[WE18]**

Mug: Wendy's Old Fashioned Hamburgers. This 3¹³⁄₁₆″ ceramic mug features the well-known Wendy's sign and trademark in red, white, and black. This mug probably dates from the early to mid-seventies and, like Wendy's issues in general, it is not often encountered. **[WE25]** Value: $3–$5.

"Where's the beef" (1984). A 5" round-bottom glass with a black line drawing of Clara Peller. The famous words "Where's the beef" are in red letters above her head encircled by a balloon. The reverse is blank, but the right side is identified with "© 1984 Wendy's Exclusive Licensee Pro Sports Inc." One of many Peller promotional items produced. **[WE30]** Value: $4–$6.

"Where's The Beef?" (1984). A 5⅞" glass in white, black, and pink issued by Wendy's during the "Where's the Beef" advertising blitz. "Where's The Beef?" in large black-outlined capital letters with small question marks in pink, pink and black, and black and white gives way on the right to Clara Peller's picture in black and white. Then, to the right of Clara, appears the answer to all of these questions: "At [Wendy's logo]/Wendy's/of/Course" in pale pink lettering amidst a field of small question marks. Under Clara's picture are the words: "© 1984 Wendy's/Exclusive Licensee Pro Sports Inc." As collector glasses go, not old, but definitely not easy to find. **[WE35]** Value: $5–$7.

"Where's The Beef?" (1984). A taller, (6³⁄₁₆") variation of the glass above, but there are some design differences. The colors here are brown, white, and grey. "Where's The Beef?" appears in large brown-outlined capital letters. Slightly below the question mark is a drawing of a hamburger with a Wendy's square beef pattie extending well beyond the confines of the bun. To the right of this drawing is a drawing of Clara Peller identical to the one on the smaller glasses (above), but this time the drawing is brown and white. Below Clara appear the words: "© 1984 Wendy's/Exclusive Licensee Pro Sports Inc." Near the bottom of the glass below Clara the word "Wendy's" appears in grey, and it appears again under "Where's The Beef" on the other side. A brown and white band encircles the glass at the top. It is immediately noticeable that the question marks which appear as background on the earlier glass are missing on this one. Like the glass above, unusual and hard to find, though a great many of both must have been produced. **[WE40]** Value: $5–$7.

World's Fair (1982). A red and black 5⅝" glass issued by Wendy's for the 1982 World's Fair in Knoxville, Tennessee.

One side has "Wendy's" in black letters superimposed over the same word in red. The other has a red World's Fair logo with the words "The 1982/World's Fair/Knoxville, Tennessee" in black under it. A simply designed glass, but not often encountered. **[WE45]** Value: $4–$6. (*See also Dr Pepper*)

Whataburger

Yellow Rose Pitcher (1986). A 9" pitcher with a leaded glass window design in yellow, green, white, and black. In the center of the window there are three yellow roses, and to their left in black appear these words: "WHATABUR-GER/the burger that was born/and raised in Texas, wishes/our great State a happy/150th birthday/1836–1986." **[WB1]** Value: $5–$7.
(*See also Coca-Cola*)

The Wizard of Oz

The Wizard of Oz (Fluted Bottom Set). A set of six 5" glasses with fluted bases featuring characters from the Wizard of Oz story. The title, "The Wizard of Oz," and the individual character's name appear in white at the top of the glass on both front and reverse. The scenes on the glasses are wraparound, and they depict motifs from the story in various pastel colors (one color per glass). Near the bottom of each glass, "© Baum." appears, but there is no other writing and no date. These glasses are hard to find, and assembling a set requires persistence. Value: $8–$10.

Dorothy **[WO1]**
Lion **[WO2]**
Scarecrow **[WO3]**
Tin Woodman **[WO4]**
Toto **[WO5]**
Wizard **[WO6]**

The Wizard of Oz (Plain Bottom Set).

A set of six 5" glasses with plain bottoms and featuring the same Wizard of Oz characters listed above. These glasses are also difficult to find. Value: $8–$10.

Dorothy **[WO7]**
Lion **[WO8]**
Scarecrow **[WO9]**
Tin Woodman **[WO10]**
Toto **[WO11]**
Scarecrow **[WO12]**

The Wizard of Oz (Wavy Lines on Bottom).

This set of six 5" glasses features the same Wizard of Oz characters that appear in the two sets above. The glasses in this set have four wavy lines which

encircle the base of each glass. Near the bottom, each glass has "© S & Co." Like the other Wizard glasses, these are hard to find. Value: $8–$10.

Dorothy **[WO13]**
Lion **[WO14]**
Scarecrow **[WO15]**
Tin Woodman **[WO16]**
Toto **[WO17]**
Wizard **[WO18]**

The Wizard of Oz (Fluted Bottoms).

This fluted bottom set has a slightly different cast of Wizard characters. At the top of the glass, "The Wizard of Oz" appears on one side, and the character's name appears on the other. Near the bottom appears the "S & Co." copyright information. Like the others, hard to find and hard to assemble a set. Value: $8–$10.

Dorothy **[WO19]**
Emerald City **[WO20]**
Flying Monkeys **[WO21]**
Glinda **[WO22]**
Winkies **[WO23]**
Witch of the North **[WO24]**

Wonderful World of Ohio

The Wonderful World of Ohio. A set of 5$\frac{3}{16}$" glasses celebrating various attractions in the state of Ohio. The glasses are white with an array of colors. The subject of each glass is on the front with the words "The Wonderful World of Ohio" near the top in a combination of colors, and the title of each glass appears near the bottom. On the reverse there is round (2" diameter) section of road map showing the location of the site in question, and below that a brief account of each site appears within a rectangular frame. These colorful glasses are undated, and the number of glasses in the set is unknown at this time. Value: $1–$3.

Cincinnati Skyline [WW1]
State Capital Columbus [WW2]
Air Force Museum Fairborn, Near Dayton [WW3]

Old Man's Cave, Hocking State Park [WW4]
Memorial at Fallen Timbers, Maumee Near Toledo [WW5]
Campus Martius Museum, Marietta [WW6]
Perry's Victory Memorial, Lake Eire [WW7]
Fort Recovery State Memorial, Greenville [WW8]
Cleveland Lake Front [WW9]
Pro Football Hall of Fame, Canton [WW10]

Ziggy

Giantburg (1972). This 6⅝″ giant-capacity fountain glass has a panel featuring Ziggy examining a small hamburger on a large bun. Above him is the word "Giantburg," which must be a joke of some kind, since the burger is anything but giant. On the reverse there is the standard black and white Ziggy name, underneath which there are the words: "By Tom Wilson/© Universal Press Syndicate 1972." This giant glass is rather plain, but if you like Ziggy at all, you'll like this rather unusual one. **[ZG1]** Value: $3–$5.

Milk Glass Tankard—World's Worst Skier (1977). This 5¼″ milk glass tankard shows Ziggy skiing down a hill backward. On the reverse there are broken skiis and ski poles, and a white plaster cast and the words "World's Worst/Skier" in black. At the bottom right of this picture are the words: "Ziggy TM/© Universal Press Syndicate 1977." **[ZG5]** Value: $2–$4.

Hi-ball Tumblers (1977). The glass shown is one of a set of "8–11 oz. Decorated Beverage Glasses" produced by Federal Glassware (Set T 2152) in 1977. These glasses are for adult drinks, and the numbers on the glasses are intended to help partiers keep track of their drinks. Each number is a different color, and because Ziggy's efforts to avoid confusion are so humorous, we quote his words from all the glasses in the set:

1 (Green) You're The One!! **[ZG10]**
2 (Blue) That's You! **[ZG11]**
3 (Red) If You're Number 3 . . . You're Gonna Have To Really Try Harder! **[ZG12]**
4 (Orange) If Your Number Is Not 4 . . . You've Got Someone Else's Drink! **[ZG13]**
5 (Yellow) If Your Number Is Not 1, 2, 3, 4, 6, 7, Or 8 . . . Then This Is Your Glass! **[ZG14]**
6 (Brown) Your Number Is Six . . . Unless, Of Course, You're Holding The Glass Upside Down . . . In Which Case Your Number Is 9 **[ZG15]**
7 (Plum) This Is Your Lucky Number! **[ZG16]**
8 (Butterscotch) No Matter How You Look At It . . . You're Number 8 **[ZG17]**

Have a Happy! (1978). A blue $3\frac{1}{16}''$ Christmas glass, featuring Ziggy standing on a sled next to a birdhouse on a tree limb. White snowflakes encircle the glass, and to the left of Ziggy and to the right of the tree the words "Have a/ Happy!" appear in red. Below this scene in red are the words: "Christmas is Sharing." In black to the right and slightly above the word "Sharing" are the words: "Ziggy TM © Universal Press Syndicate 1978." A small animal stands at the base of the tree looking at Ziggy, and a small red bird appears to be sitting on the limb next to the birdhouse. **[ZG20]** Value: $2–$4.

Hello world! (1979). A $3\frac{7}{8}''$ juice glass with "Hello world!" near the top in red and Ziggy parting some long-stemmed hearts to peer out at us. These heart "plants" continue around the entire glass. On the reverse in small black print are Tom Wilson's name and "Ziggy TM/ © Universal Press Syndicate 1979." **[ZG25]** Value: $1–$3.

. . . it looks like LOVE!! (1979). On this $5\frac{1}{8}''$ glass, Ziggy is pictured holding a black umbrella under a sky of small falling hearts which go all the way around the glass. Beneath him in black writing are the words: " . . . it looks like LOVE!!" Tom Wilson's name is located to the left of Ziggy, just under the bottom-most hearts. On the reverse below the deluge of hearts are these small black words: "Ziggy TM/©.Universal Press Syndicate 1979." This glass is for wholesome beverages, and though its message is naive, at least it is understandable! **[ZG30]** Value: $1–$3.

Zodiak

Beverly Zodiak Series (1976). A set of twelve 4¾" astrological sign glasses identical in color and design to the Arby's 6¼" set, but differing in shape and size, this set having a wide bottom and a narrow mouth. All other content is the same as the Arby's set, including the "Beverly" signature and the "K.M.A. 1976" copyright date. Collectors interested in astrology will want both sets. If you actually go out looking for these, they are hard to find! Value: $1–$3.

Aries (the Ram) **[ZO1]**
Aquarius (the Water Bearer) **[ZO2]**
Cancer (the Crab) **[ZO3]**
Capricorn (the Goat) **[ZO4]**
Gemini (the Twins) **[ZO5]**
Leo (the Lion) **[ZO6]**
Libra (the Balance) **[ZO7]**
Pisces (the Fishes) **[ZO8]**
Sagittarius (the Archer) **[ZO9]**
Scorpio (the Scorpion) **[ZO10]**
Taurus (the Bull) **[ZO11]**
Virgo (the Virgin) **[ZO12]**

Index